subtle
energy

subtle energy

AWAKENING TO THE UNSEEN
FORCES IN OUR LIVES

WILLIAM COLLINGE, PH.D.

WARNER BOOKS

A Time Warner Company

Grateful acknowledgment is given to the following:

The International Society for the Study of Subtle Energies and Energy Medicine to reproduce figures 7–14. From Dean Radin and Jannine Rebman, "Lunar Correlates of Normal, Abnormal and Anomalous Human Behavior," *Subtle Energies* 5, no. 3, pp. 220–224. Used by permission.

HarperCollins Publishers, Inc., for permission to reprint the poem by Starhawk on page 105, from *The Spiral Dance*, Tenth Anniversary Edition, copyright © 1979, 1989, by Miriam Simos.

The Institute of HeartMath, Boulder Creek, CA, for permission to reproduce the Freeze-Frame Technique® on page 270.

Bethe Hagens, Ph.D., and William S. Becker for permission to reproduce their "Rings of Gaia" illustration.

Warner Books, Inc., 1271 Avenue of the Americas, New York, NY 10020
Visit our Web site at http://warnerbooks.com

 A Time Warner Company

Printed in the United States of America
First Printing: January 1998
10 9 8 7 6 5 4 3 2 1

Library of Congress Cataloging-in-Publication Data

Collinge, William.
    Subtle energy : awakening to the unseen forces in our lives /
William Collinge.
        p. cm.
    Includes bibliographical references and index.
    ISBN 0-446-52017-9
    1. Self-realization—Miscellanea. 2. Force and energy—
Miscellanea.   I. Title.
    BF 1999.C682   1997
    133.8—DC21   97-6221
                                                        CIP

Illustrations by Susan Hoffman

Book design and composition by L&G McRee

NOTE TO THE READER

This book includes case examples and descriptions of alternative ways of dealing with health problems. Such examples are illustrative only and are not intended as medical advice. You should consult your health care professional for individual guidance with specific medical problems. Also, names in stories and case examples have been changed to protect privacy.

CONTENTS

LIST OF TABLES AND FIGURES   ix

FOREWORD by Emmett E. Miller, M.D.   xi

ACKNOWLEDGMENTS   xv

CHAPTER 1. Subtle Energy: Medium of the Spirit   1
  By any other name • Finding our way

CHAPTER 2. Embodiment: Our Energetic Anatomy   23
  *Our vital energy • The biofield • Flowing rivers of energy • Pools and
  points • Energy centers • Being "in sync" • The five elements • The mind
  and subtle energy*

CHAPTER 3. Spiritus Mundi: Subtle Energies in Nature and the
  Environment   59
  *The Rings of Gaia • The paths of the dragon • Power places and sacred sites
  • The cocoon of life • When mother earth shakes • Celestial influences • A
  positive spin on negative ions • The dance of wind and water: feng shui •
  Man-made electromagnetic fields • Remembering the earth*

CONTENTS

CHAPTER 4. Two or More Together: Subtle Energies in
Relationships   109
On the same wavelength • In the family crucible • The doshas and relationships • What happens when we touch? • What's love got to do with it? • Relating sexually • Influences from afar • The power of the group

CHAPTER 5. In-Spiration: The Breath-Energy Connection   143
Breath and spirit • The way of the West • Anatomy of the breath • The breath and health • Breathwork: tool for transformation • The breath in meditation • Tending the fire

CHAPTER 6. Sustenance: The Care and Nurturing of Our Vital
Energy   173
Timing is everything • The balance of activity and rest • The energetics of food • The fire within: digestion • Energetic herbs and supplements • The tao of exercise • Energy practices • Balancing with earth energy • Sex and vital energy

CHAPTER 7. Courting the Spirit: Subtle Energies in Prayer,
Meditation, and Healing   225
Filled with the spirit • Rapture and ecstasy • Chanting; the power of resonance • The mind-heart connection • The energetics of posture and concentration • When the light shines • Energy and healing • Collective intention • Evidence for healing through touch and prayer

NOTES   273
APPENDIX: RESOURCES   291
INDEX   295
ABOUT THE AUTHOR   303

LIST OF TABLES AND FIGURES

———

TABLES   PAGE

  1. Some Equivalent Terms for Biofield   18
  2. Tastes, Foods, and Their Energetic Effects   192

FIGURES

  1. The Human Aura   29
  2. Meridians and Acupuncture Points   31
  3. Chakras and *Nadis*   37
  4. The Rings of Gaia   64
  5. Needles of Stone   71
  6. Earth's Geomagnetic Field   76
  7. Solar Radio Flux vs. Lunar Cycle   84
  8. Barometric Pressure vs. Lunar Cycle   84
  9. Psychotic Behavior vs. Lunar Cycle   85
 10. Death by Suicide vs. Lunar Cycle   85
 11. Total Deaths vs. Lunar Cycle   86
 12. Crisis Calls vs. Lunar Cycle   86

FIGURES

		PAGE
13.	Mutual Fund Residuals vs. Lunar Cycle	87
14.	Lottery Percentage vs. Lunar Cycle	87
15.	Overlapping Energy Fields	111
16.	Sexual-Energetic Communion	131
17.	The Complete Yogic Breath	163
18.	The Microcosmic Orbit	167
19.	Yoga: Opening the Channels	209
20.	*Tai Chi:* Following the River	212
21.	Prayerful Hands: Completing the Circle	242
22.	Collective Intention and Laying On of Hands	255
23.	Therapeutic Touch	262

FOREWORD

This book comes at a very opportune time. The enormous changes taking place planetwide are having profound impacts on our individual lives. We are turning our attention more and more to the quest for the full flowering of human potential, and the world stands poised at the edge of a new awakening in many ways.

The thirst for information about alternative ways of thinking, feeling, and being has led to such a profusion of new ideas that to try and grasp them all is a bit like trying to get a drink from a fire hydrant. One of the more exciting but perplexing areas of emerging knowledge—a subject that has suffered from too many confusing and incomplete efforts to explain it—is our understanding of energy and our nature as beings of energy. I'm reminded of the story of the five blind men trying to describe an elephant, when each was only in touch with one part: one was holding the tail, one a leg, one an ear, one the trunk, and another a tusk. Each had a handle on a piece of the truth, but none had the full picture. In the following pages, however, you will be introduced to the full picture.

Many cultures, including our own before it became obsessed with technological progress, have had great respect for the subtle and unseen forces in life. Ancient healers would first develop a great sensitivity to an individual's mental, emotional, physical and spiritual makeup, and then suggest relatively subtle changes in diet, herbs, and healing rituals to bring them back into harmony. Such sensitivity has fallen prey to the rampant technology of our time and the sledgehammers of modern medicine.

It was in my practice of medicine that the full significance of subtle energies became apparent. People were aware of extreme symptoms of system breakdown (headaches, heart attacks, cancer, ulcers) but were unaware of the more subtle indicators and changes that forewarned of such serious problems. I found that by teaching people how to become more deeply attuned to themselves and their environment we could markedly affect the speed and depth of their healing responses. Unfortunately, people often don't pay careful enough attention to the subtle aspects of their experience, including the effects of thoughts and emotions on their physical bodies.

It's not surprising that it has taken so long for Western culture to rediscover and accept the influence of subtle energies in our lives. Our basic orientation has always been to dominate and control. After all, Columbus did not come to the New World to learn from its inhabitants, but to take from them. The movement west was not inspired by a desire to learn of a new ecosystem, but for the lure of material wealth. And since the industrial revolution we have worked hard to support our hubris so that we could find ultimate health and fulfillment through science and technology. But there is a great deal missing if we fail to see and experience on a daily basis what connects us to the earth and to all of life.

This book provides a fascinating and illuminating

overview of the field of subtle energies, in its many diverse aspects. Dr. Collinge, like a master painter, dips his brush briefly into each, then applies it skillfully to the canvas, and right before our eyes a masterpiece appears: the magnificent dance of the energies of earth-body-mind-spirit-cosmos. To catch a glimpse of this is to have a hint of what is possible. To see it clearly will enable you to more fully appreciate how each is a facet of the whole and a reflection of the one Spirit that moves through all things.

EMMETT E. MILLER, M.D.

ACKNOWLEDGMENTS

This book is a product of many years of learning and sharing with friends, teachers, colleagues, students, and clients. I particularly wish to thank Abigail Platt, my partner and consort, for her love, wisdom, and patience. Others who contributed include Jeffrey Cram, Ph.D., Sierra Health Institute; Richard Pavek, the Shen Therapy Institute; Rollin McCraty, the Institute of HeartMath; William Tiller, Ph.D., Stanford University; Penny Hiernu, T. M. Srinivasan, Ph.D., Jeff Levin, Ph.D., and Jerry Wesch, Ph.D., the International Society for the Study of Subtle Energies and Energy Medicine; Candice Fuhrman, my literary agent; Colleen Kapklein, Warner Books; Harvey-Jane Kowal, Warner Books; Joann Davis, formerly of Warner Books; Sona Vogel; Henry Reed, Ph.D.; Larry Dossey, M.D.; Elmer Green, Ph.D.; Efrem Korngold; Harriet Beinfield; Janhavi Morton; Ellen Raskin, Flowing River Institute; Jannine Rebman and Dean Radin, Ph.D., University of Nevada; Minor Davis, National Geophysical Data Center; Bethe Hagens, Ph.D., Union Institute; Hector Ramos, the Pranic Healers Association; Willie Lansing;

Karen Carroll; Stanley Krippner, Ph.D., Saybrook Institute; the Venerable Ayya Khema; Frank Echenhoffer, Ph.D.; Richard Gerber, M.D.; Kylea Taylor; Roger Jahnke, O.M.D.; Daniel Benor, M.D.; Emmett Miller, M.D.; Annabel Gregory; Robert Winquist; Elizabeth Stratton; Bill Thomson; Katherine Metz; Rev. Samuel Celovsky; Janet Quinn, Ph.D., R.N., University of Colorado School of Nursing; Kenneth M. Sancier, Ph.D.; and my illustrator, Susan Hoffman. With so many having contributed to this effort, there is a good chance I have inadvertently left someone out, and if so I apologize, for your help is greatly appreciated as well.

May all beings be happy.

CHAPTER 1

SUBTLE ENERGY:
MEDIUM OF THE SPIRIT

Look, it cannot be seen—it is beyond form.
Listen, it cannot be heard—it is beyond sound.
Grasp, it cannot be held—it is intangible.

—LAO-TZU[1]

There must have been a hundred people across the room between them, but she felt something, turned, and their eyes met. . . .

Walking down the street in a strange city, he felt a sudden pull to enter a certain café. There sat an old friend he hadn't seen in ten years. . . .

After lying facedown on the earth for twenty minutes, she realized that all her tension and depression had left her. She felt rejuvenated and infused with fresh energy. . . .

Real forces are moving within our bodies and the world around us—unseen, unheard, and some undetected by even the most sensitive scientific instruments. In recent years researchers have coined the term "subtle energy" to describe these forces. While an understanding of subtle energies has been part of many cultures and spiritual traditions for millennia, Western science is only now beginning to acknowledge they exist. They have become the focus of study in disciplines as diverse as physics and psychology, engineering and medicine.

Some of these energies are known and recognized by physics, while others cannot be explained by science—yet we experience them as no less real. In this book you will discover how subtle energies affect your life every day—from your body to your environment, your relationships, your spirituality, and even your health. Recognizing the presence of subtle energies, and learning to work with them, offers us new means of self-mastery and living a harmonious and fulfilling life.

THE SPIRIT-ENERGY CONNECTION

Earlier this century, Albert Einstein showed through physics what the sages have taught for thousands of years: everything in our material world—animate and inanimate—is made of energy, and everything *radiates* energy. The earth is one enormous energy field—in fact, a field of fields. The human body is a microcosm of this—a constellation of many interacting and interpenetrating energy fields.

But why does energy take the patterns that it does, and what holds them in place? Through his efforts to answer this, Einstein became a deeply religious man. He concluded that the continuously unfolding and dynamic nature of the universe could be understood only as the work of a higher guiding intelligence of another dimension. Indeed, the perennial wisdom of humankind holds that our physical world is

2

embedded within a greater, transcendent dimension—that of Spirit or the Absolute.

The world's spiritual traditions share the understanding that energy and spirit are intimately intertwined. Energy is the "raw material" of which Spirit is continually forming our physical reality. Energy is the medium in which Spirit moves through our world, the bridge between Spirit and matter.

The following description of this relationship was offered by the late Indian mystic Swami Muktananda. While he refers to Spirit or the Absolute as Kundalini, his message could easily find expression through most any tradition simply by substituting Holy Spirit, Great Spirit, Lord, or many other names:

> [The Kundalini] creates the universe out of Her own being, and it is She Herself who becomes this universe. She becomes all the elements of the universe and enters into all the different forms that we see around us. She becomes the sun, the moon, the stars and fire to illuminate the cosmos which She creates. She becomes the prana, the vital force, to keep all creatures, including humans and birds, alive; it is She who, to quench our thirst, becomes water. To satisfy our hunger, She becomes food. Whatever we see or don't see, whatever exists, right from the earth to the sky is ... nothing but Kundalini. It is that supreme energy which moves and animates all creatures, from the elephant to the tiny ant. She enters each and every creature and thing that She creates, yet never loses Her identity or Her immaculate purity.[2]

As you will see throughout these pages, subtle energies are an integral part of an evolving paradigm of life: *we are beings of energy, living in a universe composed of energy.* In this chapter I will present an overview of subtle energy phenomena, the scientific basis of which will be explored in more detail later. Let us begin with a journey into the heart.

SOOTHING THE HEART

Maggie is an eighty-one-year-old woman living in a retirement village. She is relatively self-sufficient in her private apartment and still cooks many meals for herself. During a recent physical exam her physician expressed amazement at the progress of her heart. Over her last several exams she had shown an increasingly irregular heartbeat, and her physician was concerned that a serious problem was developing. When the physician queried her about the improvement of her heart, Maggie could not explain why it had changed.

"The only thing new is the dog," she stated. Four months ago Maggie's daughter gave her her dog to care for while she accompanied her husband on an extended consulting trip in another state. "I spend pretty much all my time with him," explained Maggie, "and we've become pretty close."

It is common knowledge that pets are beneficial to the health of the elderly living alone. Usually the explanation that is given is that the psychological companionship improves the person's morale and will to live. This is important, but there is perhaps a more compelling explanation for the health benefits of pet ownership.

Researchers at the Institute of HeartMath in Boulder Creek, California, have found that feelings of love and tenderness affect the heart energetically. The heart is by far the most powerful of several energy centers in the body. When feelings of caring and love are accessed, the beating pattern of the heart shifts to become more even and regular. This in turn alters the electromagnetic field of the heart, which then brings tremendous benefits to the person on all levels—body, mind, and spirit. In fact, as we shall see, love itself is a subtle energy that can have potentially powerful effects throughout the body and even on other people. The dog didn't soothe Maggie's heart; she did it herself by accessing these feelings.

THE MAGIC OF A KISS

Two-year-old Amy runs across the living room floor, stumbles, and falls. There is an immediate eruption of screaming and crying, but within seconds after her mother picks her up, holds her close, and kisses her, she is playing again contentedly.

This is a scene we have all probably witnessed many times. We take for granted the soothing, nurturing connection between mother and child. Yet what actually are the ingredients of that connection? What transpired in that moment of solace for Amy that allowed her to shift her state so instantaneously?

On the surface it may again look simply like a psychological transaction. Her rhythm was severely disrupted in a flash, leaving her in a state of confusion and fear. Mother came along and gave her an infusion of reassurance that she is safe and loved, and Amy then resumed where she left off.

Energetically, however, there's much more to the story. Because of their history together, Amy and her mother have a deep affinity for each other's energy fields. Being held and kissed, she is reconnecting with the energy field to which she has been entrained from conception onward, to this moment. For Amy, it is the experience of being reimmersed in the energy field that is the ground of her being. It's a simple matter of connecting with her source—like hitting a reset button. However, the source is actually a rich and complex mixture of her mother's electromagnetic field and many subtle fields of vital energy emanating from her heart and other energy centers throughout her body.

There are many other ways we can be energetically connected as well. Many of us have had experiences where we were so attuned to another person that we actually uttered identical statements at the same time or knew what the other person was about to say. In chapter 4 I'll explain research findings that show that we indeed become energetically connected to the people we are closest to, so much so that our brain waves may react to things that happen to them even though we are far removed from the situation.

Likewise, there is scientific evidence that when we are part of a group, such as a prayer group or meditation group, we become part of a shared energy field that can have a powerful impact on us. This was illustrated in the case of Ralph, a forty-five-year-old attorney who had been suffering from a liver ailment that could not be helped by his doctors. He began working with a shaman who used collective visualization. That is, the shaman would have four of his assistants sit closely around Ralph, about two feet away, commingling their energy fields with his. They would then chant and visualize for about twenty minutes. After several months of these weekly treatments, Ralph's symptoms were completely gone, and his blood tests all came up normal.

A Risky Business

Our energetic connections with others can also carry some risk. Katherine has been a successful and highly regarded psychotherapist for fifteen years, specializing in the treatment of people with depression. Over the years she has developed a very compassionate perspective and has even come to view love as a component in the healing work she is doing with these people. She often ends her sessions with giving her patients a hug as a gesture of her support and caring for them as human beings.

Recently, however, she has encountered an obstacle all too common in her profession: burnout. She starts each day with plenty of energy but feels dragged out and depleted at the end. She is feeling a decline in enthusiasm for her work but still believes it is her right calling in life.

Katherine decides to learn more about energy by taking a class in *chi kung*. *Chi kung* is the ancient Chinese tradition of energy cultivation. The mother of all the martial arts, it teaches how to generate more energy and conserve what you have.

It comes as a shocking revelation to Katherine that in *chi kung* there is a principle that when you touch another person there is an exchange of energy. Furthermore, energy will move from the person with the highest energy to the one with the lowest energy. Her teacher is adamant that she should stop hugging her patients and keep her energy for herself. With some experimentation Katherine realizes that indeed her teacher is right. Her practice of hugging her depressed clients has been draining her of vital energy.

She has adopted a new style of working in which she no longer ends her sessions with hugs and finds herself having more energy at the end of her workday.

INTIMACY AND ENERGY

I need to change my pattern of attraction to women, thought Martin after another sad ending. On reflecting back upon the significant women in his life, he realizes that his pattern is to be drawn to certain specific qualities: a somewhat submissive and insecure personality packaged in a slender, waiflike figure. His relationships of late have come to a similar fate: his own judgmental nature seems to be overbearing, and he hurts his partners unintentionally with side comments critical of their ideas and with his sometimes overwhelming sexual energy.

Indeed, what Martin is experiencing is a classic problem in relationships that is the result of incompatible *energetic types*. We can complement or conflict with others depending on our unique energetic nature, and Ayurveda, the ancient energy-based "science of life" from India, helps explain why. In this case, Martin's energetic nature is strongly *pitta*, meaning that he has a lot of the fire element in him.

This makes him naturally more "inflammable," with a propensity to be both judgmental and passionate. The women of his attraction pattern, unfortunately, are strongly of the *vata* type. They are naturally more easily thrown off center, more vulnerable, and more insecure. Unless they are both aware of their tendencies and compensate for them, putting a *pitta* and a *vata* together is asking for trouble.

What Martin needs to discover is that his *pitta* nature is more naturally complemented by a mate whose energy is more *kapha*, since these people are more solid, resilient, and able to balance his fire with their grounded, softer qualities. As we shall see later, the guidance of Ayurveda can be very practical in understanding the subtle energetic dynamics of relationships and even in choosing a mate.

As Martin has shown, how our relationships with others are played out is based on much more than our personality and relationship history. Our individual energetic nature is perhaps a more telling influence. Anna and Frank, whom you'll meet again later, found that it can be altered in some rather surprising ways.

Both, like Martin, are fiery characters with strong *pitta* energy. This quality of their energy makes them a little more volatile and sharp with one another. One of the most effective ways they have found to reduce conflict between them has nothing to do with relationships or psychology per se. Rather, simply by eating foods that do not aggravate this fiery nature but soften it instead, they are able to keep their relationship on a relatively even keel.

While it doesn't sound like a sophisticated form of marital therapy, their strategy is to enjoy an occasional sweet together, make sure they eat plenty of green leafy vegetables, and include beans and pomegranate in their diet. These food choices are understood in Ayurveda to help "pacify" their *pitta* natures. They also agree to minimize their intake of yogurt and cheeses, salty foods, and hot, spicy foods—particularly around times of stress or conflict—which would aggravate their *pitta* energy. To smooth the way for a successful relationship, Anna and Frank are applying an age-old yet simple understanding of how foods affect our energetic nature in subtle ways.

Sexual Healing

"You wouldn't believe me if I told you," replied Rafael to his physician, who wondered why he was doing so much better. "Let's just call it my secret cure." A year ago Rafael had been diagnosed with chronic fatigue syndrome and had to go on disability from his job as a building contractor. He had all the classic symptoms, including an immune system in disarray, inability to concentrate, short-term memory loss, and debilitating fatigue after the slightest exercise. At one point, trying to "push through," he jogged once around a quarter mile track and was then in bed for a week.

Since conventional medicine had nothing to offer, Rafael turned to Chinese medicine for whatever insights he could gain about building his vital energy. The acupuncture and herbs were helpful, but he believes that what saved him was an old secret from Taoist lovemaking practices: ejaculation control. For the past three months he has been making love several times per week without ejaculating, taking advantage of the powerful healing potential of sexual energy.

This principle, which will be discussed at length later, explains how sex can serve to either deplete or build our energy level. Long considered a secret of spiritual adepts, it is an example of the power we have to cultivate our vital energy if we want to. His wife found it a little difficult to understand at first but now is quite pleased with the results of his having learned this practice.

HE LOST WEIGHT WITHOUT CHANGING HIS DIET

In addition to sexual practices, our diet also affects subtle aspects of our energy. Willard has been learning about the relationship between his vital energy and his eating patterns. He has been struggling for many years with a tendency to gain weight. He has tried dozens of different diet and exercise regimes, but nothing has seemed to stick. As soon as he lets up on a plan, the pounds come back on almost immediately. He sees the handwriting on the wall—that as he gets older, his metabolism will continue to slow down, and he's likely to gain even more weight. With a history of heart attack in the men in his family, he is especially motivated to find a new relationship to food that really works for him.

Upon consulting with a practitioner of Ayurveda, Willard learns that in many ways he has indeed been on the right track. The consultant is impressed that he has in general been eating the right foods for his situation. However, Willard soon discovers that there's more to diet than *what* you eat. Equally important is *when* you eat.

He learns that his vital energy goes through a sequence of specific phases in each twenty-four-hour period, and there are optimal times for eating and digestion that directly affect weight gain or loss. Willard comes away with an understanding of how to lose weight without changing his diet, simply by changing the timing of his meals.

When Spirit Enters

A woman is sitting silently in the fourth day of a meditation retreat and suddenly has an orgasm. A man in that same retreat suddenly sees an explosion of light behind his closed eyelids and feels filled with a delightful sensation of bliss. During a Pentecostal worship service, a man feels overcome by the Holy Spirit and begins alternately weeping and laughing uncontrollably.

Energetic experiences that we have during spiritual practices can be both surprising and exciting. Every spiritual tradition has a way of accounting for the energetic phenomena that occur during devoted spiritual practice. The common theme is that an infusion of energy can come into the body, often accompanied by flashes of light and waves of heat. These are experienced as moments of "in-spiration"—entry of the Spirit—when energy from another dimension seems to be moving through us.

A less sensational but still fascinating impact of spiritual practice is one involving the methodical chanting of prayers. A group of Benedictine monks who had been chanting daily for years suddenly stopped the practice. Soon thereafter they began experiencing low energy, sleep disorders, and other health problems. All their symptoms disappeared when the chanting practice was reinstated.

How could chanting have such profound effects on the body? It turns out that chanting affects our energetic anatomy on several levels, from the electrical potential of our brain to the energy passing through energy centers throughout our body. Millions of people are now learning through the popularization of Gregorian chant music that this practice can serve as a delightful means of self-generation of energy.

LIFE ON EARTH

Subtle energetic influences from the earth, the moon, and the sun affect our lives as well. A mutual funds investor times his investments to coincide with a certain phase of the moon. His associates think he's loony, but he seems to be uncannily successful at what he's doing. Now researchers have found that for some unknown reason, mutual fund profits do in fact follow the lunar phases. This is not the only effect of the moon, however, as research has also found links to mental hospital admissions, suicides, and even lottery payouts.

This is one example among many showing that the energies of the moon and the sun are involved in a cosmic dance that can influence our behavior and play a role in our lives each day. Then, on a more down-to-earth level, there are the energies of the earth herself. Our home planet radiates its own energy field in which we are immersed our entire lives. We feel its pulsations, and we are affected by its moods.

Some energies surrounding us in our environment—such as the geomagnetic field—are known to science, but others remain the province of esoteric tradition. The notion that the earth is a living entity, with its own subtle energetic anatomy, has given rise to some very practical insights as to the nuances of life on earth. For example, Judith and Stanley have recently moved into a new home. Ever since the move, they have been having difficulty getting to sleep in the same bed together and have had to resort to separate bedrooms. They get along well in all areas of their relationship but for some reason just can't get to sleep together. They can't put their finger on it, but something seems to be "off" energetically.

Stanley has heard about *feng shui*, the Chinese art of working with subtle energies in the physical environment to create harmony and peace in one's surroundings. He decides to call in a *feng shui* consultant to evaluate their new home and see if anything can be done to improve the bedroom.

The consultant immediately notices that suspended from the ceiling in their bedroom is a large beam that runs lengthwise over the bed, splitting it down the center. The beam is a divisive force energetically, he explains. They decide to shift all the furniture in the room, moving the bed under a clear area of ceiling. After doing this, they discover that their sleep is harmonious and undisturbed.

IN THE HANDS OF A HEALER

Subtle energies are taking center stage in the quest for new healing technologies. The laying on of hands and other ways of working in the energy field without physical contact are enjoying a renaissance and are now being validated scientifically.

The power of energy-based healing is illustrated in the story of Jane, who had a hysterectomy five months ago. She has been unable to lie on her stomach ever since because of pain from the adhesions. She decides to go to a pain clinic and see what might be done to help her cope with the discomfort. She is introduced to Edith, a nurse who is also a biofeedback technician and pain control specialist.

Edith has a variety of ways of working with people, based on what her own intuitive guidance tells her in the moment. With Jane she decides to use a technique called off-body Therapeutic Touch. This involves no physical contact with Jane and no counseling. Rather, Edith simply focuses her attention on the energy field surrounding Jane's body and moves her hands through it.

After just one session Jane remarks, "I could feel the adhesions just melt. The pain was dissolved."

Another example is that of Shawna, who had received a head injury from an automobile accident and was having an ongoing problem with headaches. She went to another practitioner who worked in her aura, about two to three feet away from her. Shawna could feel the pain being "pulled" out of her head.

"I could swear I just had surgery," she said afterward, "because it felt as if something had been removed from that area."

The practitioner later explained, "I was aware of the experience of energy shifting, and I felt something come into my hand. I was trying to pull it out. She didn't experience any more pain in her head after that."

COUPLED TO THE COSMOS: OUR SUBTLE PERCEPTUAL ABILITIES

The energy healers who worked with Jane and Shawna were relying on their own abilities to perceive another person's energy field. Through practice and study, they have developed the abilities to detect qualitative changes and irregularities in energy. These are not unique gifts to them, however, as we are all capable of such sensitivity.

These abilities can be applied in some other very practical ways as well, outside the realms of healing and interpersonal relations. For example, a farmer had built a two-acre water pond at great expense but could not keep it full. Somehow the water kept seeping away, so he called in a dowser to consult. The dowser walked the entire perimeter of the pond with a pair of dowsing rods. At one point he put a stake in the ground with a little red flag on it. He told the farmer that if he'd dig down sixteen feet under this flag, he'd find where the pond was leaking.

The next day the farmer brought in a back hoe and dug straight down sixteen feet, where he found a gravel deposit, the source of the leak. After he sealed it with clay, the pond filled up.

We all have a remarkable capability to sense energies that may not be detectable by technological means. Each of us has, in effect, a subtle perceptual system that we often rely upon without even being aware of it. When we are aware, however, we can use these abilities for some very practical ends.

But what exactly are we perceiving? In the worldview of Western culture, which is based on what we think of as our physical reality, any kind of energy must be measurable by scientific instruments in order to be taken as real. According to conventional physics, there are only four kinds of energy in existence: electromagnetism, gravity, and two subatomic forces called the strong force and the weak force. Yet, consistent with the worldviews of indigenous cultures, ours, it appears, is a multidimensional reality, one in which we experience a whole *spectrum* of energies, some from the physical dimension and some from beyond. Indeed, Dr. Kenneth Klivington of the Salk Institute observes that many spiritual traditions "invoke the existence of previously unidentified forms of bioenergy that may interact [with the body's electrostatic] fields."[3]

How can it be that we are able to sense energies that the most sophisticated technology cannot detect? The answer lies in the human perceptual system itself. In *Beyond Biofeedback*, researcher Dr. Elmer Green of the Menninger Foundation states that

> [some energies] have not been detected with scientific instruments because these instruments have no parts above the [physical] level. Humans have all the parts and can therefore detect a greater spectrum of energies. Instruments are made of minerals, and lack the *transducer* components needed for detection.... In other words, living beings are coupled to the cosmos better than scientific devices, which are, after all, quite limited tools[4] (emphasis added).

Green introduces here a key term that will be referred to often in this book. A transducer is a device, like a microphone, that converts a signal from one form of energy to another. It appears that our ability to detect and work with subtle energies is based on a transducer system that involves our endocrine glands, our nervous system, and our own biofield—*to which these systems are coupled.* Of course, our biofield is itself a subtle phenomenon not measurable by technological instruments. It is the presence of our biofield that makes us alive, and when we die it is no longer present. In a sense, you could say our biofield *is* life, and it follows that *any living system* is a transducer because it bridges the physical dimension and the subtle realm beyond.

BY ANY OTHER NAME

As can be seen in the previous stories and in Muktananda's description of the world of energy at the beginning of this chapter, one of the challenges in the study of subtle energies is that the vocabulary can be very imprecise. Words are used very differently by different spiritual traditions, as well as by different scientists in the field.

Indeed, every culture has its own words to refer to this elusive force. Richard Pavek of the Biofield Research Institute in Sausalito, California, advocates the term "biofield" because it captures the meanings of *life field, life force,* and *life energy;* in essence, it names that elusive energy that must be present for life to exist. Pavek has also assembled the terms that are used in other cultures (see table 1).[5] It should be noted that these terms are commonly used to apply not just to the human energy field, but also to that of animals, plants, and the earth herself.

TABLE 1. SOME EQUIVALENT TERMS FOR BIOFIELD

Term	Source
Ankh	Ancient Egypt
Animal magnetism	Mesmer
Arunquiltha	Australian Aborigine
Bioenergy	United States, United Kingdom
Biomagnetism	United States, United Kingdom
Gana	South America
Ki	Japan
Life force	General usage
Mana	Polynesia
Manitou	Algonquin
M'gbe	Hiru pygmy
Mulungu	Ghana
Mumia	Paracelsus
Ntoro	Ashanti
Ntu	Bantu
Oki	Huron
Orenda	Iroquois
Pneuma	Ancient Greece
Prana	India
Qi (chi)	China
Subtle energy	United States, United Kingdom
Sila	Inuit
Tane	Hawaii

Term	*Source*
Ton	Dakota
Wakan	Lakota

One leading subtle energy researcher, William Tiller, Ph.D., an Emeritus Professor in Stanford University's Department of Materials Science, recounts the story of a meeting he once had with Muktananda. Tiller wanted to have a high-level conversation about the nature of subtle energy and get some validation for his ideas. Unfortunately, as he recalls, Muktananda could respond only with poetry.

"We have the language of apples and we want to talk about oranges," Tiller states, "so we will stumble, and we will have to be patient because we are going to have to learn a new language. The metaphysical language is not good enough because it is imprecise. You can use that language, but it will be vague. The problem is not in knowing, it's in articulating. At the point in space and time where we are, we have a certain language, a certain symbology, that we use to describe the known. There are many other possibilities."[6]

FINDING OUR WAY

That some subtle energies can be measured by technology, while others can be sensed only by the more elegant human perceptual system, poses an interesting dilemma. Our Western scientific tradition holds that unless something can be measured by the current technology, it does not exist. By this logic, of course, brain waves did not exist until the invention of EEG equipment.

In matters of spirit and energy, human experience must take primacy over science. In the words of the famous psychologist William James earlier this century, "[Science] might one day appear as having been a useful eccentricity rather than the definitely triumphant position which the sectarian scientist at present so confidently announces it to be."[7]

As we prepare to venture more deeply into the world of subtle energies, I have identified six principles that will guide our way. The principles are as follows:

1. *We are beings of energy.* When we think of our anatomy, we ordinarily think of our bones, muscles, organs, and other physical tissues. However, we also have an *energetic* anatomy. It is composed of multiple, interacting energy fields that envelop and penetrate our physical body, govern its functioning, and extend out into the world around us. This anatomy serves as a vehicle for the circulation of vital energies that enliven and animate our lives.

2. *The earth herself has an energetic anatomy, similar to our own, which influences our own energy field.* The entire earth and biosphere in which we live is one gigantic living organism, with its own metabolic and energetic qualities. Energy centers, energy channels, and energy fields emanating from the earth—as well as from plants and animals—are in many ways analogous to our own. By understanding the energetic life of this vast system of which we are a part, we can learn to live in a greater state of harmony and balance.

3. *Our relationships with other people are shaped by the interactions of our energies.* Our relationships are based on more than just psychology and family history. The energetic states that we bring to one another can introduce dynamics that are even more profoundly influential. Simply by touching another person, we influence what happens in their energy field. We can come to understand the impact of our own energy on others, and theirs on us, so as to relate with great clarity and effectiveness.

4. *Through the simple act of breathing, we traverse the boundary between the physical and the spiritual every moment.* There is no life activity more important than the simple act of breathing. It is our most immediate and intimate connection to the life force in every moment of our lives. It is a direct link to many expressions of subtle energy and spiritual attunement and a doorway to profound states of harmony and peace.

5. *We are each capable of sustaining and cultivating our vital energy.* Our vital energy has a metabolism that we can come to understand and work with. Through attending to the nourishment we take into our bodies, our patterns of rest and activity, and our practice of disciplines of energy cultivation, we can learn to become the stewards of our vital energy.

6. *Meditation, prayer, and healing are rich with subtle energy phenomena that represent contact with the spiritual dimension.* Many experiences we have during these practices can be taken as direct evidence of a state of communion or communication with Spirit. Healing abilities are present within us all, and we have been unknowingly using them throughout our lives.

It is my intention to provide you with ways to explore

these phenomena as directly as possible. The remainder of this book is devoted to how we can work with and benefit from subtle energies in everyday life, achieving rewards in health, harmony, and peace.

CHAPTER 2

EMBODIMENT:
OUR ENERGETIC ANATOMY

Human beings represent the juncture between Heaven and Earth, the offspring of their union, a fusion of cosmic and terrestrial forces. . . . Sustained by the power of Earth and transformed by the power of Heaven, humanity cannot be separated from Nature—we are Nature, manifest as people.
—HARRIET BEINFIELD AND EFREM KORNGOLD[1]

For my daughter, Rosalea, nursing was one of the highlights of her life for the first few years. I have many photos in which various states of bliss and ecstasy are apparent in her face during this primal exchange. While naturally we associate the image of a mother nursing a child with themes of bonding, intimacy, closeness, and oneness, what we don't see is that more than milk and love are being transferred as the child is cradled in the mother's energy field.

Of the four energies recognized by Western science, the one most commonly associated with our energetic anatomy is electromagnetism. Our electromagnetic qualities have been studied using magnetometers and other devices, and as you'll see later, such instruments have found that electromagnetic phenomena are associated with energy points and channels throughout our body.

The new science of neuromagnetics shows us that we are magnetic beings. Crystals of magnetite permeate our brain cells,[2] and the pineal gland, the "king gland" that regulates the endocrine system, just below the crown of the head, has a unique magnetostatic sensitivity.[3] There is also magnetite throughout the rest of the body, and this is why there is literally a magnetic connection between the mother and the child.

According to subtle energy researcher Robert Becker, M.D., we actually have a magnetic sense, which he believes may be the basis on which our brains function.[4] One can easily imagine how a child and mother can be in a state of magnetic resonance simply by virtue of their evolution in each other's energy fields.

In other species there are practical uses of the magnetic sense for survival. It is a popular theme in children's movies to see abandoned or lost pets finding their way back home across unknown territory. It is also well-known that animals such as migrating birds or fish return to their spawning grounds and can navigate over great distances with the help of magnetic field receptors in their brains.[5] It is theorized that these animals are able to tune in to the magnetic field of the earth to determine location and direction.

Does our magnetic sense explain why some of us have a better sense of direction than others? Even more intriguing, what role might this sense play in the energetics of our interpersonal relationships? Given the state of our knowledge of subtle perceptual abilities, our magnetic sense may well be just a precursor of a variety of such abilities yet to be discovered. I will often be referring to our magnetic nature later in this and other chapters.

OUR VITAL ENERGY

What is the difference between the body of a person who is alive and that of someone who died just an instant ago? The magnetite is still there, their blood chemistry is the same, their nervous system is still intact, and the structures of their bones, muscles, and organs are all unchanged. What has changed at the moment of death is nothing that the physical sciences can recognize as being part of our material reality. It is clear that some mysterious kind of animating force has departed.

Clearly life is imbued with an energy from beyond the electromagnetic, beyond the physical dimension. In Chapter 1 I noted the many names that have been used for that animating force that surrounds us, penetrates us, and makes us alive. In this discussion I will settle on vital energy.

Western cultures tend to consider this animating force unfathomable, and references to it are conspicuously absent in conventional medicine. On the other hand, the world's indigenous cultures have long been cultivating a working understanding of the ways and nuances of how this animating force manifests within us.

Other cultures have long embraced the notion that we are primarily energy beings and that in addition to our physical anatomy, we have an energetic anatomy. The mapping of our energetic anatomy is an interesting challenge because it involves a marriage of modern science and the world's spiritual traditions. The more science learns through research, the more its understanding comes into alignment with what has been taught in other traditions down the ages.

Our vital energy is not just an amorphous, random collection of energy. Rather, it seems to take the form of a distinct field that surrounds our body. This is another place where our language is less than fully adequate, as we bridge the boundary between physics and metaphysics.

THE BIOFIELD

Imagine for a moment that you are sitting ringside at a boxing match. There is a tremendous flurry of vigorous activity in the ring just a few feet away from you, and you are so close that you can sense the energy being radiated by the two fighters. Now imagine sitting in the back row of the balcony far above the event. How would you experience the fighters' energy differently? Now imagine you are watching the event on television, even further removed from the live experience.

Like other kinds of energy fields, the human energy field is strongest at its source and fades with distance. In this regard it behaves similarly to other fields recognized in physics. Other names for our energy field are the "biofield," "bioplasmic energy body," or "aura." No doubt you can think of people you know who seem to radiate stronger energy than others, as if their energy field is somehow bigger or more potent. In fact, we have many expressions in our language for this, such as when we describe someone as unusually "radiant," or a "high energy" person.

Another way our field is like other fields in nature is that it seems to have qualities of polarity, positive and negative, north and south. According to Richard Pavek of the Biofield

Research Institute, "Polarity between the hands and between different bodily regions appears to be equivalent to polar differences in electromagnetic fields."[6] Many traditions of energy healing, including Pavek's Shen Therapy, think of the right hand as the giving hand and the left as the receiving hand. In fact, a whole school of energy healing called "polarity therapy" was developed by Randolph Stone in the 1950s.[7]

SEEING IS BELIEVING

There is strong consensus among experts in the study of the biofield that the inner part, which extends about two to four inches from the surface of the skin, is the most visible and has the same shape and contours as the physical body. By "visible" I mean it can be seen under certain lighting conditions and with a certain amount of preparation in the observer. (See the exercises at the end of this chapter.)

We are all capable of seeing this, and your first experience of doing so will no doubt be very compelling, as was mine. I remember sitting in a large meeting room of a hotel in a course being led by the energy healer Mietek Wirkus. The participants sat against opposite walls about fifty feet away. The lights were dimmed and the windows heavily curtained. As I stared across the room at those on the other side, I relaxed my eyes, blinked as little as possible, and tried not to focus.

Gradually, as my eyes became more and more tired, it was as if they "gave up" struggling to see anything. It was at this moment of surrender that I began to see a glowing aura extending a few inches around the other people. The moment I tried to see it more clearly, it would disappear, but when I relaxed completely again it would reappear.

The explanation I was given for why I could see this was

that when the eyes become fatigued they cease having control over the visual process, and the "third eye," our intuitive faculty for seeing subtle energies, opens. Since that time I have also noticed, with less effort, the auras of plants and trees, which are particularly easy to see around dusk.

AURA PHOTOGRAPHY?

Can the human aura be captured on film? In recent years technology has evolved that captures aspects of the human energy field on both still photographs and video.[8] The equipment includes a combination of biofeedback sensors that you hold in your hands, a computer, and a special camera or video recorder. However, what is being captured on film is not the actual aura, but rather your electromagnetic field. The video capability is most interesting and may someday even have diagnostic value, because you can see changes in color, shape, and size of the field as a result of changes in moods and thoughts, hands-on healing, acupuncture, prayer, and other interventions.

As explained previously, technology does not have the transducers that we humans have in order to be able to perceive subtle energies from dimensions other than the physical. The human aura is much more involved than just the electromagnetic field. It comprises energies that are not electromagnetic and are not of the physical dimension.

A FIELD OF FIELDS

Our energy field has several subtle layers, called "subtle bodies," each encasing the others within it like a series of Russian dolls. As with other aspects of subtle energy, the vocabulary is inexact and some terms are used differently by different teachers. Clairvoyants and energy healers most commonly refer to a sequence of subtle bodies from the skin outward, as follows:

The "etheric body" (in England, the "blueprint field") is in the shape of the physical body and is believed to serve as a template from which the physical body is formed. Also called the "vital layer" or "thermal body," it can be detected with infrared cameras. Second is the "emotional body," usually described as the field of emotions and feelings surrounding us. Third is the "mental body," also called the "causal body," where thoughts, mental processes, and visual imagery reside. Fourth is the "astral body," associated with the heart and intuition. Fifth is the "etheric template," which contains the information to perfectly form the etheric body. Sixth is the "celestial body" and seventh is the "ketheric body," both of which are associated with spiritual attunement.[9]

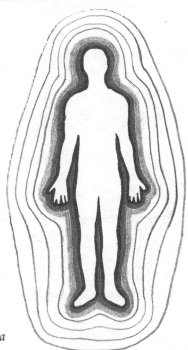

Figure 1.
The Human Aura

It is certainly not important to understand the esoteric details of the subtle bodies. What is of value, I believe, is understanding that the physical body is encased within, and fully penetrated by, an energy field that influences what happens on the physical level.

That the biofield influences what happens in our physical body is well proven by studies of energy healing, such as Therapeutic Touch, a form of healing in which the practitioner touches only the energy field of the recipient and not the physical body. Such healers commonly report that they can actually feel and see changes in the energy field as a result of using these techniques. They can also see changes caused by our moods and thoughts.

SUBTLE DIAGNOSIS

Energy healers can diagnose changes in our medical status by detecting irregularities or imbalances in our energy field. For example, a study by Dr. Susan Wright published in the *Western Journal of Nursing Research* explored whether disturbances in a person's energy field can be verified independently by different Therapeutic Touch practitioners. She studied a group of fifty-two chronic pain patients to determine whether the practitioners could independently agree on the location of energy field disturbances in the patients.[10]

Wright found that there was indeed a highly significant level of agreement among the experts as to the location of pain conditions, solely on the basis of their assessing the energy field of the patient with their hands. In addition, studies in this and other forms of energy healing have found that techniques such as smoothing, clearing, rebalancing, or otherwise working with the energy field can speed wound healing, reduce acute and chronic pain (including in burn victims), and help other conditions.

FLOWING RIVERS OF ENERGY

We've all had times when we felt as though our energy were "stuck" or not "moving" or "flowing" properly. These expressions have literal meaning because our vital energy is not just radiated outwardly but has patterns of circulation through us, via many rivers and tributaries. For thousands of years Oriental conceptions of our energetic anatomy both from China and India have shared the understanding that there are pathways along which our vital energy flows through our body, analogous to the unseen network of underground streams in the earth.

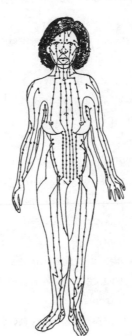

Figure 2.
Meridians and
Acupuncture Points

In Chinese medicine these pathways are called our "meridians," and in India they are called our *"nadis."* The geography of these pathways forms the basis of acupuncture and Oriental medicine. We now have scientific evidence that the map described in the ancient texts is indeed accurate. Our meridians emit light and can actually be seen with infrared photography.[11] Researchers have even found evidence that illness is associated with emission of less light from the meridians and that acupuncture increases the amount of light emitted.[12]

The AMI Breakthrough

The Japanese subtle energy researcher Hiroshi Motoyama has developed a machine that has been successful in locating and measuring energy flowing through the meridians. It is called the "AMI," an acronym for "apparatus for meridian identification."[13] The AMI is an extraordinarily sensitive device that measures the flow of ions through "ionic stream beds" in the interstitial layer of tissue just beneath the surface of our skin. The patterns of flowing ions detected by the AMI correspond with the geography of the acupuncture meridians recognized for thousands of years.

This flowing stream of ions is not our vital energy, or *chi,* itself. Rather, it is a parallel electromagnetic effect and indicator of the flow of *chi.* This is consistent with the idea that our energetic anatomy includes "octaves" of energies stacked one on another, from subtle to dense. Thus the strength of the flow of ions through a certain point, or meridian, is considered an indirect indication of the strength of the *chi* flowing through that stream bed.

It works simply by attaching electrodes to specific points

on the person's hands and feet and touching each electrode with a short, weak electrical pulse. In a ten-minute session the AMI can give a complete evaluation of the condition of a person's meridian system and the corresponding internal organs fed by those meridians. It can identify predisease states where *chi* is excessive or deficient and can even document the energetic effects of acupuncture, meditation, and other treatments.

According to Gerald Livesay, Ph.D., dean of research at the California Institute for Human Science in Encinitas, California, which is the American center for Motoyama's research, the accuracy of the AMI's output has been confirmed by experts using the traditional diagnostic methods of Oriental medicine such as pulse diagnosis. Research has also shown that it can detect changes in a person's energy flow while the person is receiving energy healing treatments, such as that from a *chi kung* healer.[14] While the AMI has previously been a very expensive, esoteric investigative device, it is now becoming available for wide distribution as a diagnostic tool in medicine.[15]

POOLS AND POINTS

In Chinese communities each morning you'll often see people out in the open practicing *tai chi* and *chi kung*. One of the movements you may notice is a vigorous massaging or rubbing of the ears, and this is for a very good reason. The ears have a high concentration of acupuncture points that can stimulate the flow of vital energy throughout our body. You can experience this for yourself right now by setting down the book for a minute. Pinch your ears between your thumbs and fingers and vigorously squeeze, rub, and massage them. The increased heat and sense of alertness you will feel are direct indications of increased flow of energy. (I encourage you to do this for a full minute now to experience the full effect.)

As our vital energy flows through us, it forms hundreds of tiny whirlpools along the way. In Chinese medicine these are our acupuncture points; in India, our *marma* points. These points can function somewhat like gates, where the flow of the stream can be modulated. To have acupuncture needles inserted into these points, or to have them touched or manipulated, can have a profound effect on the overall circulation of vital energy through your body. Indeed, acupuncture has been proven effective in pain control, reducing symptoms of disease, and even curing drug abuse and alcoholism.

The hundreds of energy points that pepper the surface of our body have distinct electrical characteristics. For example, studies in China have found them to have much higher electrical conductivity and higher amplitude of the electric current wave than other points on our body.[16]

What then of the current fashion statements of piercing the ears, nose, lips, navel, genitals, or other areas of the body with metal objects? It does not take much imagination to see that adorning the body in such a way may interfere with the harmonious, balanced circulation of one's vital energy, particularly if key acupuncture meridians are being constantly blocked or stimulated.

ENERGY CENTERS

While our acupuncture points could be thought of as tiny energy centers, we also have several much larger energy centers. These are major centers of both electromagnetic activity and the pooling and circulation of vital energy and are recognized in indigenous cultures the world over. In the Huna tradition of Hawaii, they are called *"auw"* centers; and in the Cabala, they are the "tree of life" centers. In the Taoist Chinese tradition the term is *"dantien,"* and in yogic theory they are called "chakras."

The energy center that all traditions acknowledge at the core of our energetic anatomy is the heart, and this is also recognized now by modern science. The power of the heart is revealed in the experience of Harold, who has just finished viewing a film of Mother Teresa serving the poor and dying in the slums of Calcutta. While films with emotional themes have always moved him, he is particularly touched by the depths of love, compassion, and selfless service—*agape*, or pure altruistic love—revealed in this documentary. With tears in his eyes he describes the sensation of his heart feeling "more open" and adds that the vague feelings of depression that had been lingering for several months seem to have lifted.

Harold's feelings are not uncommon, but what has happened on an energetic level? Watching that particular film triggered a cascade of subtle energy phenomena that profoundly affected his body. Scientists now know that our heart creates the body's strongest electromagnetic field and that with deep feelings of love, compassion, and caring this field actually expands and strengthens.

Each beat of our heart produces a wave of electromagnetic energy that pulses outward in all directions. One of the effects of opening our heart is that the pattern of these waves becomes more *coherent.* That is, while there is normally a degree of irregularity in the wave pattern from one beat to the next, when we feel love the waves become dramatically more uniform and consistent.[17]

According to research conducted at the Institute of HeartMath in Boulder Creek, California, this more refined, coherent wave pattern reflects greater balance and harmony in our nervous system[18] and is also associated with improved immunity.[19] Through the simple experience of watching a film, Harold literally transformed the energetic environment of his entire body.

Our heart's energy field influences every cell of our body throughout our lifetime. Mystics have always maintained that the heart, rather than the brain, is the center of our being. As Alice Bailey states: "The soul, seated in the heart, is . . . the central nucleus of positive energy by means of which all the atoms of the body are held in their right place. . . ."[20]

The energy field of Harold's heart actually radiates beyond his physical form to those around him. As we all know, being near someone who is feeling love or tenderness, like a nursing mother or a child petting a puppy, feels very different from being in the presence of someone in a state of agitation. When we are in a coherent field, our own energy naturally coheres in response, leaving us more peaceful and calm.

THE CHAKRAS

In yogic theory, the heart is in the middle of seven main centers called the "chakras," which are vertically aligned up the center of the body from the base of the pelvis to the top of the head and are connected by the *nadi* system. There are three major *nadis:* the *shushumna,* which goes up the center of the spine, and the *ida* and *pingala,* which weave their way up through the body, crisscrossing at the chakras. Chakra theory gives us a comprehensive understanding of the role of the major centers in our energetic anatomy, so I will focus further on it here.

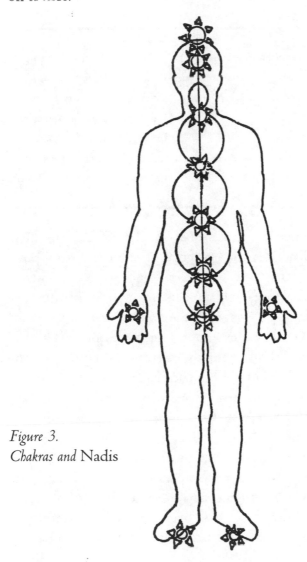

Figure 3.
Chakras and Nadis

Our chakras are like spinning disks or spheres of energy and function like portals or gateways through which energy enters and leaves our body. Each chakra governs and energizes a particular part of our physiology as well. The locations of the chakras, and their presumed "couplings" to our physical systems, are as follows:[21]

First chakra	Location: perineum	Influences: urogenital system
Second chakra	Location: just below navel	Influences: urogenital system
Third chakra	Location: solar plexus	Influences: digestive system
Fourth chakra	Location: heart	Influences: circulatory system
Fifth chakra	Location: throat	Influences: respiratory system
Sixth chakra	Location: forehead	Influences: central nervous system
Seventh chakra	Location: crown of head	Influences: central nervous system

Scientific Evidence. Hiroshi Motoyama found the first objective evidence for the existence of the chakras by positioning copper electrodes a small distance from the body in front of the chakras.[22] His conclusions were verified by Dr. Valerie Hunt at UCLA through the more conventional means of using EMG (electromyograph) electrodes placed directly on the skin. Hunt actually detected regular, high-frequency signals coming from the chakra points.[23]

Motoyama has also developed a device called the chakra instrument, which detects the number of photons (units of light) being emitted from the locations of the chakras. The more active a chakra is, the more photons it emits. An advanced meditator or other person whose chakras are "awakened" will emit unusually high numbers of photons from the chakras. This has been verified in laboratory studies with meditators in a darkened room. Motoyama also found that by concentrating the mind on a certain chakra, people can dramatically increase the level of photons being emitted.[24]

As with the acupuncture points and meridians, the energies that we can measure coming from the chakras are not vital energy. Rather, they are "secondary effects" of the presence of vital energy—in a sense, its imprint in the physical domain. The chakras can be thought of as transducers of higher dimensional energies into physical energies.

There is a great deal of popular literature about the nature of the chakras. Obviously, most of this is based on yogic theory or direct experience by mystics, healers, and students of subtle energy. Still, the consensus is remarkable. Next I will describe some of the more important characteristics of the chakras.

Spinning. One of the more fascinating features of our chakras is their spinning. Each chakra is like a spinning turbine but is spinning in two ways simultaneously. There is a force spinning in a clockwise direction and another force spinning in a counterclockwise direction, and both forces occupy the same space. This, of course, is hard for us to imagine because we cannot fathom two whirlpools of water in the same space. According to Hector Ramos, a teacher of *pranic* healing in Berkeley, California, there is a dynamic balance between the two directions of spin within the chakra. One direction is associated with receiving or drawing energy into the chakra and the other with releasing energy out through the chakra.

Whether this dynamic balance swings in one direction or the other—that is, more energy is coming out than is going in, or vice versa—is determined by many factors. One is our conscious intention to give or receive through that chakra, such as when giving to or receiving healing from another person. Healers who work with energy directly always set their intention in mind first before entering the recipient's energy field. The intention may be to send or channel fresh healing energy out their hands into the other person, or it may be to absorb some negative energy from the other person and then release it into the ground.

Another factor in the balance of the spinning is our general level of physical health. If we have been exercising, sleeping, and eating well, we may have what others would describe as "radiant health," and this cliché would actually be an accurate representation of what is happening with our energy: we have an abundance of energy that is naturally over-flowing without any conscious intention. On the other hand, if we are depressed or sick, we are like a sponge and will absorb energy from those around us who have an abundance. Indeed, this is why it feels so good to be around others who have a lot of energy: it raises our own.

This is also why some therapists and health care practitioners get "burned out." They may have entered their work with an abundance of enthusiasm and energy, but they were unable to protect and conserve their own vital energy effectively, and it was absorbed or drained from them in their constant contact with people who were sick or had low energy.

Therapists and healers who are successful in maintaining their own energy often have a routine of self-protection before the healing encounter. This may be as simple as a prayer for self-protection or a visualization of a protective sheath of white light surrounding their body. They also have a heightened awareness of the reality of the need to balance work with play and pleasure, replenishing their own vital energy regularly.

Opening and Closing, Expansion and Contraction. Each chakra is a dynamic vortex or portal to the outside world that, while constantly spinning, releasing, and receiving energy, can be relatively more open or more closed at different times and in different situations. Our daily experience of these principles is embedded in our language, as we have coined certain phrases to express them.

For example, the term "tight-assed" reflects a closed base chakra, suggesting a state of holding on as a result of rigid attitudes that are really an expression of underlying fear of change. On the other hand, the ability to "let go" and have a more open first chakra indicates a willingness to move through fear rather than contract around it and hold back.

For the second chakra, matters of opening and closing are commonly associated with sexual trauma or dysfunction. Impotence in men is understood in terms of a closing off of the flow of energy through the sex center. Vaginismus in women—the literal closing off of the vagina through muscular contraction around it—is an even more obvious expression of this theme. "Letting go" sexually suggests an ability to enjoy sex and have a full "flow" of energy through the sex center.

We have all experienced having a "knot in the stomach," which is an indication that the third chakra is closed and tight. Perhaps you can recall a movie in which a policeman or military officer walks up to someone's door to tell of the death of a loved one. You can imagine the feeling of contraction against the blow of this information, which may first be felt in the pit of the stomach as a clenching or holding sensation. It is as if we are attempting to armor ourselves from an external blow to our vital organs. We feel a great deal of our vulnerability in the abdomen—an exposed, soft area of the body that is not protected by bony structures. Another expression of this vulnerability is the notion of "feeling kicked in the stomach."

The heart center is another obvious point of dynamic closing and opening. "Closed-hearted," "open-hearted," "warm-hearted," "cold-hearted," "soft-hearted," and "hard-hearted" are all qualities that we have experienced in ourselves or others. The vulnerability we feel in our heart is expressed in the notion that a heart can be "broken," which reveals our intuitive awareness of how much our emotional well-being resides in that energy center. Anyone who has experienced a broken heart can understand why a person who has recently suffered a loss would tend to "close" it to a degree as part of a healing process.

There are, of course, countless other expressions attributing various qualities to the heart, such as the "angry heart," "good-hearted," "bad-hearted," "a joyful heart," "striking fear in the hearts of men," "a jealous heart," "an evil heart" (of which "mean-spirited" is a variation), and "kind-hearted." But perhaps the strongest image of contraction associated with the heart is the feeling of having "a dagger in the heart"—a sense of woundedness at a point of deep emotional vulnerability and from which we must contract.

We have all experienced opening and contraction of the throat chakra by struggling with a "lump in the throat." At times of great sadness or the "welling up" of emotion, it is as if the throat is the shaft of a well that penetrates downward through the energy centers below, and emotional energy "wells up" and has to pass through the throat center in order to be released through the organs of expression above—the mouth through sound and the eyes through tears. The opening of the throat chakra is also experienced through singing, and we have all been "choked up" while singing particularly poignant or emotionally charged songs, such as in religious settings. I used to feel a lump in my throat while singing my school's alma mater song before football games.

The opening of the third eye center is at the core of our concerns about understanding others and being understood. Do you "see" what I mean? Can you "see" the other person's point of view? Can you "see" the big picture, or are you taking a "narrow point of view"? Do you have "tunnel vision" or a "myopic" view? It's all a matter of "perspective," and we prefer to be around people who can see things our way. This is all directly associated with being "open-minded" rather than "closed-minded" or "narrow-minded."

The crown chakra is a little more obscure in terms of everyday expressions of language, because we are not a very spiritually based culture; but there are a few. Such phrases as "an enlightened attitude" or an "inspired vision" suggest an infusion of light or spirit from above into our thinking. We seem universally to accept the top of the head as a point of transit of Spirit into the body. This is particularly apparent in religious traditions in which we are "blessed" by a religious authority placing his or her hand on the top of our head. You do not see them touching other energy centers for religious purposes. The sprinkling of "holy water" is also directed to this energy center.

The Palm Chakras: Extensions of the Heart. There are many smaller chakras throughout the body, and the chakras in the palms of our hands come into play in many symbolic ways. When we receive a wound or injury, such as a bump on the head, why do we instinctively place a hand on it? Such a gesture not only provides some physical protection in the form of a barrier against further trauma, but it also brings the chakras in the palm of our hand directly into contact with the injured area. In the chakra system, our hands and arms are considered extensions of our heart chakra, and our hand chakras radiate the healing and soothing energies of our heart. A similar principle is at play when spiritual healers practice the laying on of hands, yet this is something all of us have done in our lives countless times without thinking about it.

When we shake hands with another person, we are in a sense directly contacting the pathway to one another's heart. When we touch a person on the shoulder, it is as if we are touching them with a conduit through which energy can flow from our heart. And in times of grief or loss, such as the loss of a loved one, we may touch a person's belongings or some other symbol of his life, as if to "reach out" in search of another heartfelt connection. A graphic image of this was a photo of Rob Stein, former chief of staff of Commerce Secretary Ron Brown, who died in a plane crash in Croatia, standing with head down and arms outstretched, his palms resting on Brown's casket.

THE WINDOWS OF THE SOUL

Have you ever had the sense that someone was staring at you, only to turn around and see that you were right? What were you sensing? Could it be you were feeling an energy that was impinging on you from the other person's eyes?

The eyes are small chakras that are very important to our experience each day. The pupils, with their disklike shape, even look like chakras. They expand and contract, open and close, to regulate the amount of light, which is of course a kind of energy coming in. But the eyes also send energy out. Research in the former Soviet Union found that the eyes emit electromagnetic radiation,[25] which, as we have seen, is but the lowest of multiple "levels" of energy moving through us.

As in the Chinese saying "Where the mind goes, the *chi* follows," vital energy is released and directed outward through the eyes. When we fix our gaze on something, our mind is in a sense being sent out through the eyes, carrying our energy with it. The "cold stare," the "evil eye," or the feeling that someone is "looking right through me" all reveal qualities of energy that we can send with the eyes. Likewise, we can also send love, appreciation, and acceptance.

When we make eye contact with another person, it is a very revealing experience, both for them and for us. It is a form of both self-disclosure and vulnerability: we are "revealing" our energy as it comes out through our eyes, and we are receiving the other's, as the eyes function as portals through which energy can enter. The other person can literally pierce our boundaries, as their energy enters us through our eyes. This is why eye contact can sometimes be so uncomfortable. By turning away, or by closing our eyes, the final defense, we escape this exchange and protect our vulnerability.

BEING "IN SYNC"

When Joe Montana broke the record for consecutive pass completions without a miss, everyone said he was "in sync." When Michael Jordan scores forty points in a basketball game, he's described as "in sync." We know when we're "on" and when we're having an "off" day. But what does it really mean to be "in sync"? This is an expression that we all understand intuitively, and it has a real basis in our energetic anatomy.

As you've seen by now, we are a system of energy centers.

I'm going to introduce a mechanical term here to help explain what happens when our energy centers work together. Anything that produces a rhythmic, cyclic pattern of movement or energy is an "oscillator." A pendulum clock, a spinning hula hoop, a Frisbee flying through the air, a merry-go-round, a gyroscope, the engine and wheels of a car, a pumping heart, our brain waves, and our chakras are all oscillators. In the case of the human body, our oscillators produce electromagnetic output as well as rhythmic waves or pulsations of vital energy, or *chi*.

ENTRAINMENT: GETTING YOURSELF TOGETHER

What is fascinating about oscillators is that they can become entrained with each other. This was discovered accidentally in 1665 by the inventor of the pendulum clock. He had a room full of clocks and found that over time they would all "entrain"—that is, they would all start swinging together synchronously. When he interrupted this pattern so they swung randomly, within an hour or two they would all "sync" back up again.

Entrainment means that the frequency of the pulsation or movement of two different oscillators comes together. It happens at all levels of nature, from atoms to cells. Flocks of birds and schools of fish moving synchronously are examples, and there can also be entrainment between people, such as when the heart rate energy wave of a mother and nursing infant become entrained. And entrainment between two or more people can be particularly helpful in situations demanding teamwork, with each person functioning as an oscillator.

This is what we are experiencing in those special moments

when we feel in total harmony, peace, and balance within our bodies and our surroundings. When all of our systems are in sync there's a feeling of seamless integration, ease, and gracefulness as we are able to perform perfectly and efficiently at whatever we are doing.

When Your Heart Leads the Way

In a room full of pendulum clocks, all the other clocks will entrain to the one with the biggest pendulum, for it is putting out the strongest pulsation of energy. Likewise, in the human body, the heart is our most powerful oscillator, and as such it is capable of "pulling" our other oscillators into entrainment with it.

In terms of electromagnetic power, the heart produces about 2.5 watts with each beat, enough to power a night-light or a small radio. The amplitude of the electrical wave produced by the beating heart is about fifty times that of our brain waves, and the heart's magnetic field is about a thousand times stronger than that of the brain. It's enough power that, according to Rollin McCraty of the Institute of HeartMath, our electrocardiogram can be measured in every cell in our body, from the toe to the ear.

McCraty and his colleagues have also found that the effects of our thoughts and emotions on the heart can be seen in the wave forms that show up in our electrocardiogram.[26] When we are under a lot of stress or experiencing depression, anxiety, or frustration, the wave pattern becomes more irregular and incoherent. We may experience such a bodywide sense of disharmony and imbalance among all our oscillating systems—feeling "out of sync."

When we are in a state of calm and peace, the heart's

energy wave form is smoother and more coherent. This tends to bring our other oscillators into entrainment, promoting optimal health and well-being. Our heart even pulls our brain waves and oscillating cells in our digestive system into entrainment. Head, heart, and gut are literally in sync. The researchers have found that this state brings corresponding increases in clarity, buoyancy, intuitive awareness, and inner peace.

As you might expect, our heart signal does not stop at the skin, but radiates into the space around us. The field of the heart can actually be measured four or five feet away with a magnetometer. Since the wave forms of this field change with our thoughts and emotions, you can see how it is possible that with our magnetic sensitivity, we can sense "bad vibes" or "good vibes" from someone around us and why we feel uncomfortable around someone who is angry or agitated, depressed or fearful. We are all transmitters and receivers.

To this point we have been exploring structures of our energetic anatomy. Now I would like to turn to a consideration of the subtle qualities of our energy.

THE FIVE ELEMENTS

Roger is known to his friends as a fiery character. He has red hair, a pinkish complexion, and a volatile temper, yet he can also be passionately loving and loves to laugh and dance. Roger has a lot of the element called "fire."

Think back for a moment to your high school science class. Perhaps you can recall a large poster hanging on the wall with rows of numbers and abbreviations, called the "Periodic

Table of the Elements." You learned that there are over a hundred elements, types of atoms that are considered the building blocks of matter. To Western science, the world is composed of the elements of the periodic table. In the Oriental view, which sees the universe as an energetic domain, an analogous usage of the term "element" is applied to different aspects of our vital energy.

In the ancient Indian science of Ayurveda and its offspring, the Taoist Chinese system, the energetic universe is made up of five elements. The interworkings of these five elements explain all life processes and govern what actually happens in our body. Because of their unique characteristics and how the elements interact with each other, they are given symbolic names from nature.

While there is a great deal of similarity between the two systems, Ayurveda and Chinese medicine use slightly different names and meanings of the elements. In Ayurveda they are called earth, water, fire, air, and ether. In the Chinese system they are called earth, water, fire, metal, and wood. I will use the Ayurvedic vocabulary in this discussion.

Just as you will find the periodic table of elements on the wall in any chemistry lab, you will often find charts of the five elements on the office walls of practitioners of Oriental medicine. However, unlike the elements of matter, they are not unrelated and separate building blocks. Rather, they are weaving together constantly, complementing and balancing one another.

A good analogy for the relationships among the five elements can be found in the structure of a plant. As explained by David Frawley and Vasant Lad, "The root corresponds to earth, as the densest and lowest part, connected to the earth. The stem and branches correspond to water, as they convey the water or sap of the plant. The flowers correspond to fire, which manifests light and color. The leaves correspond to air, since through them the wind moves the plant. The fruit corresponds to ether, the subtle essence of the plant. The seed contains all five elements, containing the entire potential plant within itself."[27]

The relationships among the elements are the focus of the world's traditions of energy-based medicine, including Chinese medicine and Ayurveda. The five elements need to be flowing in a smooth and balanced way with one another for optimal health, and turbulence or imbalance among them is considered the underlying cause of disease and unhappiness. For example, a person like Roger, with an excess of the element fire, is more vulnerable to high blood pressure and heart attack.

The influences of the elements are felt in all areas of life, including our personality, relationships, interests, preferences, nutritional needs, mental and emotional proclivities, and health.

GETTING PRACTICAL: AYURVEDA AND THE *DOSHAS*

As the four-thousand-year-old "science of life" from India, Ayurveda offers us a very practical way to understand the workings of the five elements in our daily lives. In Ayurveda they are organized into three dynamic functional pairings, known as *doshas*. The three *doshas* are *vata* (ether and air), *pitta* (fire and water), and *kapha* (earth and water).

Each of us has all three *doshas*, and the interweaving of the *doshas* governs our physiological and psychological functions. In fact, together they determine our personal metabolism and our mind-body type. The unique pattern that they take in each of us at our conception is called our *prakriti*.

50

Some of us have a *prakriti* in which there is a clear domi-
nance of a single *dosha*—either *vata*, *pitta*, or *kapha*. Others have
a slightly more complex *prakriti* in which there are equal influences of multiple *doshas*, such as *vata-pitta*, *pitta-kapha*, *vata-kapha*;
and still others have the most complex, where all three are
equally strong. The influences and qualities of the individual
doshas are described briefly in this section, and a questionnaire
to determine your own *dosha* is included in the exercises at the
end of this chapter.[28]

Vata is considered the lightest of the *doshas*. As such, it represents easy movement, at all levels and in all ways. *Vata*
governs the movement of cells circulating in the body, the
movement of fluids and materials through the cells and
through the body, the activity of organs and muscles as they
perform their functions, the motor and sensory functions of
the person as they move through the world, and the
movement of thoughts through the mind.

People in whom *vata* predominates tend to be active, alert,
and restless. They need to be involved in movement and
activity in order to feel in a state of harmony. They usually
have a lot of energy, though they may not be doing anything
with it. They are often fiddling, doodling, and moving
around. They tend to disperse or sometimes waste energy. In
the same way, a *vata* person is more likely to disperse money
easily. *Vatas* may fritter it away at a flea market and may even
dispense with a large inheritance rather quickly. A *vata* person
may prefer to be an artist or musician rather than an
employee of someone else. *Vata* disperses.

Pitta is transformative energy. The digestion and transformation of food into energy, and ultimately into the tissues of
the body, is considered a *pitta* function. *Pitta* governs the
digestive functions, body temperature, and other metabolic
functions. Fire is a good symbol to represent this *dosha*.

Pitta people are often involved in transformative kinds of activity, taking one thing and changing it into something else. They may also have fiery qualities in their personality, such as a lot of anger, irritability, a red face, aggressiveness, or competitiveness. *Pittas* would be more inclined to budget their money and transform it into useful things or projects to improve their standard of living. They make good CEOs. *Pitta* transforms.

Kapha is the densest element, providing the physical structure and contents of the body. Comprising earth and water, it represents accumulation and the formation of dense structure. *Kapha* is what heals wounds, fills spaces, and brings physical strength and resiliency to the body. *Kapha* is bodily tissue, fluid, and substance.

Kapha people tend to be heavier, slower moving, and more solid and have greater muscular strength. They may also be more stable and grounded, with a more steady, tranquil personality. They would tend to hold on to money and would be more likely to be wealthy because of their tendency to accumulate. *Kapha* people don't like to move around much, and they tend to make good middle managers. *Kapha* accumulates.

As you might well imagine, the *doshas* have a lot of impact on how we relate to others and on the quality and balance of our relationships. I will discuss this in more detail in chapter 4.

THE MIND AND SUBTLE ENERGY

Imagine that you are sitting down at the end of a long, hard, stressful day, really feeling depleted. Now imagine that when going through your mail, you find a letter from a long-lost friend to whom you had lent some money many years ago. Your friend has won the lottery and is now repaying your kindness a hundredfold with an enormous check. What kinds of changes would occur in your emotional and energetic state?

Perhaps the most important aspect of all in our energetic anatomy, and one so obvious it is often overlooked, is the mind. We have all experienced the mind as a source of energy, but it seems to operate outside the laws of the physical world. Indeed, it can be found nowhere in physical space, yet its influence can be felt everywhere throughout our physical and energetic anatomy.

The mind can be used as a tool to direct the flow of vital energy through the body, as in *chi kung* and *tai chi*. Certain repetitive or passionate thoughts can also cause a "pooling" of energy in the various chakras. Any sex therapist will attest to the power of fantasy in drawing energy to the second (sexual) chakra and creating physical sexual arousal.

Having loving feelings, as in the case of Harold's story earlier, changes the energy of the heart chakra. Research from the Institute of HeartMath proves that feeling love and sincere appreciation increases the coherence in the heart's energy wave pattern, altering the electromagnetic field emanating from the heart.

There is no doubt that these "energetic events" are happening in the body, but they are being orchestrated by our consciousness. Studies in biofeedback have also shown that the mind can be used to control many body functions such as skin temperature, pain, and healing of bodily tissues.[29]

BUT IS THE MIND "ENERGY"?

It depends on how you define "energy." If energy has to originate from a source that is based in the physical time-space dimension, like one of the four kinds of energy recognized by physics, then mind is not energy. It cannot be captured or measured, nor can it even be localized to the brain tissue.

However, if you take a broader view of the meaning of "energy" and define something as energy by virtue of its capacity to produce effects, then the mind certainly qualifies. As you will see later in this book, there are many instances where from a distance away, far beyond the reach of our energy field, our mind can influence other people and the growth of plants. I will be telling you about the proven effects of prayer over hundreds of miles.

The confusion over whether mind should be considered as energy is easily resolved if we accept that mind is "non-local"—that is, it is not confined to our physical time-space reality, but straddles across multiple dimensions of reality. Its home is in a higher dimension, one that encapsulates our physical time-space dimension but is not confined to it. That higher dimension has been called by many names, such as "the field of consciousness," "the higher mind," "the One Mind," "the Divine Mind," and others.

The mother who instantly knows that her son has been wounded in a war half a world away, the parent who suddenly knows that a child has been injured in a car crash, or the lover who feels a pain in her heart as she senses that her beloved is being unfaithful at this moment are all tapping into that higher "mind field" to know things at a distance. We can also influence events and even send information to someone at a distance, as has been proven in ESP experiments and studies of the effects of long-distance prayer.

In this book I will be taking the perspective that mind is energy, but of a special, higher order—one that can influence other energies by our conscious intention. For now, let us expand our focus to the energetic anatomy of the earth herself.

EXERCISE

Feeling Your Own Energy

One exercise for feeling energy involves placing your hands in the air in front of your body, facing each other, about three or four inches apart. Let them be curved naturally, as if you are holding a ball. Now concentrate your attention on the space between your hands. Note any sensations you feel. Usually the first sensation noticed is the warmth being radiated by the hands toward each other.

Now experiment with very subtle movements of your hands, just a fraction of an inch, very slowly, closer and then farther apart. Do this a few times and see if you notice any other sensations. You may feel as if you are working with a spongy ball, compressing it and allowing it to expand. Or you may notice a sensation of tingling or vibration. To some people it feels as though the fingers of opposing hands are connected by rubber bands that are being stretched as the hands move apart. Others describe this as a sensation like taffy being stretched between the hands. Move your hands slowly apart and together in a variety of ways, but always keeping some space between them and noticing what sensations are there.

Each hand has minor chakras in its palm and fingertips. These chakras are radiating energy that can be felt in this exercise. At first your mind may tell you, I'm just imagining this, and it may take some time and practice to convince yourself that the sensations you are experiencing are actually palpable evidence of the energy coming from your hand chakras.

EXERCISE

Feeling Energy of Another

This exercise is done with a partner. Begin by pressing your left thumb hard into the center of the palm of your right hand, and the right thumb into the left hand, to stimulate those chakras. Your right hand will be your giving hand and the left your receiving hand. Then sit facing your partner and place your giving hand in the air, facing down over the receiving hand of your partner, which is facing up. Likewise, the partner places his giving hand in the air, facing down over your receiving hand.

Now sit patiently and notice what sensations arise. You may begin to experiment with subtle, slow movements of your hands to explore the sensations, but without touching. After a while discuss what you have been noticing.

Some people experience the sensation as being like what you feel when you put your hand out the window of a moving car to play with the wind. Or it may feel like a spotlight shining on you or like playing with a spongy rubber ball, or it may be just a general sensation of tingling, warmth, or vibration.

EXERCISE

What Is Your Dosha?

Following is a list of the tendencies associated with each *dosha* described in Ayurveda. Use this to help you determine your predominant *dosha(s)*. Simply total the number of items that apply to you for each *dosha* to get an idea of how strongly each is represented in your energetic nature and where imbalances may lie.[30]

Vata Tendencies

I often feel restless, unsettled.
My sleep comes slowly or is easily interrupted.
I tend to overexert.
I'm easily fatigued.
I tend to be constipated.
I feel anxious and worry too much.
I'm underweight.

Pitta Tendencies

I tend to be demanding or critical.
I'm a perfectionist.
I get frustrated or angry easily.
I have sensitive skin.
I get irritable and impatient easily.
My hair is prematurely gray or thinning early.
I don't tolerate hot weather well.

Kapha Tendencies

I often feel complacent or dull.
My skin is oily to normal.
I tend to have slow digestion.
I feel lethargic.
I can be possessive, overattached.
I tend to oversleep.
I'm overweight.

CHAPTER 3

SPIRITUS MUNDI: SUBTLE ENERGIES IN NATURE AND THE ENVIRONMENT

I simply quiet my mind and try to feel the response of my body. I tune into an instinctual awareness of the quality of the energy that permeates a place, a sensory intuition that extends to people, animals, trees, and even rocks.
—JEAN SHINODA BOLEN, M.D.[1]

Fifty miles north of San Francisco in western Sonoma County there are several swaths of redwood forest gracing the hills that separate the wine country from the ocean. Just outside the small town of Occidental is an area where the redwoods are particularly dense. One day my friend Steve, who lives near one of these groves, invited me and another friend to "come and see the cathedral" nearby.

Not knowing what he was talking about, we followed him to a grove that from the outside looked like any other with many tall, straight redwoods that, as always, evoke a feeling of stillness and majesty in their presence. However, upon entering the grove, we came to a stand of twenty-four trees in a perfect circle of about fifteen feet in diameter. "My feeling is that these are the third generation," explained Steve. "The original tree in the center died out long ago, then those sprouting up from its roots made a circle around it. They later died out, and we now have their descendants."

The center of the circle is like a big bowl, as the root structures of the surrounding trees seem to be elevated above ground level. On one side, seven trees are joined together at the hip, forming a redwood wall that goes up about six feet, with their roots forming an altar in front.

We all sat down in the bowl and could sense that this is indeed a very distinct power spot. The energy emanating upward through the center of the cathedral had a quality of profound stillness, softness, and strength—it was an amazing place to just sit quietly.

Time seemed to stand still, and to speak would have seemed like a violation. My sense was that the circle was like a vortex that acted like a funnel for the energy radiated by the earth upward through the cathedral. But the length of the trees as they reached upward into the sky seemed to add something to the equation—as if the trees were like conduits, transmitters, or acupuncture needles on the earth's surface, connecting it to the sky.

Perhaps all trees serve this same function, joining heaven and earth.

The pleasant feelings that arise from being in nature come from more than simply the fact that we are resting our minds and exercising our physical body. The healing powers of nature work primarily through the medium of energy to have their rejuvenescent effects on our own energy.

In the ancient Oriental healing tradition of *chi kung* (a form of meditation on the circulation of vital energy), many of the practices involve tapping into the vital energy of nature. It can be drawn up through our feet and legs from the earth, from the air through our breath and the palms of our hands, from trees through direct contact by our hands, and even through our hair with the help of visualization.

One popular exercise is to tap into the energy of a tree by standing facing it and placing your hands on each side of the trunk. While holding this position, you visualize drawing the energy of the tree in through your hands, circulating it through your body, and releasing it back into the earth through your feet. A variation of this is to imagine drawing it in through your left hand, circulating it through your body, and releasing it back into the tree through your right hand, completing a circuit between your heart and the tree.

The principle of vital energy coursing through energetic pathways and vortexes is present throughout nature. Just as science has confirmed that humans and animals have meridians and points that emit light and have higher electrical conductivity, plants also have an energetic anatomy. This was shown when researchers inserted acupuncture needles into the stems of soybean plants and found the temperatures in the veins of the leaves increased, indicating that more vital energy was flowing through the plant. Clearly plants are like conduits or transmitters of energy from the earth.[2] Plants are well-known also to radiate their own biofields, as can be seen in the aura that can be captured on film.

THE RINGS OF GAIA

Does the earth itself have an energetic anatomy similar to our own? This idea has inspired poets and visionaries for millennia. Many civilizations have indeed shared the understanding that the planet is embedded within an energy field or subtle energy body. This field is commonly thought to take the form of a complex web of energy lines running through the earth and across her surface, forming a spherical, gridlike matrix.

To anthropologist Bethe Hagens of Union Institute Graduate School in Cincinnati, the geometric form of this grid represents "the etheric skeleton of the earth, the morphogenetic field for its creation."[3] Others have referred to it as an organizing lattice or matrix of cosmic energy. In the words of author Richard Leviton, it is "the spiritual link for the blending of cosmic and terrestrial energies . . . more like Mother Gaia's exterior skeletal energy structure, her prototypal design and predetermined matrix of energy and light from which her physical body was manifested."[4]

Archaeologists have found that many ancient cultures shared such a "geometric worldview," with a very sophisticated understanding of spherical geometry. This theme is amazingly consistent across traditions. For example, a Lakota Sioux creation story refers to "the fifteen hoops" in forming the earth, and these circles are used in their cosmological diagrams. Plato described the earth as a spherical "hexakis icosahedron," a geometric figure based on fifteen circles of equal size, intersecting sixty-two times and forming 120 identical right triangles on its surface.

The Egyptians, from whom Plato got his geometry, built

the Great Pyramid of Giza on what they determined to be the "orienting" ring, one of the five hoops that pass north and south from pole to pole. Its longitudinal (east-west) position fixes the locations of the triangles, intersections, and other fourteen rings around the globe. Why Giza was chosen as the orienting site is a mystery, but it is interesting that it is the geographic center of the earth's continental land masses.

Hagens refers to the great circles forming the etheric grid as "the Rings of Gaia," after the Greek goddess of earth. In addition to the major rings, minor rings of the same symmetry and size can be calculated passing through and connecting all the major intersections. This process can continue infinitely, filling in all the spaces in the web in such detail that the lines and intersections over the smallest local area can be mapped out.

Does this etheric structure offer us any hints as to whether the earth has chakras? This is an intriguing question, because as you follow the north-south rings from pole to pole, you always encounter exactly seven intersections with other major rings (including the polar intersections themselves). Should these intersections turn out to be chakralike vortexes of energy, they would serve as very interesting backdrops for some of the mysteries and events associated with their locations.

A partial list of these areas includes Easter Island in the South Pacific, with its megalithic statues; the Pyramids of Giza; the Bermuda Triangle; Iwo Jima, site of the pivotal World War II battle; the Hawaiian Islands; Findhorn in Northern Scotland, site of the famous spiritual community; Kiev, near the Chernobyl nuclear accident; the ruins of Macchu Picchu in Peru; the Gulf of Alaska, site of the Exxon Valdez oil spill; the southwest United States, an area rich in native American wisdom traditions; the Galapagos

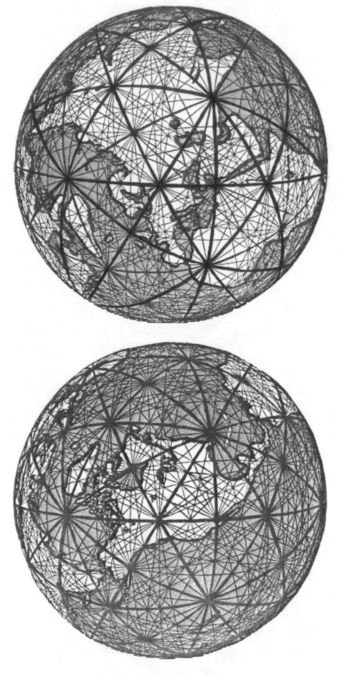

Figure 4. The Rings of Gaia (courtesy Bethe Hagens, Ph.D.)

Islands, with their rare species of life; Lake Baikal in Siberia, the world's deepest lake; and South Africa, site of the monumental struggle of apartheid.

THE PATHS OF THE DRAGON

While the Rings of Gaia may define the earth's etheric body on a grand scale, another common understanding across cultures is that there are small, local lines of etheric energy flowing through the environment. Sometimes they are straight, and sometimes they snake their way through the countryside. Like subtle meridians, or *nadis*, these are called "ley lines" or "telluric currents" in the West, and *lung-mei* in China (for "the paths of the dragon" or "dragon currents"). Ley lines have even been described in the cultures of the Pacific islands, whose lore includes oceanic navigation by following energy currents across the surface of the water.

As John Michell explains in *The View over Atlantis:* "The Chinese believed that *lung-mei* extended all over the world, and this belief is everywhere supported by the evidence of local tradition. In Australia and North America the dragon lines are creation paths, haunted by the gods and by the great primeval serpent, the ancestral guardian of all living things. In Ireland they are the roads of the fairies. In some parts of the world they can still be seen from the air, although their origin is obscure and even their very existence is no longer remembered among the people through whose country they run."[5]

Michell adds that such lines often have "some further quality known only to the native magicians. American

Indians, particularly the Hopi of the Southwest, appear to use them as cables of mental communication. In China they . . . run between astronomical mounds and high mountains."[6] Western science has yet to discover and measure this aspect of the earth's energetic anatomy. Yet to people who live close to the earth, her lines of energy have real, perceptible consequences, as revealed in the following passages.

Taming the Dragon

On a farm in rural eastern Iowa, a farmer was perplexed as to why his calves who were held in a certain pen would not thrive as well, were sick more often, and developed rougher coats of hair than calves placed in other pens nearby. When he moved them out of the pen, they would do much better, but when he returned them the problems would recur.

"So I happened to tell him what I knew, and he had me come out," explains Willy Lansing, another farmer living near the small town of Hopkington. Lansing uses the ancient art of dowsing to locate lines of energy and work with them. "When I come out to a place I take my flags on wire and walk clean around the whole site with my dowsing rods. I ask to be shown any negative energy lines affecting this farmstead. When I find one I'll stick a flag in there and continue on around the site and compare one side to the other. I find where the lines are entering and leaving the area, and then I correct them."

To "correct" them Lansing places wooden, six-pointed stars at the points where the energy lines enter and leave the site. Resembling the Star of David, each star functions as a vortex. The pattern of joints in the construction of each of these shapes determines the "positive" or "negative" spin on the energy that flows through it, depending on how the star is oriented at the site.

"I hang them up, positive and negative, on each line that needs it. . . . In those pens where the calves were doing bad, there were two negative energy lines crossing right in the center, and right where they crossed over was your hot spot," he continues. "After I treated them, they became the best pens. The calves' coats got shiny and their weight gain picked up."

Lansing recounts another story of a farmer growing alfalfa for hay. He would routinely have his crop tested by a lab to determine its protein content and thus whether he needed to supplement his cattle's feed with extra protein. The farmer discovered that when the hay was tested out in the field, it would be 20–21 percent protein, but after it was moved to his barn, the protein levels would be only about 13 percent.

Lansing dowsed the area around the barn and found two lines of negative energy going north and south and one going east and west through the barn. "Once we tuned the negative energy lines in there, the very next test that came back was 21 percent protein," he states. "The cattle looked very different afterward. Before the tuning they were a pretty rough-hair-coated herd. They're just shining today, and have gained weight much faster."

A SUBTLE PERCEPTUAL ABILITY

Dowsing has actually been a traditional method of following lines of earth energy in many indigenous cultures for millennia. In one Native American tradition, medicine wheels were laid out on the surface of the earth over subterranean water domes that have been found through dowsing. The spokes of the wheels represented the streams of water flowing outward from the domes. In other cultures it has been used to locate sacred sites—power points where lines of energy converge.

While the outward action of dowsing appears to be similar in all uses—holding some form of wand and walking over the ground being scanned—the conscious intention of the dowser seems to determine what is picked up. As explained by Lansing, "You get what you ask for when you dowse. That's why when I walk around an area I ask for any harmful energy line that's affecting that family, that building, or whatever. I try to keep it simple."

The parallel here between people who can sense the energy fields of other people and those who sense earth energies is an obvious one. Lansing is quick to point out that it's not the rods that are doing the detection, it's the person. "The rods are responding to *your* energy. You do get into your higher self when you dowse," and it is the higher self that responds by moving the rods. Dowsing can be used to detect lines of geomagnetic energy, the locations of mineral deposits, and, of course, veins of water.

AN ANCIENT SOLUTION FOR A MODERN DILEMMA

The mystery of dowsing has taken on a whole new importance in modern times. One of the dramatic changes in the earth as a result of population growth and urbanization is a decrease in the water supply. About eighty countries have water shortages now serious enough to threaten crop production. In addition to the skyrocketing demand, water shortages are also a result of available resources being contaminated by pollution from industry, domestic waste, and farm chemicals.

The search for underground water is a multibillion-dollar industry worldwide. Yet the best technology available is not as successful as dowsing, an age-old method that relies simply on the human perceptual system to make the wand respond when over a water source. In fact, dowsing for the underground streams in the earth is even more accurate than infrared photography from satellites.

Dowsing under Scrutiny. To respond to the life-threatening problem of water shortages in arid parts of the world, the German government launched a ten-year project to explore whether dowsing is really a viable method. The outcomes were striking. For example, the dowsers achieved an overall success rate of 96 percent in 691 drillings in Sri Lanka. Researchers concluded that based on geological experience in that area, a success rate of 30–50 percent would be expected from conventional techniques alone.[7]

According to physicist Hans-Dieter Betz, who headed up the project, "What is both puzzling yet enormously useful is that in hundreds of cases the dowsers were able to predict the depth of the water source and the yield of the well to within 10 or 20 percent. We carefully considered the statistics of these correlations, and they far exceeded lucky guesses."

The dowsed sites were in regions where the odds of finding water by random drilling were extremely low, and the dowsers were able to locate underground sources, often over one hundred feet down, whose streams are so narrow that misplacing the drill site by a few feet would yield a dry hole. Such precision is far beyond any known geological indicators.

What could account for such success? What are the energies involved? Betz has hypothesized that it is more than just some unknown biological sensitivity to water that underlies the phenomenon of dowsing. He suggests that subtle electromagnetic gradients may result from the fissures through which the water flows beneath the surface, and these create changes in the electrical properties of the rock and soil. The dowsers somehow sense these gradients with their subtle perceptual abilities.

An alternative explanation, in keeping with our earlier discussions of the "layering" of energies from different dimensions, is that the vital energy of the earth herself is being detected as it flows through its *nadis,* or meridian system.

POWER PLACES AND SACRED SITES

What we call sacred sites are often points of palpable energetic experiences. The most prominent of such points on the body of the earth are mountains. These are places where the earth's energy is channeled upward, and to be on top of a mountain gives a feeling of being uplifted by this energy. In the language of the five elements, mountains embody the fire element with their upwardly thrusting shape. The fire element represents transformation, and mountains are cherished for their ability to bring clarity of mind and perspective, in a sense "burning off" confusion. In addition, volcanoes are easily seen as chakralike vortexes through which the earth vents her fire from time to time.

Places where the earth's energy lines converge are also

often considered power centers. Throughout the British Isles, legends abound of unseen tracks of energy linking the stone circles and other sacred sites of Great Britain. Sacred places on the earth where people have worshipped for thousands of years are often held in the esoteric traditions as places of confluence of lines of energy flowing through the earth.

The British dowser Tom Graves studied ley lines intersecting and moving through ancient sacred sites such as Stonehenge in England. He concluded that these sites functioned like telephone exchanges, moving energy along the ley network, and that the large sharp stones piercing the skin of the earth functioned as acupuncture needles, adjusting or purifying earth's vital energy as it flows along its pathways.[8]

Figure 5. Needles of Stone: Avebury, England

The points where these lines converge are recognized as energy centers or vortexes where energy is felt particularly strongly. These are places where your own energy can be lifted up and altered states of consciousness seem easily attained.

My own pilgrimage to one such power spot, the Glastonbury Tor in southern England, was a memorable experience. It was a cold, windy, midwinter day when my friend Annabel and I arrived at Glastonbury, a small, quaint town shrouded in the mysteries and traditions of the Chalice Well and ancient Avalon. Positioned just outside the town, the tor is a peculiar and mysterious sight indeed, a rather large, knoblike hill standing out in a region of relatively flat plains. One cannot escape wondering whether the tor was natural, man-made, or formed by supernatural forces. Sitting atop the tor is the tower of St. Michael's Church, the remainder of which was destroyed in an earthquake.

Upon ascending the tor on the terracelike paths that spiral around it, we began to encounter fierce winds. The positioning of the tor in relation to the flat plains for miles around created an aerodynamic effect—like the wing of an airplane, with the wind accelerating tremendously in order to pass over the top. When we finally entered the tower, Annabel's long hair shot straight up as if we were in a wind tunnel.

It was an eerie feeling to sense the incredible aerodynamics of this site, knowing at the same time that it is situated atop a convergence of two famous ley lines: the Michael Line, reaching from St. Michael's Mount in Cornwall, southwest England, and the Mary Line, which sometimes parallels it and sometimes snakes across it at several points on their shared journey across the southern reaches of the country.

Each intersection along the way is marked by a church or other symbol of their union.

FROM THE BREAST OF THE MOTHER

One common perception among the world's spiritual traditions is that wells and fountains are considered holy or sacred points on the anatomy of Mother Earth where her deep healing and restorative energies can be accessed from the surface. This is illustrated by author Mara Freeman in reflecting on Celtic traditions: "The sacred well as a miraculous irruption of spiritual power, or *numen,* into the everyday world was also, it seems, viewed as the nourishing breast of the earth-mother. . . .

"A strong instinctual feeling for the numinosity of sacred waters remains in the modern soul, even if it prompts only the casual toss of a coin into a 'wishing-well.' . . ."[9] Indeed, there is an unspoken sense of mystery and reverence when we immerse ourselves in a natural spring, as if we are somehow acknowledging our source.

Living Water. Freeman's words are more than just beautiful prose, for they actually reflect qualities of water from within the earth. In the 1950s the German naturalist Theodore Schwenk conducted studies comparing water from natural sources in the ground to water from taps. What he found was that groundwater in its natural state is indeed more alive. By developing a new method of water analysis called the "drop picture" method, Schwenk was able to see and photograph the complex, subtle patterns of flow *within* drops of natural spring water. Such water naturally tends to undulate and spiral more than tap water, creating visible patterns Schwenk called "rosette forms." Polluted or tap water does not have these complex patterns.

Researchers from Schwenk's Institute for Flow Research and the University of Freiburg recently conducted an interesting study of this concept. By examining water drop flow patterns in water taken from a point in the Black Forest where the streams were polluted, they found that the lively patterns of flow had disappeared—only to reappear in water taken from farther downstream.

The life-giving nature of "flowforms" in water, as they are called, derives from their ability to actually assist in the oxygenation of water as it moves, thus making the water a more vital resource for living things.[10] It makes perfect sense that untainted water that is in movement is also more highly oxygenated, therefore naturally carrying more vital energy—more *prana*, or *chi*, which is carried in the air.

THE COCOON OF LIFE

When a team of Russian cosmonauts returned to earth after having spent over a year in space, their doctors were startled to find that they had lost nearly 80 percent of their bone density. This problem has since been remedied in spacecraft by including strong artificial magnetic fields on board, but it illustrates how important the earth's magnetic field is to life.

Like the human body, the earth radiates an energy field outwardly, called the "geomagnetic field." This is a "DC," or "direct current," unidirectional field of magnetic energy that originates in the earth's core and radiates out beyond the atmosphere. It serves as a supportive cocoon, a vibrant and stimulating energy medium within which all of life exists.

The strength of this field varies in different locations depending on the topography of the internal layers of the earth, as well as mineral deposits near the surface. Figure 6 shows these variations across the surface at sea level. (The contour lines refer to increments of ten thousand "nano-teslas," the unit of measure of strength of the field.)

As you can see, there are extremes. For example, the geo-magnetic field is twice as strong over North America and Russia as it is over Brazil, an area known to geophysicists as the "Brazilian low." The effects of this aberration on humans—given our magnetostatic sensitivity—are not clearly known, but one can only wonder whether the *joie de vivre* characterizing the culture of Brazil (it has been reported that Brazilians know how to party) and the conservatism of North America and Russia are in any way related to this phenomenon.

The Brazilian low has, however, been found to affect sensitive instrumentation in orbiting satellites. For example, every time the Hubble Telescope passes over the region, scientists have to send its delicate instruments into a "sleep mode" because otherwise they malfunction.

Regardless of where you are, there are subtle changes in the strength of the field with the time of day. If you've ever worked a night job and discovered how difficult it can be to sleep during the day, you may have experienced one of the effects of the day/night cycle.

The field is always slightly stronger on the night side of the planet, away from the sun. This is because radiation from the sun is "pushing on" and compressing the earth's field on

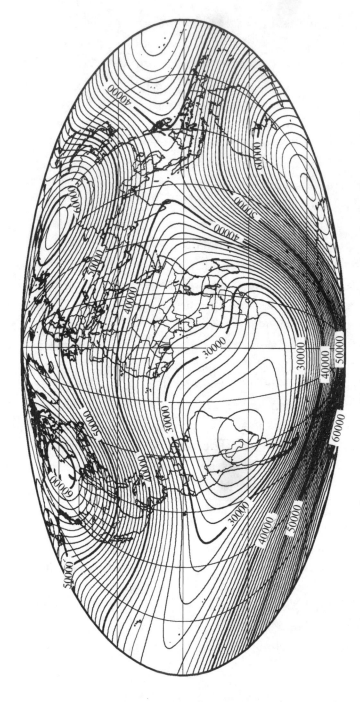

Figure 6. Earth's Geomagnetic Field (courtesy National Geophysical Data Center, 1997)

the daytime side. Although the earth's field extends out into space in all directions, when it meets that coming from the sun, it does not reach out as far. Its lines of "flux" (magnetic energy) are not as long—and therefore not as strong—as they are on the nighttime side, away from the sun. Thus the magnetic field passing through our bodies at night is stronger, with longer lines reaching out into space than in the daytime. A stronger field is more conducive to health, as I'll explain later, and this helps make sleep at night more refreshing and healing than sleep in the daytime.

The earth's geomagnetic field has a kind of long, slow metabolism in which its overall strength builds and then diminishes in cycles of five hundred thousand years. Scientists have determined that we are approaching the end of one of these cycles within the next thousand years. Over the last four thousand years, the strength of the geomagnetic field at the surface has declined by about 90 percent— from 4.0 gauss down to 0.4 gauss. This has been discovered by studying variations in the degree of north-south orientation of magnetic deposits in stratified layers of the earth.[11]

A Mystery Solved

In the late 1950s in Japan, a period of rapid and explosive industrialization of the country's economy, doctors began to see a peculiar syndrome of low energy, insomnia, and generalized aches and pains. After an exhaustive and fruitless search for a common cause, a group of insightful researchers determined that these people all spent large amounts of time in metal buildings and were thus being shielded from the earth's natural magnetic field.

The disease was labeled "magnetic field deficiency syndrome," and symptoms were alleviated by the external application of magnetic fields to the patients' bodies. Today magnetic healing is surprisingly popular in Japan and has become a significant part of mainstream medicine in that nation.[12]

We are only now beginning to realize that magnetic fields, and particularly a negatively charged field such as that of the earth, are essential and can have a health-promoting effect on the body. Yet at the same time that the earth's field is naturally waning, we have exacerbated the situation by distancing ourselves farther from it.

But how can the earth's field affect our bodies? The answer lies in the fact that any magnetic field produces an increased level of activity in the "charged particles" that make up the physical body. It's as if all our atomic particles buzz around faster and interact with more zest. A magnetic field is like a generator, generating more energy and spin in the atomic particles that are present within it. Chemical reactions, healing, and other cellular activity are all accelerated in the presence of a stronger field, and thus they are naturally improved slightly at night because of the slightly stronger field.

The overall decline in the earth's geomagnetic field may be a factor in the evolution of today's chronic and degenerative diseases. We already know that pollution, bad diet, stress, and artificial electromagnetic fields are important pieces of the puzzle, and the body needs all the help it can get with these adversaries. It's interesting to consider that our ancestors at the time of Buddha and Jesus were living in a much stronger geomagnetic field than we are today. With no cure in sight for such maladies as cancer, chronic fatigue syndrome, fibromyalgia, and Alzheimer's disease, we may need to expand our paradigm of what matters in health, to consider magnetic field therapies.

TURNING BACK THE CLOCK

Would re-creating the geomagnetic conditions of four thousand years ago help? Dr. Dean Bonlie of Alberta, Canada, an engineer and magnetic therapy researcher, has invented and patented a system of using magnetic sleeping pads that simulate the earth's field of the era. His devices are being evaluated by researchers at the University of Alberta, and preliminary findings indicate that people suffering with a variety of chronic ailments appear to receive medical benefit. Meditators have also reported that their meditations are more powerful when done while "cocooned" in one of these fields.[13]

WHEN MOTHER EARTH SHAKES

It was a warm October afternoon when Madeline was driving west with her infant son toward the beach along the Sonoma coast in Northern California. About three miles from the ocean, the thought "earthquake" suddenly popped into her head. She immediately stopped the car, turned around, and went home. Two hours later, the Loma Prieta earthquake struck the San Francisco Bay Area, collapsing freeways and killing several dozen people.

"I don't think about earthquakes a lot," she states, "but

when it comes into my thoughts, I know there's going to be one, especially if there's a strong feeling with it."

Madeline describes the feeling she refers to as one of "pressure—in my brain, in my belly, in my third chakra, everywhere, like an 'energetic' pressure."

For many years Jennifer has been known among her friends and family to have premonitions of impending shakes, which have for the most part been accurate. At age seven she was trapped in an elevator during an earthquake in Southern California, and it was after that experience that her special ability seemed to develop.

What are Madeline and Jennifer picking up?

EARLY WARNINGS

Animals living in nature are attuned to the geomagnetic field of the earth, and they can sense subtle changes in it. It is common to hear of snakes unexpectedly appearing on the surface of the earth, dogs barking, and horses and cattle becoming agitated just before a temblor.

The reality of these subtle energetic signals from the earth has recently been confirmed scientifically. In the 1970s, Dr. Marsha Adams, a biologist doing research at Stanford University Medical School in Palo Alto, California, was studying the effects of cardiac drugs on chicken embryo hearts. In the course of this research she stumbled across the discovery that the earth's occasional emission of low-frequency electromagnetic signals influenced how the hearts responded to the drugs. Certain detectable signals released by the earth were found to cause a pattern of signals that *occur shortly before and after earthquakes.*

Adams and her Stanford colleague Dr. Anthony Fraser-Smith subsequently built a prototype earthquake prediction system called the EAR (electromagnetic activity report) system, which has had some surprisingly impressive results. Based on the subtle patterns of geomagnetic signals, the EAR system is able to estimate the largest probable earthquake in the coming week, accompanied by a list of potential locations ranked in order of likelihood for the occurrence of the largest earthquakes. The researchers believe it may soon become very feasible to pinpoint the time within seventy-two hours and the location within fifty kilometers of future devastating earthquakes.[14]

This is another case where the human perceptual system may serve us well and even supplant our reliance on technology, if we can learn how to attune as some individuals have to subtle signals from within the earth.

CELESTIAL INFLUENCES

BY THE LIGHT OF THE MOON

As a kindergarten teacher, Monica has observed over several years that for the two or three days leading up to a full moon the children become easily overstimulated. "They'll twitch and fidget, and they don't have control over their own actions. There's not necessarily more hitting, but perhaps more exuberance," she states.

"They're not comfortable in their bodies. They become more frenetic. When they're lying down resting, they're so wiggly that they may kick each other, and at the end of the day they can't stand still to say good-bye. We have to take extra care to hold their energy. Then when the full moon passes, they're immediately back to normal."

Monica's experience illustrates how fluctuations in the geomagnetic field can have real effects on feelings and behavior. The activity of the earth's energy field is affected by solar radiation reflected off the surface of the moon. Like a giant celestial mirror, the moon reflects solar radiation toward the earth, and the full moon and new moon represent extreme swings of a pendulum of this input, subtly altering the earth's energetic environment.

With a full moon the maximum amount of solar radiation is reflected toward us, and this radiation meets the outer boundaries of the earth's field somewhere out in space. Where this meeting takes place, there is a "compression" of the earth's field, which alters the earth's energetic environment at the surface. With a new moon, there is no such compression, and the earth's field is able to expand fully out into space.

BUT IS IT REAL, OR IS IT LUNACY?

Is there a real basis in our ages-old fables and folk wisdom about the effects of the moon on human experience? Various studies over the years have brought mixed results, but recently a highly sophisticated approach to this research was taken by scientists at the Consciousness Research Laboratory at the University of Nevada—Las Vegas. Drs. Dean Radin and Jannine Rebman examined public records of human behavior and the lunar phases throughout the calendar year 1993 in the Las Vegas area, with some fascinating results.

As expected, they found that the amount of solar radiation hitting the earth parallels the phases of the moon. More interesting, however, were the following findings over the twelve-month period:

1. Barometric pressure rose with the waxing moon, then dropped rapidly at the time of the full moon. Meteorologists know that such rapid drops of pressure are often associated with disturbances in weather, which may in turn be related to increased violence and disturbed behavior.
2. In admissions to the psychiatric ward of the local county mental health department over the year, there was a pattern of a sudden rise in psychotic behavior on the day of the full moon.
3. Suicide rates increased almost in lockstep with the waxing moon, then declined rapidly three days before the full moon.
4. Death rates overall dropped about six days before the full moon, peaked about two days after it, then dropped again six days after the full moon.
5. Crisis calls to "911" showed an abrupt increase on the day of the full moon.
6. The mutual funds market was found to lag the lunar cycle by about five days, as residuals (profit) shot up at the peak of the cycle. This indicates that mutual funds should be purchased a week before the full moon and sold on the full moon.
7. Average lottery payouts for six U.S. state lotteries were found to be lowest on the day of the full moon, suggesting an inverse relationship with lunar phases.[15]

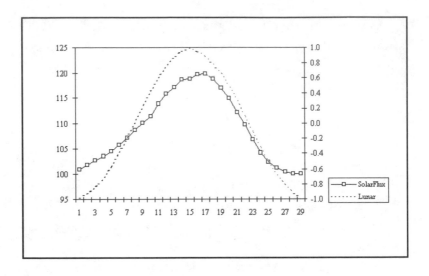

Figure 7. Solar Radio Flux vs. Lunar Cycle

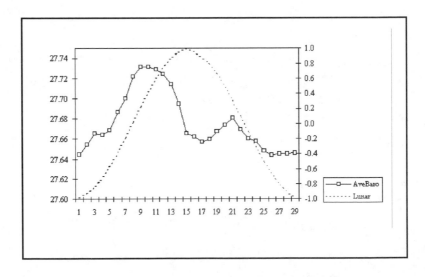

Figure 8. Barometric Pressure vs. Lunar Cycle

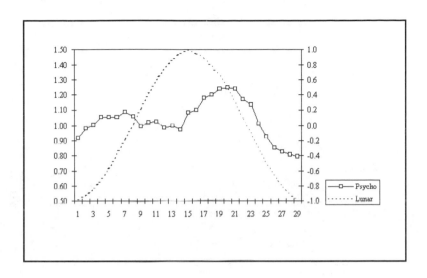

Figure 9. Psychotic Behavior vs. Lunar Cycle

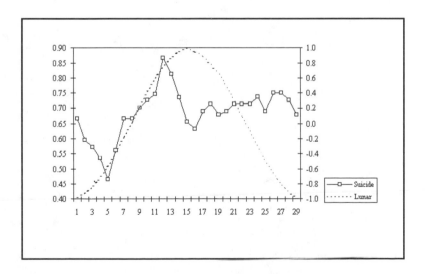

Figure 10. Death by Suicide vs. Lunar Cycle

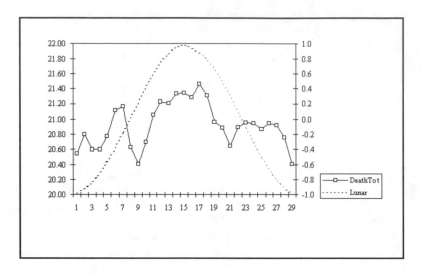

Figure 11. Total Deaths vs. Lunar Cycle

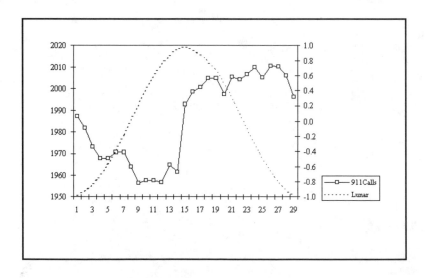

Figure 12. Crisis Calls vs. Lunar Cycle

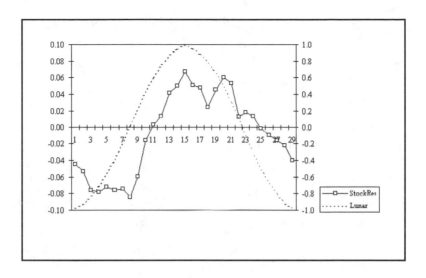

Figure 13. Mutual Fund Residuals vs. Lunar Cycle

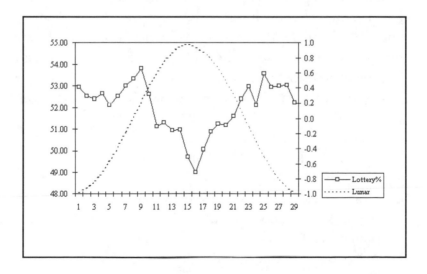

Figure 14. Lottery Percentage vs. Lunar Cycle

Radin and Rebman conclude that these findings support our popular beliefs about the influence of the moon on human behavior. But what about the actual *magnitudes* of the effects? These statistical trends are based on large numbers of people. While they are significant, they are also quite subtle. Thus, the impact for a given individual is difficult to measure, and for practical purposes may be negligible in most cases.

WHEN THE SUN SHINES BRIGHTER

In addition to its indirect effects via reflection off the moon, the sun "agitates" the earth's field with sunspot activity. Sunspot activity causes intense magnetic explosions on the sun that shower additional solar radiation on the earth, in turn disturbing our geomagnetic field. Researchers have found more behavior disturbance in patients on psychiatric wards,[16] higher admission rates to mental hospitals,[17] and higher rates of violence and even homicide[18] during periods of geomagnetic disturbance.

On the other hand, days when the earth's magnetic field is most *quiet* are when paranormal experiences like mental telepathy, clairvoyance, precognition, and apparitions are much more likely to occur.[19] This was shown in a study of mental telepathy during dreams. Subjects were instructed to dream about a picture that was unknown to them in a distant room and then describe the picture the next day. Researchers discovered that the most accurate descriptions of the picture were developed during dreams that took place when the earth's geomagnetic activity was lowest.[20]

These findings point to a new area of research on the horizon: the relationships between optimal mental performance and geomagnetic influences. How are our creativity and lucidity affected by the phases of the moon and geomagnetic activity? And can we plan the timing of our creative pursuits to take advantage of these influences—using something like "geomagnetic weather reports"? According to the eminent parapsychology researcher Dr. Stanley Krippner of San Francisco's Saybrook Institute, these are logical questions, and the answers may even help explain such phenomena as the extreme mood swings of some exceptionally creative people.[21]

LET THERE BE LIGHT

Sunlight is an essential nutrient to life on this planet. Unfortunately there are myriad ways in which we separate ourselves from natural light—buildings, tinted windows, sunglasses, and sunscreen, to name a few. We have only a fraction of the exposure to natural light that our ancestors had. In recent years another obstacle has been added in the form of warnings of the link between skin cancer and overexposure to sunlight, particularly with regard to the deterioration of the protective ozone layer; yet there are real health consequences to not getting enough natural light.

Natural light is an important factor in our health by way of its stimulating effects on the hypothalamus and pineal gland and the resulting impact on our hormonal and neuroregulatory systems. "Malillumination," a term coined by the photobiologist John Nash Ott, D.Sc. (Hon.), has been linked to conditions as diverse as malabsorption of certain nutrients,[22] fatigue, tooth decay, depression, seasonal affective disorder (SAD), hostility, suppressed immune function, strokes, hair loss, skin damage, alcoholism, drug abuse, Alzheimer's disease, cancer,[23] and even loss of muscle tone and strength.[24]

Ironically, there is even evidence that extreme lack of exposure to sunlight may contribute to the form of skin cancer called melanoma, which is often associated with fears of *over*-exposure. A study of 4.6 million U.S. Navy personnel found that melanoma occurred most frequently in sailors who worked *inside*. It turns out that sunlight is needed for the body to manufacture vitamin D, which *suppresses* the growth of melanoma cells.[25] Thus it may be counterproductive for fair-skinned people, who are naturally at greater risk for melanoma, to avoid sunlight altogether.

In a similar vein, an important study published in the prestigious *International Journal of Epidemiology* compared the incidence of fatal ovarian cancer in northern and southern latitudes within the United States. Women living in the more southern latitudes, where they received more sunlight, were found to have a much lower likelihood of dying from ovarian cancer. It was concluded that sunlight may be a protective factor for ovarian cancer mortality, probably because of the protective action of vitamin D.[26]

One of the little-known effects that air pollution has had on the natural environment is a reduction in light reaching the earth's surface worldwide. The Smithsonian Institution has reported that there has been a 14 percent loss of overall light intensity over the past sixty years. Scientists at the Mount Wilson Observatory in California estimate that farmlands have lost 10 percent of average sunlight intensity and there has been a 26 percent decrease in the ultraviolet part of the spectrum. This reduction in sunlight is suspected as a factor in increasing crop diseases and infestation.[27]

In the Realm of the Planets

What do we know about the subtle energetic influences of other planets? How can they possibly influence us, and is there any real scientific basis for astrology?

Generally astrology gets no scientific support. However, there does seem to be one nagging, troubling set of findings that just won't seem to go away. The French researcher Michel Gauquelin has found through exhaustive statistical analysis of birth records that famous athletes are more likely than others to have been born when the planet Mars is either on the rise from the earth's horizon or past its upper culmination in the sky. He calls this "the Mars Effect."[28] Gauquelin's findings have been confirmed by the German researcher Suitbert Ertel, who examined the data on several thousand athletes prominent in their sports.[29]

To their distress, critics have been unsuccessful in finding any flaws in this research. Yet the Mars Effect is only the piece of Gauquelin's work that has gained the most attention. He has also conducted studies on people in other professions and occupations. Jupiter was found to be linked statistically to success in politics, cinema, theater, and journalism; Saturn with the sciences; and the moon with writing. He found that Mars also plays a significant role in predicting prominence of military leaders, chief executives, and physicians.

There seems to be no possible explanation for these findings in terms of the laws of physics, which would have to rely on energy from the electromagnetic spectrum or from gravitational influences. Even if such subtle influences could be detected, how could they affect human performance?

The explanation must lie somewhere in another dimension beyond the physical. Most likely the physical planets themselves are not the *source* of influence. Rather, they are but parts of a "cosmic clock" whose positioning in the heavens merely reveals *larger archetypal influences at work in the background*. In other words, the positioning of the planets is a *result* of a patterning of energies based in another dimension, and it is these energies, which we have yet to understand, that influence the human being's development.[30]

A POSITIVE SPIN ON NEGATIVE IONS

Perhaps you can recall sitting on the rocks beside a waterfall, breathing in the fresh, moist air, and the feelings of exhilaration, relaxation, and peace that arise. Or perhaps you have had similar feelings at the seaside, by a river, or even when walking out into nature after a powerful rainstorm. Somehow the body seems to want to absorb something in the environment at times like these.

Are these pleasant, refreshing feelings simply the result of the psychological cues in these situations? Certainly the images of flowing water or the cleansing effects of a rainstorm are attractive metaphors for healing and renewal in the subconscious, and simply focusing on these images can lead to the relaxation response and greater feelings of peace. However, there is also an energetic basis in the environment for these experiences. When water moves or flows it releases negative ions (negatively charged atomic particles) into the air.

Scientists have recently discovered that being immersed in a field of negative ions actually alters our own energy field and hence our moods. Researchers at Columbia University and the New York State Psychiatric Institute conducted a study testing the effects of negative ions on people suffering from seasonal affective disorder, a mood disturbance sometimes called the "winter blues" and associated with lack of adequate sunshine. They used a generator to release negative ions around the patients and found that with a half hour of exposure they had significantly reduced symptoms and elevated mood.

This may be explained as a result of the impact of the negative ions on our own electromagnetic field. Being immersed in a field of negative ions seems to have a balancing effect on our energy. Emotions that had been stagnant or stuck seem to flow and be released more easily, thereby allowing our mood states to lift. It is as if the metaphors of "cleansing" and "washing away" that we associate with moving waters have a real basis in their impact on the field of emotional energy that surrounds and penetrates our body.

THE DANCE OF WIND AND WATER: *FENG SHUI*

James and Dorothy had had their house on the market for nine months. A couple of contracts to buy had fallen through, and they were in danger of losing the opportunity to buy another house they had fallen in love with. They consulted a *feng shui* practitioner, who had them place some crystals in opposite corners of the house and clean out a centrally located closet. They also put a rug in the closet, hung some crystals inside it, and put a crystal under their bed. Within twenty minutes of making these changes, an agent showed up who declared that she knew this was the house for a new client. The next day the client showed up and made an offer that came through. The buyer commented to my friends later: "I knew it was the house for me when I saw that closet."

To the Western mind, this could be called mere coincidence. However, to Katherine Metz, a *feng shui* consultant in the art of placement in Los Angeles, "the universe is responding to what we ask for. *Feng shui* is the *asking*, and it is using the physical environment to do the asking. We are one with the environment, inseparable from it. We begin by asking for what we want ourselves, and then when we use the environment we add power to that."

Feng shui is an ancient Chinese tradition that offers practical guidelines for our relationship with the earth. It is the Chinese art of designing one's immediate environment in order to establish both inner and outer harmony. Its goal is to create a state of balance between the energetic forces within you and those of the environment. The term literally means "wind and water" in Chinese and stems from ancient agricultural practices that recognized the impact of the five elements and natural forces in the surrounding environment on the success of crops.

From its origins in this agricultural context, the principles of *feng shui* were extended to inform the placement and positioning of buildings, architectural design, landscaping, the use of colors inside and outside, and even the placement of furniture in rooms. The principles are grounded in an understanding of the five elements as they weave their way through nature and through our bodies.

Feng shui is used for such diverse purposes as choosing a building location, choosing the directional orientation of a building, placing plants and shrubs around a building, placement of doors and windows, and arrangement of furniture. The purpose of all of this is to bring the physical environment into harmony with the surrounding natural circulatory patterns of vital energy.

FACING DOWNSTREAM

Alex, a physician, had to plan the building and layout of a new medical office complex on a steep hillside. He hired a *feng shui* consultant to help him integrate the building into the surrounding environment. The consultant immediately nixed a plan to have the main entrance facing up the hillside, which would be like facing upstream with the doors opening directly into the downhill flow of *chi*, like opening a floodgate.

He recommended that they place the main entrance on the more protected downhill side instead. The consultant also suggested planting some trees on the hillside above to disperse the flow of *chi*, hanging some mirrors in the entryway to deflect energies coming in from the street, and placing plants in the darker corners of the waiting room where *chi* would tend to stagnate. The incorporation of these "cures" and other suggestions resulted in an office complex with a decidedly peaceful and harmonious feeling to it.

FENG SHUI AND THE SUBCONSCIOUS

This tradition extends beyond the purely energetic domain to the psychological realm as well. Hence there are two uses of *feng shui*: the harmonizing of the five elements in the physical environment and supporting the comfort of the subconscious mind, particularly in creating peace and relaxation.

Following are a few examples of *feng shui* principles applied psychologically.

By placing your desk or sofa facing the entrance to the room, you will feel more comfortable because you will have a greater sense of control. You will be able immediately to see all energies or forces coming at you. Conversely, sitting with your back to the door will lead to unconscious feelings of being exposed and vulnerable and may make you less productive.

The amount of space on each side of a couple's bed is believed to influence the ease with which they relate. If it is equal space, there is a sense of equal access and freedom of movement within the relationship, whereas if one side is against a wall, one partner may feel "pressured."

Sleeping under a heavy beam creates a subconscious impression that there is something overhead that could fall at any time—in an earthquake, for example. We may not think of this consciously; yet by noting and addressing the concern, perhaps by convincing oneself of the integrity of the structure, the subconscious may then be able to rest more peacefully. A *feng shui* cure of this would be to hang a crystal from the beam as a symbolic gesture of dissipating any danger—the *intention* of which would also assuage the subconscious. As Metz states, "Your intention is the most powerful part of the process. It's a mystery how the placement of crystals may influence the subtle energetic environment, perhaps by influencing the frequencies of energies around."

CURES

A variety of "cures" can be used to disperse or ameliorate disharmonious or undesirable energy patterns in the environment. Examples include bright or light-refracting objects, such as mirrors, crystal balls, or lights; sounds, such as those produced by wind chimes or bells; living objects, such as plants and flowers (real or man-made); moving objects, such as mobiles, windmills, or fountains; heavy objects (to stabilize), such as stones or statues; electrically powered objects (to stimulate), such as air conditioners and televisions; bamboo flutes; and colors.

Metz recounts the case of a Chinese grandmother who was living with and caring for her grandchildren. She had diabetes and was getting worse, to the point where she could no longer take care of the children, which was hard on the whole family because both parents worked. The children loved her and were very distraught.

"I went into the house, and there were a number of things going on. As she slept in her bed and looked out the window, the very strong corner roofline of the house next door was coming right at her through the window, suggesting the element fire jutting into the room.

"Then she was spending most of her time every day sitting next to a wall that is covered with beveled mirror tiles, and she's eating there. In fact, the whole dining room was covered with these tiles, in a sense, cutting up the body. The *image* of the body is being cut up. At the entrance to the house, there is another point of another building directed at the front door, also representing fire and threat.

"For the corner pointing to her bed through the window, we put a mirror up on the outside of the house to send the reflection back to itself. We took down all the beveled mirror tile. We put a chime at the front door to stop the energy coming in from the point across the street. We corrected all those things, and her blood sugar level returned to normal.

"My job is to create spaces that heal people, that are nurturing, that make people whole and complete."

A CIRCLE AND A SQUARE

In *feng shui* the geometry of spaces and structures is also influential. Circles serve as funnels or vortexes for the movement of energy, and squares serve to settle it and organize energy. I experienced both of these dynamics in the writing of this book. The first phase of gathering information and "throwing it into the blender" was done in a round room, a fourteen-foot-diameter yurt. This shape is very conducive to creativity because it is a natural vortex for earth energy emanating upward. As the energy is in effect "funneled" upward through the circle, it also circulates or spins, and this vortical action stimulates ideas and creativity.

However, such a round structure is not so conducive to *organizing and ordering* things. Hence, when it came time to do the final organization and editing of the book, I found myself compelled to move to a rectangular-shaped room. Squares and rectangles are a form well-known in sacred geometry and *feng shui* to promote organization, and I found it much easier to do the final work in this space.

MAN-MADE ELECTROMAGNETIC FIELDS

The earth's natural magnetic field has been instrumental in the evolution of life on this planet. We are enveloped in this cocoon throughout life, and the magnetic aspects of our anatomy are naturally attuned to it. However, our use of electric power dramatically alters our magnetic environment, and unnatural fields have potentially serious impact on us.

The Dark Side of Power

In 1974 epidemiologist Dr. Nancy Wertheimer set out to find a pattern that might explain the unexpected rate of leukemia deaths in a four-county area around Denver, Colorado. She found an unusually high rate of cases in dwellings that were near utility pole transformers. Upon further scrutiny, she found identical distribution patterns in the placement of high-intensity electromagnetic fields (EMFs) and dwellings in which leukemia deaths had occurred.[31]

This famous study was the first of many to link such fields to human cancer. Other research has found links to cancers of the blood, brain, colon, prostate, nervous system, lymph system, lung, and breast.[32] Electromagnetic fields have also been linked to poorer short-term memory,[33] depression, and suicide.[34] One study even found that dogs who spent 25 percent or more of their time in yards under overhead power lines had three times the risk of lymphoma than did dogs whose homes were powered by underground lines.[35]

Beyond the obviously large fields of large power transformers, research has also proven that appliances we use every day are potentially hazardous. In one study, electric blankets were shown to diminish the pineal gland's ability to produce the hormone melatonin.[36] Melatonin is important to regulation of the entire endocrine system and many organs of the body. In addition, the fact that melatonin is oncostatic—fights cancer cells—helps explain electric blanket–related leukemia.[37]

More recently, a startling relationship has been found between Alzheimer's disease and exposure to electromagnetic fields, a link even clearer than those obtained in most of the cancer studies. In three studies involving over 800 people, scientists found that those with high exposure to strong fields in the workplace—particularly tailors and seamstresses, whose machines may expose them to three times as much radiation as power line and cable workers—were three times likelier to develop Alzheimer's disease than people who did not work around electric fields.[38]

The health risks of EMFs have been debated vociferously for decades, with a curious mixture of impressive studies showing findings on both sides of the issue. Recently, however, a federal panel formed by the National Council on Radiation Protections and Measurements, funded by the Environmental Protection Agency, produced a preliminary draft of a report based on ten years' study of scientific evidence in this field. The draft report, which had no official standing at this writing, concluded that EMFs may indeed pose a risk to health and that "a significant proportion of the world's population" may face modest levels of risk. Among their suggestions were that new housing should not be built under high-voltage transmission lines and that schools and child care centers should not be placed near strong sixty-hertz fields.[39]

BUT HOW DO EMFS DO DAMAGE?

Researchers have long been looking for the biological mechanisms by which EMFs could affect health. A breakthrough is the recent discovery that our air and water are permeated with microscopic crystals of magnetite, which is the magnetic form of iron oxide. Magnetite crystals are also present naturally in our brains and other tissues. The presence of magnetic fields such as those found in residential wiring causes these crystals to rotate at about 60 times per second.

Scientists believe that when the crystals are attached to cell membranes, their rotation could contribute to abnormal cell physiology.[40]

Another explanation is that the increased cancer incidence reported in individuals living and/or working in an environment where they are exposed to higher than normal artificial electromagnetic fields may be caused by suppression of the body's natural manufacture of melatonin.[41] While usually associated with sleep, melatonin [as mentioned earlier,] is also a natural anticancer agent that has been found to inhibit several types of cancers, particularly hormonally related cancers like breast and prostate cancer.[42]

Still another angle is offered by Stanford's William Tiller, who explains that the ill effects are not caused by the mere *presence* of the field per se. Rather, they are caused by the electrostatically charged particles (photons and electrons) that are passing through our bodies. The problem is that these particles are *unpolarized*, and their behavior is chaotic and disordered as they pass through our cells.

The chaotic nature of these particles disturbs our natural energetic field, resulting in damage to the body's tissues. Hence, theoretically, if these charged particles could be made to be ordered and polarized rather than random and chaotic, they would pass through us "transparently" with no ill effects.

A POUND OF CURE?

Can electromagnetic fields be altered to achieve this? A team of researchers has been working for several years to develop devices that "condition" electromagnetic fields in just this way. The goal is to be able to "align" the charged particles in the field, much like a magnet could be used to align iron filings on a table. This ordering and polarizing of the offending particles would then eliminate their ill effects without having to eliminate the field itself.

The researchers have developed a device that can be plugged into any wall outlet in a room and create a "coherent polarizing field effect," organizing all the photons and electrons emanating from artificial electromagnetic fields within a thirty-five-foot radius. Their research has yet to be published in mainstream scientific journals. However, according to Tiller, who consulted in the development of the technology, this approach "is something that can potentially open the door to a new realm of physics.... My intuition and logic suggest that this category of devices will be an important part of humankind's future.[43]

REMEMBERING THE EARTH

"Ecopsychology" is the name for the new field of study of how our psychological well-being is tied to our relationship with the environment. The term was coined by historian Theodore Roszak, founder and director for the Ecopsychology Institute at California State University, Hayward. According to Roszak, "We have detached ourselves so [completely] from the natural environment that it is wounding our mental health."[44]

Psychologists now suspect that our degradation of the earth's natural environment may play a major role in current worldwide trends in emotional dysfunction, feelings of depression and alienation, and existential malaise. According to Michael Cohen, Ed.D., we spend nearly 95 percent of our time indoors, out of contact with nature and the very energies that supported our evolution as a species. Cohen observes that when people partake of activities in nature, many human ills improve, including eating disorders, personality disorders, prejudice, and hostility.

Harvard scientist Edward Wilson, Ph.D., goes so far as to state that we have a genetic *need* to commune with nature. He argues that a lack of contact with nature undermines our intellectual, aesthetic, and spiritual satisfaction.

In the modern way of life, we can go for months or even years without ever actually touching the earth. We entomb ourselves in buildings, we wear shoes when outdoors, we walk on synthetic floors, concrete, or asphalt, and we ride in cars, buses, and airplanes that insulate us from the energies of nature. There is always something between us and the earth.

In his book *The Sixth Extinction*, anthropologist Richard Leakey refers to the urge to get back to nature as "biophilia," or love of the biosphere. In Leakey's perspective this universal human urge is tied to both our physical and mental health, and communing with nature and her energies nourishes the human spirit.[45]

A Return to the Forest

Ecopsychology has very personal implications for each of us in our sense of satisfaction and peace in the world. This is illustrated by Dr. Sarah Conn, a clinical psychologist who teaches ecopsychology at Harvard Medical School. Conn actively inquires about her clients' reactions to the natural world, validating these reactions as important sources of energy. She also looks at what they describe as personal, inner pain not only as an expression of their unique personal history or circumstances, but also as an expression of the earth's pain. She relates the following story:

"[A] fifty-year-old man who had grown up as a poor child in Central America and had achieved financial success as an adult in the northeastern United States came to therapy after a severe heart attack. He wanted to address some basic questions about where he belonged in the world and what he needed to do next. He felt that his life was not working and that drastic changes had to be made. We focused on the bodily sensations connected with a particularly intense combination of sadness, anger, and disappointment that seemed to be associated with his current marital difficulties. When we did this, he visualized going deep into the earth and coming out in a tropical forest near a spring from which a waterfall bubbled up. His tears began to flow as he imagined sitting under this waterfall, experiencing the water as tears flowing through him. 'This is so big,' he said, 'so much more than my own personal sadness.' . . . He said he had been thinking that his next endeavor should address environmental issues, but that he was not aware of feeling so intensely about it. When we went back to the bodily sensations and an open visualization in a later session, a guide appeared who took him back to the waterfall and told him to sit in the water, to let it run through him, to feel the sadness of the world every day in order to learn how to love. He developed a vision of moving back to his Central American country, living in a compound with others, setting up a think tank on ecology."[46]

The beautiful words of the Native American poet

Starhawk offer another poignant way of reminding us of our relationship to the earth:

> Earth Mother, Star Mother,
> you who are called by a thousand names,
> May all remember
> we are cells in your body
> and dance together.
> You are the grain and the loaf
> that sustain us each day,
> And as you are patient
> with our struggles to learn
> So shall we be patient
> with ourselves and each other ...[47]

EXERCISE

Going to the Mountain

Mountain peaks and hills are concentrations of energy. They are attractive places to be because of their ways of shaping and directing energy. They seem to lift us above the confluences of various conflicting energies and place us in a relatively simple and pure energetic environment. This is why we feel "uplifted" and exhilarated when we go to a mountaintop. We have clearer thinking and a sense of inspiration when in such a rarefied energetic environment.

As an exercise, go to the highest natural point available near where you live, a high hill or mountain if possible. Looking down below, get a sense of the differences in the two energetic environments. You may sense that the higher point is a place of refined, clear, focused energy and the area below is like a bowl of "soup," with a confluence of many energies collecting and commingling.

EXERCISE

Absorbing Earth Energy

This is an exercise I first discovered in a secluded grassy area of an aspen grove near Lake Tahoe in the Sierras. It is a direct and very powerful way to absorb energy from the earth, release stress, and balance your own energy.

Find a grassy, open area, preferably on ground that has not been excavated so it will be in its relatively natural state. The exercise involves spreading out facedown on the ground, either with or without a blanket. As you lie there with arms and legs extended, all your chakras are in direct contact with the earth. Visualize an exchange taking place in which you release to the earth any stress or negativity you have been carrying. With each in-breath imagine that your chakras are receiving fresh, balanced, healing energy from the earth.

Lie there for at least twenty minutes, and you will find yourself in a very pleasant and refreshed state.

EXERCISE

A Simple Exploration

Take a walk in nature and with your hands explore the energetic qualities of rocks, live trees, dead trees, and anything else you find. Begin by placing your hand in the energy field surrounding it and seeing what you can detect. Does it seem to have an aura? Can you sense energy moving through it? Gradually move your hands closer until you make physical contact. Resting there, see what else you can sense about the energies of this part of nature.

CHAPTER 4

TWO OR MORE TOGETHER: SUBTLE ENERGIES IN RELATIONSHIPS

When two people are at one in their inmost hearts, they shatter even the strength of iron or bronze, and when two people understand each other in their inmost hearts, their words are sweet and strong like the fragrance of orchids.

—I CHING

Two strangers are attending a workshop on developing intuitive communication. They are instructed to pair off and sit in their partner's energy field for just three minutes, with eyes closed and no verbal or physical contact. For that brief period they are told simply to attempt to communicate with each other through their imaginations. At the end of the three minutes each has attained a remarkable degree of accurate insights about the other's life and has even seen identical images of being in imaginary situations together.

"When I was tuning in to my partner," states one of the participants, "I saw her with shorter hair and an upside-down bicycle. I saw her and me arm in arm. I then swallowed and swallowed and felt as if I had to cough but didn't want to. I swallowed again, but the urge was so strong, I felt as if I were choking. My eyes started to water and I had to leave the room to relieve the choking feeling. The choking and cough then left. [After the exercise] my partner then said she used to have a shorter hairstyle and she had to go to a specialist when she was young because she would swallow wrong and start coughing and choking with watering eyes. When she felt me choking, she soothed her throat as she was taught and my cough left. We both sensed swirling. The amazing thing is that I was actually choking as she used to."

How could such a detailed, accurate awareness of another's life be gleaned in three minutes of sitting together silently?

What these two people have just experienced is called "imaginal communication" by Henry Reed, Ph.D., a psychologist and researcher in Virginia Beach, Virginia.[1] Based on his work leading thousands of such encounters, Reed has found that our imagination is actually an *organ of perception* that reaches beyond the five senses. "To use a technological metaphor," he explains, "suppose that the imagination were like infrared goggles, granting night vision to see what is not ordinarily visible to the eye. Perhaps the 'eyes of the heart' exist to help us see the spirit of what is happening in a situation, an energy that is often described . . . as 'invisible forces' or 'vibrations' or simply 'feelings,' but that is no less real. . . ."

Reed uses the metaphor of a magnet and magnetic filings to illustrate how images can arise spontaneously in our imagination as a result of what we are perceiving around us. "If we sprinkle some iron filings on a piece of paper and put a magnet underneath, the filings arrange themselves in a beautiful revelation of the shape and form of magnetic waves. *Perhaps if we allow our emotional imagination to enter a situation, the situation itself will be seen to send off 'vibrations' that arrange the images of our imagination in such a way as to reveal what is going on*"[2] (italics added).

I find Reed's conception of the imagination as an organ of perception particularly crucial in understanding how we experience other people's energy. When we are in close proximity to another, our energy fields are in a state of communion, overlapping and interpenetrating. Since our mind exists in our energy field well beyond the limits of our physical body, it is "out there" to contact the mental field of the other, as well as to be contacted. The contents of our minds are thus available, in a sense, to be known by someone else, particularly if we are open to being known by that person. In this way, the images that arise spontaneously in our imagination can be taken as real perceptions of "what's out there" in the other's energy field.

Figure 15. Overlapping Energy Fields

This work illustrates what we all probably experience but are often unaware of—that on some level we routinely sense what is going on in others when we are near them, but we tend not to pay attention to those vague images, perhaps considering them as just subconscious "noise." We have not learned how to trust our imagination. Yet consider what is possible for us to experience, as revealed in the comments of a few other explorers after just three minutes of silent, imaginal communication with another:

"My partner and I could feel our energy outside of our body; meeting, actually touching, I could also feel her feelings of happiness, joy, excitement. Because of the experience we do have more of an affinity toward each other. By that I mean we both just feel closer and have more intimate sort of bonding with each other."

"We were so strongly bonded, we had to physically move ourselves back to break the bond."

"I really wanted to stay out there with my partner. I was reluctant to come back. I didn't quite enter back into myself completely. When I returned there was an extra warmth in me, all the way down to my ankles, as if the other person's body warmth was heating me up."

The space between two people—what Reed calls the "imaginal zone"—is a place where real intimacy can happen effortlessly, if both parties are willing to let go of thinking about or controlling their experience. (See the exercises at the end of this chapter for guided instruction for an "imaginal encounter.")

A Matter of Balance

We also pick up on aspects of other people's energy that they may have no conscious intention to communicate. Consider the experience of Paulann, who met two men she found equally attractive. After exchanging almost identical pleasantries with each, she felt strongly drawn to one yet repelled by the other. What was she experiencing?

In her perception, Paulann was sensing real differences in the energies being radiated by the two men. "With John, I had an uneasy feeling that the sexual energy was too strong and seemed to dominate everything else," she states. "As much as we talked about our interests, my attention kept being drawn to an uneasy, agitated feeling, as if I were somehow being invaded."

Scientists speculate that such impressions may reflect events on the energetic level. The energy field radiating from John's sex center—his second chakra—could well be dominating and unbalancing his total energy field.

"With Robert," Paulann continues, "I felt more comfortable, as if there were a kind of ease or safety with him." Indeed, while she was aware of some sexual energy, this awareness was balanced by a sense of relaxation and warmth, a feeling that he was present in his heart as well. With him she felt a "heart connection," which allowed feelings of both ease and excitement.

According to Richard Gerber, M.D., author of *Vibrational Medicine*, energy is projected outwardly as a result of a high level of *activation* of that chakra.[3] While traditionally the ability to transmit energy outwardly at will is considered a sign of advanced spiritual development, such transmission also occurs when our chakras are activated unconsciously.

AN EXPLOSION OF ENERGY

This has been the case for Michael, who several times in his life has been in a heated argument with someone when suddenly, without warning and with no physical contact, the other person inexplicably falls to the floor. This strange occurrence happens only when the energy in the argument reaches a peak. After studying with a *chi kung* teacher, Michael learned that it was an uncontrolled emission of his *chi* that was actually knocking these people over. Under stressful circumstances, his *chi* would become so aroused that it would simply explode out from his solar plexus area.

In the Orient, the controlled emission of *chi*—that is, the sending of one's vital energy to another—is a method used by *chi kung* healers. Another use for *chi* emission, however, is to overpower people. This ability is actually quite rare, and martial arts experts work for many years to cultivate it.[4] Michael, who is now studying *chi kung* formally to learn more about his energy, was apparently born with this ability.

In keeping with the age-old Chinese saying "Where the mind goes, the *chi* follows," Michael's energy followed his thought. What he was feeling so strongly in those times of conflict got translated into energy being directed outward simply by his mind. There was no conscious intention to knock down the other person, but the sheer passion of his aversion to the other caused it to happen.

We all emit energy to others without thinking of it, and this can have important consequences in our relationships. Michael, for example, was sending an extraordinarily strong burst of energy from his third chakra area, which is sometimes referred to as the "power and will center" and can be quite strong and highly energized in times of conflict or confrontation.

ON THE SAME WAVELENGTH

The previous examples illustrate what can happen in brief encounters. Over time, however, we naturally become most attuned to people with whom we live most intimately. Tom and Mary have been together for eight years, have two children, and work together in their accounting business. Over the course of their relationship they have had their share of struggles, but they have the resiliency to weather the storms. Like many other such couples, they have established a level of communication that is uncannily automatic and intuitive at times. On many occasions they start to say the same thing at the same time or anticipate accurately what the other is about to say and respond to it before it is said. How can we explain their connection?

There is now evidence that when two people are in close proximity to each other their minds actually seem to become interconnected. This was shown in an experiment where two people sat together inside a special isolation chamber. They did not communicate through any of the five senses but were immersed in each other's energy fields.

They were then moved to separate isolation chambers. When a flash of light was beamed at the first person, in complete isolation from the other, the brain wave pattern of the *second* person responded the same as the first. He "sensed" the light without actually seeing it.

This study established evidence for a kind of *direct communication* between individuals that transcends interaction through the senses *and their energy fields.* The researchers explain that when two people concentrate their attention on each other they create a shared "neuronal field" or "hyperfield" that seems to transcend physical space.

This discovery authenticates such statements as "When she hurts, I hurt" or "We are one." The researchers concluded, *The human brain is interconnected with other brains with which it has established deep, strong communication."*[5]

"NON-LOCAL MIND"

One possible explanation is what Larry Dossey, M.D., and others call "non-local mind."[6] This term refers to the understanding that our mind is not confined to our physical body, but is part of a higher "mental realm" that transcends space and time and in which we have access to potentially unlimited information.[7] The non-local nature of the mind is seemingly confirmed by cases such as the mother who knows instantly when her son is wounded in a war half a world away or the person who foresees an airplane crash and avoids boarding the doomed plane.

The nature of that interconnection—and in what dimension of reality it resides—remains to be discovered. Nevertheless, these findings also help explain how spiritual groups and communities (such as the *sangha*, which is a key part of Buddhist life) create a "collective consciousness" that nourishes and elevates the consciousness of the individual members. People from all spiritual traditions can attest to the qualitative differences that occur in group prayer or group meditation as opposed to when these practices are done privately. I'll return to this subject later in a discussion of group energy fields.

IN THE FAMILY CRUCIBLE

Not surprisingly, children are particularly sensitive to energy fields. Young children often crave physical contact, and my daughter would sometimes like to be "sandwiched" between her mother and me. Other times, however, she would complain that she was being "squashed," *even when there was no physical contact.* She truly experienced it as a palpable, concrete sensation, and while I would protest her reaction with "But I'm not touching you," she would insist with self-righteous indignation that I was.

My original impulse was to assume that she was simply acting out some kind of controlling or rebellious behavior, but after learning about our subtle energy fields, I know otherwise. This experience of feeling squashed was real to her, because she was naturally sensing the intrusion on her energy field by those of her mother and me.

Children's sensitivity is very acute, in infants especially so. Many parents have had the experience of attempting to have a "quiet" argument while their baby slept in the next room, only to have the baby awaken and start crying. Babies are open systems, with unformed energy boundaries—and they can easily feel the energy of agitation or incoherence created around them.

In my own training in family therapy, one of the underlying principles taught was that children are very sensitive to the tensions or incoherence in their parents' marital relationship, and much so-called acting out behavior is a quest to restore a sense of coherence or harmony in the family.

It is this unseen family energy field that the child is sensing. His or her behavior reveals much about the status of relationships in the family. And, in my experience, when the parents heal their marital discord, the child's acting out behavior usually diminishes.

Young children particularly may have no understanding of the true source of their pain, and it is a great disservice to focus on them as the "problem child" rather than addressing the broader context of the family as an energy system.

THE *DOSHAS* AND RELATIONSHIPS

What makes for compatibility between two people? Is it just a matter of common beliefs, philosophies, and attitudes? Is it common interests and experiences that can build empathy between them? Or is there an underlying energetic basis that has nothing to do with the psychological dimension?

In considering the psychology of relationships, we cannot escape the evidence that our basic energetic constitution influences our personality and how we relate to others. One clear and practical way to understand this influence is offered by the Ayurvedic theory of the *doshas*. As you'll recall from chapter 2, the *doshas* are three qualities of our vital energy, and certain *doshas* or combinations of *doshas* predominate in each of us, determining our "energetic type" or "mind-body type."

Ayurveda offers us some practical guidance as to how our predominant *dosha* influences our relationships, directly impacting what happens in communication, sex, and other dimensions. According to Janhavi Morton, an Ayurvedic consultant in Santa Rosa, California, Ayurveda even recommends whom to choose as a mate or work partner, and the guidance turns out to be surprisingly effective.

Following are some examples of how the influences of the *doshas* can play themselves out in relationships. Lest you get discouraged about your own situation, keep in mind as you read these that few of us are purely one *dosha* or another and that with self-awareness it is certainly possible to compensate for the influence of our *doshas* in our relationships.

KAPHA + VATA

Mark and Harriet have been reasonably happy together for fifteen years. They attribute their success to good communication and common interests. Underneath that, however, is the fact that Mark is *kapha* and Harriet is *vata*. As a result, Mark's *kapha* nature balances Harriet's tendency to be ungrounded and scattered. Her insecurity, a common trait in *vata* people, is met well by Mark's assuredness and stability. Just being in his presence calms her down, and she often refers to him as the stabilizing force in her life. His *kapha* nature is very good for her.

In return, Mark also benefits from Harriet's *vata* influence, because he needs stimulation and movement—otherwise his *kapha* nature will make him more sedentary. She likes to go out frequently to stimulating events such as concerts, dancing, and nature excursions. She also has a very active mind, which he finds enlivening and a good balance to his tendency to be calm and quiet. She is good for him in that she helps keep his energy moving. This is a good combination according to Ayurveda principles.

KAPHA + PITTA

Sharon and Paul have a little more fire in their relationship. Paul's *pitta* nature introduces the fire, and his tendency to sharpness, irritability, and anger has gotten him in trouble in previous relationships. In this case, Sharon seems to have the softness and round edges to not be so much affected. Sharon's *kapha* nature helps soothe and calm down Paul's *pitta* fire.

Kaphas are not thrown off balance very easily and are well insulated. Sharon's *kapha* brings qualities of coolness and moistness, which are good antidotes to Paul's *pitta* fire. She cools him down and is a calming influence for him.

In return, Sharon benefits from Paul's *pitta* nature. She needs some warmth and fire and gets passion from him. His fire evaporates her heavy water or moisture and lightens her up. He also stimulates her into activity, which is good because *kapha* tends to be sedentary. Paul brings mental clarity to the relationship because he is very analytical and his intellectual fire is always burning. He also brings the drive and ambition to change things. As a couple, she contributes the grounding, and he brings a transformative influence with passion and activity. This is another good combination.

KAPHA + KAPHA

Amber and John, both *kapha* predominant, consider themselves quite compatible. True, they have a lot in common, but unfortunately much of it is not so good for them. One of their favorite pastimes is watching television together at night and eating ice cream. Both are overweight, and they aren't much help to each other in bringing dietary changes or exercise into their lives. When they travel together, sampling different restaurants becomes their main pastime.

It's true that they get along well and there is a lot of stability to their relationship, but theirs could be described as a union lacking in fire and movement. The challenge for Amber and John is to help each other bring more fire and movement into their lives, which can be introduced through a specific nutritional program as well as exercise. The fact that they have the same *dosha* would make it easier for them to cooperate in terms of meal planning to eat a *kapha*-pacifying diet, as would be prescribed by an Ayurveda practitioner. They could also take advantage of their togetherness to support an exercise program to keep their energy moving. They are likely to either sink or swim together.

VATA + PITTA

Mary (*vata*) and Will (*pitta*) have been struggling for some time with their relationship. Will's *pitta* nature makes him sometimes sharp, judgmental, and critical, but Mary's *vata* nature gives her a tendency toward insecurity and ungroundedness. Slender and lithe, she often feels unprotected and wounded by his arrows. Not having a lot of substance, she becomes easily ungrounded around him as his criticism penetrates very deeply.

He apologizes and they make amends, but it is only a matter of time before his next judgment or criticism comes, which she again takes very personally. His passion seems at times overwhelming to her and burns her out—resulting in even more frustration and irritation for him.

This is not usually a harmonious combination. Both Mary and Will are in need of grounding and stability, but neither has much *kapha* to offer the other. They can compensate for their conflictual tendencies individually by taking care to eat foods that pacify rather than aggravate their particular *doshas*, which entails a slightly different diet for each. This requires some extra attention in meal planning so as to have compatible foods for each person.

They would benefit from practicing meditation or stress reduction, which will also help them remain in balance, and perhaps even from using herbal remedies suitable to their *doshas*. Counseling or psychotherapy could help Mary develop more of an inner sense of self-assuredness and groundedness and could help Will to "round his edges" and soften his judgmental nature. To flourish, their relationship would require ongoing communication and action in all these areas.

VATA + VATA

Sarah and John are both vivacious and spontaneous and generally have a lot of fun when together. They have been seeing each other for just a few months, and though they like to do the same things, theirs is a relatively unstable relationship. There is some approach-avoidance as they play out their mutual tendency for insecurity and resistance to being "pinned down." They are both runners, which tends to be imbalancing for *vatas* because it further disperses their energy.

Because they are so much alike they don't have a lot of grounding or stability to offer each other. From the point of view of Ayurveda, they are likely to be good at sharing their fears and empathizing with each other's insecurities, but their relationship, frankly, is not likely to last because of the lack of stabilizing *kapha* energy.

Pitta + *Pitta*

Anna and Frank have an intensely passionate, fiery relationship, but they tend to burn each other out. They alternate between passionate love and fighting, and theirs is a stormy marriage. During the winter months they are most at peace. The cold and snow seem to help balance their fire energy, and through skiing and other cold weather activities they do fine. As could be expected, summers and heat are worst for them, and their relationship is more volatile at this time. (It's no coincidence that civil disturbances such as urban riots, which often include large-scale burning, also occur more during the hot season.)

In order to thrive, their relationship will require accommodation on several levels. If they can learn to "fight fair," they may be able to use the fiery energy for transformation and exciting times. But they also need to be able to find balance and softness in their relationship. By a great deal of empathic communication, meditating together, and sharing a *pitta*-pacifying diet, they can make their relationship a lot more peaceful and balanced.

As you can see from these examples, anyone who is not a *kapha* benefits from being with one. Also, partnering with someone who shares the same *dosha* as you accentuates your vulnerabilities and tends not to balance you where you need it most.

According to Morton, "Fortunately, few of us are overwhelmingly one *dosha* or another. We all have all three *doshas* to some degree. If we can recognize our dominant pattern, we can at least see where our vulnerabilities lie and take them into account when considering a partner." If we understand the dynamics of the *doshas,* we can also anticipate where we are likely to go out of balance when we enter into a relationship and take steps to prevent this. Of course it also helps if we are well in balance as individuals.

It's interesting that our Western cultural preference—the idealized media image—favors *vata* or *pitta* as being a more desirable type, while *kapha* tends to be considered undesirable. Yet *kapha* contributes to good, stable, balanced relationships. The bottom line, says Morton, is that "if you're going to marry someone, marry a *kapha,* unless of course you are one."

WHAT HAPPENS
WHEN WE TOUCH?

Marianne, sixty-eight, was in the recovery room after open-heart surgery. She was full of tubes and needles when she slowly began to wake up from the anesthesia. This postoperative period is a time when people are very vulnerable to complications developing, and one of the greatest sources of concern is how a patient handles the trauma emotionally. The nurse who was assigned to watch Marianne had a practice of using the laying on of hands to calm and soothe her patients, and Marianne benefited tremendously from this. As the nurse placed her hands on Marianne's shoulder and arms, she felt a loving presence and a flood of relaxation and warmth throughout her body. Her troubled, fitful breathing became calm and rhythmic, and she went into a state of deep relaxation.

Why do we instantly feel warm and peaceful when one person touches us, yet we may bristle and cringe when touched by another? Is it purely psychological, or is something happening energetically?

An Exchange of Energy

When we touch another person we exchange energy. There is no way to avoid the fact that a kind of energetic communion takes place, even in such seemingly innocuous acts as shaking hands or touching another on the shoulder. Touch itself communicates a great deal energetically and actually influences our own energy field. This is something we all know intuitively, and there is even a passage in the Bible in which Jesus states, "Who touched me? . . . Someone has touched me, for I perceive that power has gone out of me."[8]

Some fascinating breakthroughs in understanding the energetics of touch have recently been discovered in research at the Institute of HeartMath. Since the heart creates the strongest electromagnetic field of the body (measurable from several feet away), Rollin McCraty and his colleagues wanted to find out whether our heart energy fields are really detectable at the surface of one another's bodies when we are in close proximity or actually touching.

One study involved wiring pairs of subjects up to electrodes and having them sit five feet apart. Researchers found that one person's heart energy waves (electrocardiogram output) were not detectable by the electrodes on the surface of the other person's body at that distance. However, *when they were holding hands,* each person's heart energy waves were detectable on the surface of the other's body and even affected the other's brain waves.

The researchers then wondered whether what was being picked up was being radiated through the air from the first person's heart or was being conducted, as a wire conducts electricity, through skin contact. What they found was that when one person touched the other through a latex glove, the signal was still present but was only *one-tenth as strong.*

They then did another experiment to determine whether heart energy was transferred when the subjects were sitting closely together but not touching at all. Subjects were seated three feet apart and again wired with electrodes. Indeed, their electrocardiogram output was detectable across the space between them on the surface of each other's bodies.[9] Thus we now know that the heart energy field is both conducted by physical contact *and* radiated across space between people.

When we touch or are in close physical proximity with another, there is a real transfer of energy between us. We are "touched" and no doubt "penetrated" by each other's energy fields. All kinds of contact—casual, intimate, even contact for healing purposes—involve a commingling of our energy field with that of another.

When we consider the fact that the most coherent oscillator tends to "pull" those around it into entrainment, it makes sense that we can be so moved by being in the presence of someone who radiates genuine love. Whether we are in the presence of a lover, a loving friend or a relative, a healer, or one of the world's living spiritual teachers, we are affected by the strong, coherent heart energy field being radiated, and our heart can be pulled into entrainment with the other person's. Likewise, if we are with someone who is agitated or angry, that person's *in*coherence will make it more difficult for us to be in a coherent state ourselves.

WHAT'S LOVE GOT TO DO WITH IT?

Love creates coherence. By virtue of its ability to produce such profound effects, love itself certainly qualifies as a kind of "energy." By understanding its impact on our energetic anatomy as well as on our physical body, it becomes easy to understand how being in a loving relationship can have such profound effects on our health and well-being.

It appears that the internal coherence wrought by love is the basis for the many health benefits that come from being in a loving relationship. We know, for example, that people who are happily married are healthier and live longer than those who aren't. One of the key reasons was discovered when researchers at Ohio State University studied the immune systems in 473 women and found that those in the most supportive relationships had the highest-functioning immune systems. A supportive relationship seems to act as a "buffer" against the damaging effects of stress on our health. Remember, *each individual cell* is an oscillator, and in this study, the happily married women's natural killer cells—the immune cells that fight cancer and viruses—were found to be more powerful.[10]

Getting to the heart of the matter, an Israeli study of ten thousand married men looked at the connection between marital happiness and the development of angina pectoris, an attack of painful spasms in the heart. Over the five years of the study many variables were considered, including health history, risk factors, and psychological factors. Ultimately, whether the men developed angina was predicted most accurately by their response to the question "Does your wife show you her love?"[11]

In another study researchers were perplexed as to why the heart attack rate in the small, predominantly ethnic Italian town of Roseto, Pennsylvania, was only half that of the neighboring towns. The inhabitants were mostly overweight, consumed more total fat than the average American, had a high rate of cigarette smoking, were sedentary, and had blood cholesterol levels comparable to average Americans. It turns out the only thing that distinguished them from their neighbors was that they had unusually strong interpersonal relationships within their community.[12]

The power of caring relationships also shows up in the healing effects of support groups. For example, in a study conducted at Stanford Medical School, women with advanced breast cancer who participated in a support group had *double* the survival time of those who did not.[13] The group bonding and sense of belonging apparently triggered some significant changes in the ability of the women's immune systems to respond to the cancer.

Beyond experiencing love in intimate or other supportive relationships, *altruistic* love can have profound effects as well. A team of researchers at Harvard Medical School used a film of Mother Teresa compassionately serving the poor and suffering in Calcutta. This particular film is noted for its ability to inspire feelings of altruistic love and caring. When it was shown to a group of medical students, the result was a significant boost in their immune functioning.[14]

There are many different meanings for the word "love"—romantic love (*eros*), altruistic love (*agape*), or social ties (*philia*), to name a few. Yet as diverse as these experiences may seem, they all impact our energy field and make us more coherent human beings.

RELATING SEXUALLY

Christine and Alan, both in their mid-forties, had been seeing their enjoyment of their sexual relationship decline gradually for several years. Each had been feeling more and more fatigued at the end of the workday, and on those increasingly rare occasions when they did make love, both tended to be preoccupied with their "performance," usually defined as making sure that their partner had an orgasm.

After reaching a mutual agreement that they needed to overhaul their relationship, they decided to go to Maui and participate in a workshop on tantra. In that one week their entire relationship was transformed.

"We now make love almost every morning, and we both have more energy than ever," states Christine.

"I feel like Superman," says Alan, "and I also feel that we are much closer emotionally."

SEX AND ENERGY, EAST AND WEST

This may sound too good to be true, but it's actually becoming a common experience as more couples discover some simple teachings from Oriental tantric sexual practices. Three basic teachings seem to be most impactful for Western couples. First is for men to learn to not ejaculate every time, which results in a tremendous turnaround in their vital energy in daily living. Second is for both partners to learn to breathe together and circulate their energy together, as one energetic whole. And third is to view lovemaking as a shared *meditative* experience, letting go of any goal or performance orientation.[15]

In Western culture it is a relatively novel concept to think of sex as a form of meditation or spiritual attunement, and any notion that it could be used for building vital energy would also be considered quite unusual. Yet these concerns are precisely the focus of many Eastern teachings about sex.

While Westerners tend to associate the term "tantra" with exotic lovemaking practices taught in the Orient, its more accurate meaning is the "transformation of energy." Tantric teachings of Eastern spiritual traditions are concerned with the transformation of our vital energy in all its permutations, ultimately toward the goal of spiritual attunement and enlightenment. In this context, sexual relationships and the energy that they arouse are considered resources for fueling and supporting spiritual unfoldment, not just for sex or pleasure as an end in itself.

The essence of these teachings is that when lovemaking is not goal directed (as in seeking to achieve orgasm or other pleasures), but rather takes on a more calm, relaxed, meditative quality, there is a subtle building of a charge of energy in the body. Eastern tantric traditions teach that when this powerful energy is then drawn upward to our higher energy centers with the guidance of our conscious intention and visualization, it can unite us with Spirit as well as with our beloved. Another use of this energy is to direct it into specific organs or parts of the body for healing purposes. Thus a loving partnership can contribute directly to both our spiritual unfoldment and our physical health.

In tantric lovemaking couples learn to synchronize their breathing and circulate their sexual energy through the heart. This leads naturally to coherence and entrainment with each other, and the popular metaphor "two hearts beating as one" is an allusion to this experience of "oneness." A natural outcome of this intense form of intimacy is that all the other biological oscillators involved may become entrained, both *within* each partner and *between* partners.

In effect, Christine and Alan have learned to come into entrainment and coherence with themselves and each other, in a sense forming a greater spiritual/energetic whole. Sex has become a means of energetic and spiritual communion. The ultimate coherence or entrainment to which tantra practitioners aspire, of course, is with Spirit or universal energy. Tantric practices are steps to create the conditions for this to occur, and the benefits to intimacy, health, and greater energy are a welcome bonus.

Figure 16. Sexual-Energetic Communion

THE ELECTRICITY OF SEX

Tantric teachings are based on the circulation and merging of vital energy (*chi* or *prana*) between two people. However, it is implicit that in the grand scheme of our energetic anatomy, our electromagnetic energy plays a role as well. While it may be viewed as being of a lower or denser nature than our vital energy, during intimate contact with another the two are transferred and circulated simultaneously.

In keeping with the discovery that the electromagnetic field of the heart is transmitted through touch, it's easy to see how acts of physical intimacy also allow a strong exchange of electromagnetic energy. Both kissing and sexual intercourse involve contact of moist mucous membranes, and moisture facilitates particularly strong and efficient electrical conductivity.

It is inevitable that the communion of sex engages all aspects of our energetic nature simultaneously. It is no surprise that people sometimes refer to their sexual experiences or feelings as "electric" or "electrifying."

INFLUENCES FROM AFAR

Another whole dimension to the energetics of relationships has to do with how another can affect us from a distance—what scientists call "remote influence." These are events where impact is felt on an energetic level even though the other person is physically outside our energy field—perhaps even miles away. These experiences involve an interaction of multiple dimensions of reality: the physical time-space dimension in which the sensations are felt, and the dimension of *non-local mind*, which seems to be unbounded by physical laws.

For example, Mark was standing in a long line outside a theater one night when up near the head of the line, about twenty yards away, he noticed a man who from behind resembled an old buddy from his college days. Uncertain whether it was really he, Mark kept staring and wondering.

After a few moments the man suddenly turned and looked straight at him. It was not his friend after all, and Mark was embarrassed—and also startled that the stranger seemed to feel his gaze. How can we explain this phenomenon? What did the stranger feel, and how did he know Mark was looking at him?

"He Gives Me the Creeps"

When you say you feel "the creeps" in response to someone staring at you, you are offering a surprisingly accurate description of what is actually happening energetically. In chapter 2 I mentioned that the eyes emit radiation. However, more than that is going on here. That "creepy" feeling is felt in your skin and is a result of the stimulation of your autonomic nervous system—the part of our nervous system that functions automatically. This is the kind of activation that is measured in lie detector tests, by galvanic skin response.

Scientists have long known that we can regulate our own autonomic nervous system activity, and this is the basis of biofeedback. We can learn to slow down our heart rate, influence our blood pressure, or reduce muscular tension through imagery or other mental techniques.

Now we also know that our autonomic nervous system can indeed be affected by the thoughts or intentions of others—including someone staring at us, as Mark was doing. When *another person* is able to influence our autonomic activity, this is called "alleo-biofeedback."[16] This was demonstrated in a study in which scientists placed a volunteer in a quiet room with a video-camera focused on him. The volunteer was also wired to detect his autonomic nervous system activity. Meanwhile in another room, a "remote observer" watched a television monitor that half the time was blank and the other half of the time showed the volunteer who was on camera.

In this situation, of course, there was no way the volunteer could know through his normal senses when he was being stared at. Yet, amazingly, volunteers had statistically significant elevations in their autonomic nervous system activity when they were being observed, compared with the periods when they were not.[17]

THE POWER OF INTENTION

Other research has looked at whether the observer, rather than simply staring, could actually "will" or "intend" the volunteer's galvanic skin response to change in a certain direction. Half the time the observer tried to either raise or lower it, and the other half of the time she attempted to do nothing. In twelve of thirteen experiments where influence was attempted, the volunteer's level of autonomic nervous system activity changed significantly in the intended direction.[18]

Such occurrences result from our sensitivity to the energies directed to us by others. Many experiments in the former

Soviet Union have also looked at such remote influences on others, including how we can affect other people's concentration at a distance by focusing our thoughts on them.

In one study, several people attempted to solve mathematical problems while, unknown to them, researchers mentally bombarded them with a continuous stream of numbers, emotions of panic and uncertainty, and a lack of self-confidence. The result was a significant increase in the time needed to solve the problems. Another study found that a person's reaction time could be slowed if someone else concentrated on slowing him down.[19]

We can also influence others in beneficial ways. Drs. William Braud and Marilyn Schlitz directed some fascinating research at the Mind Science Foundation in San Antonio, Texas, in this area. In one study, people seated in one room using strong positive intention and visualization were able to reduce the blood pressure and electrodermal (skin conductance) activity of subjects isolated in another room—changes that indicate reduced tension and anxiety.[20]

In another study by Braud and his colleagues, sixty volunteers took turns focusing their mental energies on a single person in a distant room. Each focus session lasted sixteen minutes. For eight minutes the volunteers tried mentally to "help" the subject in the remote room concentrate on a candle. For the other eight minutes the volunteers allowed their concentration to wander.

The recipients in the remote room did not know when the help was being sent. They were instructed to press a button each time they realized their mind had wandered from the candle. A computer charted the pattern of button presses. The findings were most intriguing, revealing that the recipients' focus on the candle was maintained best during those time intervals when the help was being sent. In addition, those recipients who had previously reported the most everyday concentration problems received greater impact from the help than those who believed that they were good at maintaining attention.

These findings confirm that our physical bodies can be influenced by distant attention from others. Researchers have concluded that we are capable of participating with others in a *field* of events that is transspatial (beyond the limitations of space or distance), transtemporal (beyond the limitations of time), and transpersonal (beyond what we ordinarily think of as the boundaries between people).[21]

THE POWER OF THE GROUP

I mentioned earlier the research indicating that we can enter into a shared "neuronal field" or a "hyperfield" with others that seems to transcend physical space and can operate at distances beyond the reach of our biofield. This seems to be particularly common with people with whom we are intimately acquainted.

However, when our energy field itself is commingling with those of others, whether they are known to us or are strangers, there is also a collective phenomenon that can happen. Since our energy field extends several feet away, another person can be twice that distance and we are connected where our fields meet. This makes it easy to understand how we can be swept up in the collective energy of a large group of people.

This was the case for Sasha, who recalls attending a Bruce Springsteen concert with two friends. While at the concert, a group of people started "the wave" surging around the stadium. "The wave" is a mass action in which people sequentially stand up, raise their arms skyward, and then sit down again.

This is done in a manner that resembles a series of dominoes rising and falling as it circles the arena, and it can accelerate in velocity as it moves around. When they saw it coming around from across the stadium, Sasha told her friends she was going to resist and remain seated when it got to them. However, when it arrived, it was as if she were swept up by an energy other than her own. To her amazement, she could not hold back from being carried up in the wave as it passed.

The formation of a collective energy field can be further illustrated by imagining two drops of water sitting near each other on a surface. Now imagine taking a toothpick and piercing the side of one drop, then drawing it over to the other drop. When they meet they flow into each other, creating one larger drop. Likewise, when we are joining energy fields with others we create a large unified field. This larger field serves as a medium through which people who are physically far apart are connected energetically.

This energetic connection also enables us to be "in sync" with others. In marching, team play, or dancing, our whole body becomes an oscillator, affecting and being affected by the oscillators around us. This same principle applies to sitting silently in meditation or prayer in a group or singing with others. When we all become entrained together, we oscillate collectively and the whole group becomes one big oscillator.

This helps explain how group experiences, cult experiences, and mass action, for better or for worse, can be so compelling. In chapter 2, I described how within the body, the heart is the largest most powerful oscillator, and it tends to pull the other oscillators or energy centers into entrainment with it. Likewise, our whole energy system can function as one big oscillator. When we are in the presence of powerful personalities such as spiritual teachers, evangelists, political orators, and even expert salespeople, we can be drawn into entrainment with them.

The indigenous people of Hawaii have a beautiful practice that is very instructive for us as to the impact of the collective energy field on us as individuals. When an individual is ill and to be treated by a kahuna healer, the patient's entire community must first assemble and undergo a forgiveness ritual in which everyone releases any resentments or ill feelings that were being held in the collective field of which the patient is a part.

This constitutes a kind of cleansing or purging of the shared field, thus allowing the group's collective intention to be as strong and pure as possible as it is focused on the well-being of the patient. It is only after this process that the healer will proceed with the healing work.

This is a true expression of the understanding that we are not living in isolation but are intimately connected to and subtly affected by those around us. The kahuna wisdom seems to incorporate what we are only now learning from research—the fact that when people join together with a shared vision, new levels of order and healing are possible. We can literally change physical reality, for we are one.

EXERCISE

Discovering Another's Energy Field

With a partner, stand at opposite ends of a large room or far apart in an open space outdoors. Focus all your attention on each other's presence, and begin walking *very slowly* toward your partner. The object is to discover when you first sense that you are contacting the other's energy field. When you detect this, stop and back up just outside the boundary, then test it again.

As a variation of this, walk toward each other simultaneously and see when each of you begins to sense the field of the other. Is there a difference?

Now try these exercises with your eyes closed.

EXERCISE

Redirecting the Flow of Energy

Sit facing a partner and place both hands in the air, facing each other. Without touching, move your hands close to your partner's hands until you can both sense the energy radiating between. Recalling that the right hand is naturally giving and the left is naturally receiving, see if you can get a sense of your partner's energy being drawn in through your left hand and your energy being directed from your right hand into their left.

Imagine that a circuit is being completed between you, with a definite direction of flow down your right arms, up your left arms, and through your hearts. Perhaps you can sense a building of momentum or a strengthening of the energy as it circulates through the two of you.

After a while, at an agreed-upon signal, using your deliberate mental intention, instantly and simultaneously reverse the direction of the flow, so that you are drawing in through the right and releasing from the left. At the precise moment that your intention shifts, you should feel a palpable sensation as the direction of the energy flow reverses. Then agree to resume the normal direction. You may play with this process a few times to get a sense of the power of intention to direct the flow of energy.

EXERCISE

The Imaginal Encounter

To facilitate your experience of imaginal communication, Henry Reed's instructions are included.[22] Begin by sitting opposite a partner, not touching, and then:

"Put your hands in your lap and close your eyes. Take a deep breath, exhale and relax . . . [pause] Notice how you are feeling, your energy level and your mood . . . Now I want you to become aware of the feeling of the presence of your partner . . . Just allow your awareness to expand now until it includes the feeling of being in the presence of your partner . . . In your imagination make mental contact with your partner . . . Psychically, making mental contact . . . Establishing a heart connection with your partner . . . As you imagine making mental contact with your partner, notice what you experience . . . Whatever it may be, simply assume it is part of the experience of being in mental contact with your partner . . . Allow the experience of mental contact with your partner to unfold now, on its own, in fullness, while you simply observe what you experience . . . I'll be silent now for three minutes while you explore the experience of being in psychic contact with your partner.

[After three minutes:]

"O.K. now, gently and gradually let go of the experience of being in contact with your partner . . . withdraw from the contact experience . . . return to yourself, into your own body, your own space, being alone with yourself . . . Notice how you're feeling now, your energy level and your mood . . . Take a deep breath, wiggle your fingers and your toes, stretch, open your eyes. Discuss with your partner what you experienced."

EXERCISE

For Lovers

Make an agreement with your partner to find out what it's like to make love once with little or no movement. This may take some self-control, so make sure you have a clear agreement beforehand.

Throughout the whole experience, resist as best you can any impulse to move outwardly. Rather, attempt simply to feel the energy that is aroused, and see what it wants to do on its own when you are not accompanying it with movement. Let this be like a form of meditation in which you simply watch the energy to discover where it goes and what it does on its own.

Synchronize your breathing with your partner, and imagine that your breathing is keeping all channels open through which the energy can circulate throughout your body.

CHAPTER 5

IN-SPIRATION:
THE BREATH-ENERGY
CONNECTION

The spiritual breeze burnishes the breast of all sorrow; let the breath be stopped but for a moment, and annihilation will come upon the spirit.

—RUMI[1]

Janet had no idea what was in store for her when she lay down on a mat surrounded by a hundred other "breathers" on the floor of the meeting hall. It was comforting to know that her "sitter" would be next to her throughout the process, and it was reassuring to know that all she had to do was breathe— nothing else.

Will I have a big breakthrough? Will I lose control? Or will nothing happen, and leave me disappointed? she thought. She had heard that this strange technique called holotropic breathwork had made a powerful impact in the lives of her friends, and she was always looking for new ways to reveal and heal the wounds of her troubled life.

Janet was not disappointed. About midway through the session she was suddenly aware of the presence of her father, who had died fourteen years before.

"He appeared to me as if his face were the whole sky. It was a very tender, sweet connection between us, even to the point of feeling him lean down and kiss me gently. This was well into the session, and was a complete surprise to me.

"I didn't really 'see' any of this, it was more of a kinesthetic sense. I could feel his presence, I knew how big his face was. It just filled the sky. And the message I seemed to get from him was 'I am with you,' which was acknowledged with the sweet kiss.

"Then my sister came along," Janet continues. Her sister had died in a car crash just three years ago. "She had always been an extremely sensitive person. When she appeared she told me that she had *had* to leave this life, that her emotional pain was just too great. She was telling me this so I would understand.

"She also said, 'What you're doing right now is what *I* needed.' And since that time she has come to me during several breathing sessions.... There is always such a peaceful feeling about her presence, and a really deep sense of love.

"These sessions are my healings. I really hadn't known how much grief I had in me, but during my breathwork I wept for hours over both of these deaths. I can remember one session where I sat up the whole time and just wept. It freed up an enormous amount of energy, and then I was flooded with feelings of compassion for every father and daughter who had ever lost each other, every family that has experienced a loss, every child who didn't get a chance to be born, or was born into a place who couldn't accept them...."

Janet's experiences show the potential of the breath to profoundly alter our energy and transform us on many levels. I will discuss the technique she was using in more detail later, but her story reveals how the power of the breath helped her to access another dimension of reality, as well to unearth, feel, and release long-held emotions.

Like her, we all have within us a simple mechanism that can fill us with more energy than we know what to do with, take us to the heights of ecstasy, and help us to feel the presence of Spirit, release physical pain and tension, unburden us from years of grief or sorrow, calm our mind, and bring us inner peace. It is so simple and easily available that we overlook it, choosing instead to search for more complicated and expensive ways to accomplish these things.

BREATH AND SPIRIT

The breath is at the center of all spiritual and religious traditions, literally and symbolically. In the Judeo-Christian tradition this is expressed in Genesis 2:7, "And God formed man of the dust of the ground and breathed into his nostrils the breath of life, and man became a living soul," and there are over ninety other references to the "breath of life" in the Bible. The East Indian word *prana* means both air and the sacred essence of life; in ancient Greek, *pneuma* means both air and the spirit or essence of life; and in ancient Hebrew, *ruach* means both the breath and the creative spirit.

In the Sufi tradition, the exalted place of the breath is revealed in the words of the twentieth-century teacher Hazrat Inayat Khan, who stated:

"The subject of breath is the deepest of all the subjects with which mysticism or philosophy is concerned, because breath is the most important thing in life. . . . [It] is the result of a current which runs not only through the body, but also through all the planes of man's existence . . . the current of the whole of nature. . . . It is one breath and yet is many breaths."[2]

The unity of breath and spirit is implicit in our language, in that the Latin word *spirare* is the origin of both spirit and respiration. *Spirare* itself originally meant simply "to breathe." And it is easy to see that *expiration* means "exit of spirit," the opposite of *inspiration*.

Clearly the process of respiration can be thought of as literally *respiriting*, or drawing in a maintenance dose of spirit to keep us alive. When we inhale, we are opening ourselves up to life energy to flow into us and nourish and enliven us.

In yielding to the irresistible impulse to inhale, we are opening up and exposing the deepest recesses of our body to whatever is out there—be it life-giving oxygen or toxic or even deadly fumes or gases. Yet we have no choice but to live in this perpetual state of vulnerability, trusting the unknown. It is a form of ongoing surrender, and no matter how independent or self-sufficient we may think we are, this is a profoundly intimate form of communion with existence.

THE WAY OF THE WEST

In Western culture the breath has been treated simply as a mechanical, metabolic function for maintenance purposes only. Unfortunately there are many forces throughout our lives that encourage us to minimize or restrict our breathing. Our relationship to breathing begins at birth, and for too many of us it was a traumatic beginning. In the words of the famed natural childbirth physician Frederick Leboyer, "Whether we cut the umbilical cord immediately or not changes everything about the way respiration comes to the baby, even conditions the baby's taste for life. If the cord is severed as soon as the baby is born, this brutally deprives the brain of oxygen. The alarm system thus alerted, the baby's entire organism reacts. Respiration is thrown into gear as a response to aggression.

"Entering life, what the baby meets is death. And to escape this death it hurls itself into respiration. The act of breathing, for a newborn baby, is a desperate last resort. Already the first conditioned reflex has been implanted, a reflex in which breathing and anguish will be associated forever. What a welcome into this world!"[3]

Beyond what we experienced at birth, as we grew up we were socialized in a culture that inhibits strong displays of emotion and aliveness. Full breathing has the effect of "potentizing" our experience of our emotions and our vital energy.

Can you recall being told as a child, "Quit your crying or I'll give you something to cry about"? If so, you probably learned very quickly that the surest way to do this was to stop *breathing*. To stop crying we had to stop feeling, and to do this we stopped breathing. We *lived* the intimate relationship between breath and emotion, between breath and life. We learned to stop feeling—in effect, to stop our lives—by stopping the breath.

Fortunately there is a way we can reconnect with our feelings—including suppressed and unexpressed feelings we still carry from the distant past, as well as feelings we want to experience in the here and now. All we have to do is breathe and keep on breathing *while* we are feeling them.

ANATOMY OF THE BREATH

For Gail, crossing the Golden Gate Bridge without having an anxiety attack is a major accomplishment. For fifteen years she had been suffering with an anxiety disorder that flared up especially strongly whenever she crossed bridges over open water. Thousands of dollars' worth of medication and years of psychotherapy had not succeeded in resolving her difficulties. What allowed her to make this turnaround?

"I finally learned that breathing made all the difference in the world in controlling the attacks," she states. "It took a lot of practice, but I learned that when I felt one coming on, I would immediately bring my attention to my breath. It amazed me to discover that I had actually been *holding* my breath, suffocating myself without knowing it. *No wonder* my body wanted to go into a panic state.

"As I would consciously start taking long, slow, deep abdominal breaths, I could feel that my body was being 'resuscitated.' Then and only then could I deal with mental images and self-assurance about the safety of where I was. Before that, the suffocation would overwhelm me and no amount of insight or self-talk would work."

I have heard many patients with anxiety disorders or chronic illnesses report that they had no idea how shallow their breathing was and that they often were holding their breath. The reality is that we can spend our lives literally lingering close to death if we are not breathing fully. When our vital energy is being cut off, it is the wisdom of the body to respond with panic.

THE BREATH AS THE REGULATOR OF OUR ENERGY

Gail's breathing is what governs her vital energy on a moment-to-moment basis. With it she determines the amount of energy moving through her, she controls where it is concentrated in her body, and she can even activate or stimulate specific chakras. She can fan the flames of emotion and passion, or she can cut off the fuel to such feelings.

This grand regulator of our vital energy is unique among our bodily functions, in that it is both voluntary and involuntary. That is, it can be orchestrated consciously or it can be left to the body, in effect on "automatic pilot." This is when our subconscious, with our hidden fears of our feelings or of meeting life fully, can drastically influence our breathing patterns.

WHERE HEAVEN AND EARTH MEET

The Taoist and yogic theories of the meridians and *nadis* both take the perspective that the breath is breathed into these energetic structures. In other words, there is a parallel process happening when we breathe—the air is being drawn into our lungs, but the vital energy it carries is simultaneously being drawn into these subtle energetic pathways.

As the famous yoga teacher Swami Rama Prasad explains in *The Science of Breath*, the two main *nadis, ida* and *pingala*, actually flow through the nostrils and terminate at the nasal septum (see Figure 3 on page 37). The *ida* flows through the left nostril, and the *pingala*, the right. When both nostrils are equally open, we are in a state of balance between these two *nadis.* When this balance exists, the third major *nadi*, the *shushumna*, which goes straight up through the spine, becomes fully open.[4] This understanding helps explain how when we draw in a breath, we are drawing in spirit—literally *in-spiring* and *re-spiring* ourselves.

Take a long, deep breath in right now through your nostrils, and imagine that you are inhaling directly into the *nadis*, drawing vital energy directly into this bodywide system of energy channels.

In the Oriental traditions, breathing represents a communion of the material and the spiritual. In Taoist theory the exhalation is considered the yin part of the breath, and the inhalation is yang. Thus each breath is a microcosm of the universe, in the sense that the two opposite polarities that make up the universe find perfect balance. It is impossible to only breathe in without breathing out or to breathe out without breathing in. The continuous flowing, dynamic balance of yin and yang is what makes harmony in all things. This function is eloquently described by Harriet Beinfield and Efrem Korngold in *Between Heaven and Earth: A Guide to Chinese Medicine:* "With inspiration and expiration the body inflates and shrinks, defining the margins of contraction and expansion, the fundamental polarities of *Yin* and *Yang. . . .* "[5]

In explaining the role of the *Lung* organ network, they add:

"In the *Lung* the *Qi* of Heaven (air) joins with the *Qi* of Earth (nutrition), forming the *Qi* that vitalizes human life. . . . With restraint and delicacy, expanding and contracting, the *Lung* collects, mixes, and scatters the *Qi,* instilling rhythm and order. . . . The activity of respiration drives the *Qi* throughout the body. This continuous bellowslike pulsation of the chest and abdomen sets the basic rhythmic pattern of all functions in the organism."[6]

The Breath as an Oscillator

Because of this rhythmic rising and falling, our respiration is one of our body's oscillating systems. Researchers have found that like our brain waves, our breathing pattern can also be pulled into entrainment with the heart when we are in a positive emotional state such as love or appreciation. Many varieties of breathing practices work directly with establishing certain oscillating patterns of the breath, bringing it into a regular rhythm with maximum coherence. This of course contributes strongly to our developing an overall state of internal coherence, wherein head, heart, and gut are in sync.

What Is a "Full Breath"?

Physiologically we have been conditioned to breathe in a shallow way, with shallow upper-chest breathing that keeps us in a constant state of underoxygenation. We rarely take advantage of the over seventy-five square yards of surface area in our lungs. Our lungs are pear-shaped, and the richest blood flow, or "perfusion," is in the lower part. When this area does not get adequate air, we end up with hypoperfusion, or underoxygenation, which of course leads to a lower overall energy level and potentially promotes illness.

The typical chest breath moves about half a pint of air, while a full abdominal breath can move *eight to ten times* that amount. Hence, to get the full benefit from our breathing we need to ventilate the lower lungs, which requires using the diaphragm. In diaphragmatic breathing, on the in-breath the diaphragm presses downward as the lower lungs expand, and the abdomen protrudes. The abdomen actually expands in all directions, not just the front. On the out-breath, the diaphragm is drawn back up, emptying the lower part of the lungs of any residue (what is not fully emptied is called "residual volume").

When my daughter Rosalea was born she gave me a fresh perspective on what it means to breathe fully. Watching a baby breathe gives a clear example of how full, complete breathing takes place. Each breath clearly begins in the belly and the entire torso appears to be breathing as one unit, with no holding patterns, no stiffness: just relaxed, full, naturally circular breathing.

THE BREATH AND HEALTH

What do you imagine would be the impact you would have on your body and your vital energy if you were to increase the volume of each breath by just 2 percent? You may be surprised to know that you actually take about a thousand breaths each hour, over twenty thousand breaths per day, over seven million per year. Such an increase would transform your blood chemistry and your energy on all levels.

One of the best reasons to do this is for its impact on your health, for every disease process is affected by the degree of oxygenation of your body. The breath is the most immediate source of energy that can be used for healing, energizing your body's self-repair processes, and reducing your vulnerability to illness.

In his famous studies of the metabolism of cancer cells, Nobel Prize winner Otto Warburg found that cancer cells thrive in an environment of oxygen deficiency.[7] It is also well-known that oxygen is toxic to viruses, bacteria, yeasts, and parasites in the body. This knowledge has given rise to experimentation in so-called oxygen therapies such as intravenous ozone and hydrogen peroxide treatments.

MATTERS OF LIFE AND DEATH

In the famous Framingham health study conducted by the National Heart and Lung Institute, several thousand people were followed over several decades to determine what factors seemed to most influence their long-term health. One factor considered was the individuals' respiratory capacity, or the simple volume of each breath.

Surprisingly, lower respiratory capacity was found to be *directly linked* to higher mortality from cardiac disease.[8] But that's not the most shocking finding regarding breathing and long-term health. In a thirteen-year study of longevity conducted in Australia, researchers found that respiratory capacity was actually *more significant than tobacco use, insulin metabolism, or cholesterol levels* in determining the length of people's lives.[9]

In my own research at the Cancer Support and Education Center in Menlo Park, California, I have found that the breath offers us a pathway to improve immune system functioning. We wanted to determine the impact of a breath therapy technique on the immune system. This technique, which I call evocative breath therapy (and describe later), is something we use in all our group programs for people with cancer and other illnesses. So as not to interrupt the normal flow of the program, we decided to take samples of everyone's saliva immediately before and after the hour-long breathing process, so we could look at the levels of the antibody immunoglobulin A (IgA).

What we found was surprising: an average 46 percent increase immediately after the breathing.[10]

IgA in the saliva is the body's first line of defense against germs entering through the mouth and nose that produce, among other illnesses, respiratory-tract infections (colds, flu, sinusitis, and so on). People with higher concentrations of IgA show a more rapid increase in antibodies to germs, making them less likely to become ill than people with lower levels of it. IgA is of course only one component of the immune system, but these results show us that breathing techniques can enhance the functioning of at least one important aspect of immunity, and quite possibly others.

BREATHWORK: TOOL FOR TRANSFORMATION

"I felt like energy was leaping from my body. I felt stuff going out all my pores and hairs."

"Breathing increased my energy. . . . It came up my spine, through my chest, and lifted me through the heart center, opening it and giving me tremendous energy in my hands, like electricity and lightning bolts. My body, hands, and arms enclosed a large, golden, healing energy bubble."[11]

"The energy continued moving in my body. I had the awareness that nothing would ever be the same for me again. That nothing in my life would ever be the same."[12]

These comments all come from people reporting their experience during holotropic breathwork, the same technique used by Gail in the opening story to this chapter. This is one of a variety of ways of working with the breath for inducing altered states of consciousness that can lead to transcendent and life-changing experiences. The special power of breathwork, as explained by Kylea Taylor in *The Breathwork Experience*, is that the "breath is our key to reconnecting with aspects of life from which we have become split off."[13]

While there are a variety of forms of breathwork, this "reconnecting" is commonly facilitated by the use of three ingredients: hyperventilation, music that evokes strong feelings, and the simple encouragement just to feel and allow whatever comes up during the experience.

Much of modern breath therapy is influenced by the original work of Stanislav Grof, M.D. A psychiatrist and founder of the transpersonal psychology movement, Grof coined the term "holotropic" to describe nonordinary states of consciousness that have a spiritual or transcendent quality.

He had observed that the world's aboriginal cultures as well as spiritual traditions have developed many ways of evoking such states. For example, baptism was originally a forced near-death experience (via near drowning) that brought the recipient into contact with another dimension of reality. Modern societies have of course diluted this ritual to where it is now only symbolic rather than experiential.

Other cultures have used smoke and near asphyxiation to provoke similar experiences. Prayer, fasting, vision quests, and extremes of solitude or sleep deprivation are other means for accessing such states, which in indigenous cultures have been ceremonialized as rites of passage through the normal transitions of life.

Grof discovered the therapeutic value of accessing nonordinary states of consciousness through his research in using LSD psychotherapy with mental patients. Through this work he found that what conventional psychiatry called mental illness or psychopathology is often more accurately understood as psychospiritual crises, rooted in the need we all have for holotropic or transcendent experience. In fact, Andrew Weil, M.D., in *The Natural Mind,* argues that the need to experience transcendent states is more powerful than the need for sex.[14] Interestingly, Western industrialized societies are the only societies that do not have a socially approved means of accessing such states.

It was during the course of his research that Grof found that patients could access nonordinary states through use of full and rapid breathing and that this could supplant the use of LSD. Thus holotropic breathwork was born and now occupies a distinctive place in the human potential movement.

THE MYTH OF "HYPERVENTILATION SYNDROME"

One of the great contributions of Grof's work is a new understanding of what hyperventilation is and is not. Some clinicians over the years have assumed that the tensions and sensations people have in their hands, arms, or other parts of the body during hyperventilation (sometimes called "tetany") are caused by undesirable or even dangerous changes in their biochemistry. For these symptoms they have coined the term "hyperventilation syndrome."

According to Grof, however, the so-called hyperventilation syndrome is simply a myth. Rather than being caused by chemistry, these symptoms are the result of *blockages in the flow of vital energy through the body.*

This was discovered by Grof and his associates through hundreds of holotropic breathing sessions in which people hyperventilated continuously for two to three hours and had no ill effects. Grof believes that when such energy blockages are apparent they reflect deep-seated tensions we carry in those parts of our body—perhaps because of unexpressed aggression, fears of reaching out, or some other fear of expressing oneself through the hands into the world.[15]

Hence, while some people experience spasmlike reactions during breath therapy, these reactions are a sign that significant work is being done and will pass if the person *continues* breathing. Also, after a number of sessions of the technique, people no longer go into these spasms, even though they are hyperventilating for the same length of time. This confirmed to Grof and others that hyperventilation is not to be feared, but rather can be used to release energy blocks and move more vital energy through the body.

OPENING UP

"I feel like my heart has broken open and is coming out through my eyes," remarked Alice, who was in a euphoric state after having just completed an hour-long session of "evocative breath therapy." This is a variety of breathwork that I use in my group programs for people with illness. Inspired by the work of several different teachers, including Grof and Jeru Kabbal, it uses hyperventilation and evocative music combined with guided imagery to build a charge of vital energy, arouse emotional experience and emotional release, and stimulate the body's healing responses.

What Alice's comment reveals is a common theme in all forms of breathwork: the opening up of energy centers—and particularly the heart. This is because through the connected, full, deep breathing, we are taking in an extremely large amount of vital energy. As our energetic anatomy holds this influx of surplus energy, it surges through and energizes all our channels and pathways through which it can flow. In addition, our chakras spin faster, radiating more energy and expanding. I can recall a session of my own in which it felt as though my third chakra (around my solar plexus) were the size of a Frisbee, spinning wildly with a buzzing, vibrating sensation.

The great gift of all such breathwork is that the energy aroused can shake loose stuck patterns in our energy field and open us up to greater flow of life energy. This is a kind of "deep cleaning" process and can renew us emotionally, physically, spiritually, and energetically.

THE BREATH IN MEDITATION

"We're going to have to do this without the IV Valium," warned Angela's doctor. "Can you just somehow breathe your way through it?"

Angela had been having severe stomach problems for a couple of years and was about to undergo a gastroscopy, which would involve inserting a long, three-quarter-inch tube down her throat and into her stomach to look around. The whole procedure takes about half an hour and is very uncomfortable because you have to breathe through your nose, and you have a tremendous gag reflex.

"They always use intravenous Valium to help people get through this, but my veins are really tiny and deep," explains Angela. "Three different technicians tried to get the IV into me, and they couldn't do it.

"So I started meditating, just following my breath. I had to breathe through my nose and just control it. It's what got me through the half hour, and I didn't gag at all. When I began to get anxious or feel like I was choking, I just came back to my breath. It's what anchored me and centered me, and I just allowed it to carry me through this really scary experience."

Angela's story illustrates a very practical benefit of meditation, in the form of greater ability to tolerate what's going on in her body. To do this, of course, required her to concentrate on her breath. Virtually every form of meditation, regardless of the tradition or the culture from which it came, harnesses the breath in some deliberate way.

The field of mind-body medicine has drawn a great deal from the world's meditative traditions. One result has been the discovery of the medically beneficial "relaxation response" that it creates (a state of reduced tension and blood pressure and other positive changes). This has in turn led to meditation being considered a legitimate medical recommendation for people with illness. I will go into more detail about energetic aspects of meditation in chapter 7, but for now I will summarize the role of the breath.

It is universal that in meditation the primary use of the breath is to help soothe or calm the mind and body. Typically the instructions pertaining to the breath involve

- using deep, slow, regular breaths.
- directing the breath into the abdomen.
- using the breath as the focus of the mind.

For example, in the traditional Buddhist practice called Vipassana, or "mindfulness meditation," the basic instruction is to put all your attention on fully experiencing each breath and allow all other thoughts, feelings, or sensations to pass by while you maintain this focus.

The Buddha's instructions appear remarkably simple, but upon trying them, one quickly discovers the power of the mind to interfere:

> O Monks, there is a most wonderful way to help living beings realize purification, overcome directly grief and sorrow, end pain and anxiety, travel the right path, and realize nirvana. . . .
>
> One goes to the forest, to the foot of a tree, or to an empty room, sits down cross-legged in the lotus position, holds one's body straight, and establishes mindfulness in front of oneself.
>
> Breathing in, one is aware of breathing in. Breathing out, one is aware of breathing out. Breathing in a long breath, one knows, "I am breathing in a long breath." Breathing out a long breath, one knows, "I am breathing out a long breath." Breathing in a short breath, one knows, "I am breathing in a short breath." Breathing out a short breath, one knows, "I am breathing out a short breath."[16]

The impact of meditation on our energy is not so much a matter of building it up as it is of balancing and maintaining it. Through regular meditation practice it becomes a habit to breathe more continuously and regularly throughout our day. We become more acutely aware of our breath each moment, even when not meditating, so that in the long run the breath becomes a reliable, steadying force in daily life. Then, as in Angela's case, we can call upon it to help us through trying times.

TENDING THE FIRE

In five minutes Henry will be on live television being inter-
viewed about a book he has just published. Aware that he has
only a short time to make a lasting impression, he wants to
do everything he can to be "on" for that brief period. In the
secluded hallways of the studio he goes through a series of
breathing exercises to "pump up" his energy. He first does
some *chi kung* postures to feel grounded to the earth. He
inhales deeply and visualizes drawing energy up through the
soles of his feet, through his legs, and into his body to his
vital organs. He can actually feel a buzzing sensation as he
concentrates on circulating the energy throughout his body,
reinforced and accentuated with each breath.

Next he "charges himself up" by directing a series of full,
deep breaths into each chakra in sequence, beginning with the
first. As he directs the breath into each chakra he imagines it
spinning and glowing with greater intensity, radiating greater
energy. He senses this as a "packing" process, as if he is
packing each chakra with more vital energy.

By the time he is summoned to go on the air, he is radiant,
confident, clearheaded, and feeling very strong and vital, all
of which shows in his face and comes across through his
voice.

If you want to lift your energy at any time, the easiest way
is to use your breath. It's not unlike working on a fire with a
bellows. As you direct the pumping of air toward the base of
the fire, you see a direct increase in the intensity of the blaze.
Likewise, as you feed your vital energy with more oxygen, you
will burn brighter. Your energy field will be bigger, your emo-

tions or passions will be felt more clearly and strongly, and you will radiate more energy outwardly.

The best-known practices for energization are *pranayama* from the yogic tradition and *chi kung* from the Taoist tradition.

PRANAYAMA

In the ancient yogic texts, references to breathing techniques go back four thousand years and there are hundreds of breathing practices within the yoga tradition, summarized under the rubric of *pranayama*. *Prana* literally means "life energy," and *yama* means "to lengthen." Hence the terms together are taken to mean "to enhance life energy through lengthening or deepening the breath." The yogis taught that shallow breathing leads to disturbances of emotion, mind, and body, and full breathing leads to peace, health, and quietude.

The Complete Yogic Breath. Perhaps most fundamental to *pranayama* is the "complete yogic breath." You can experience this right now by exhaling slowly as you focus on different parts of the lungs. First empty the lower lungs by contracting the muscles of your abdomen. Now empty the middle part by pulling in the ribs slightly, and then slightly contract your chest and shoulders.

Now, draw in a long, slow breath, reversing this sequence. First the belly expands ... then the rib cage ... and finally the chest. At the top of the breath you may notice your collarbones lifting slightly. Now repeat the process a couple of times.

As you can see, the emphasis is on the thoroughness of emptying and then the fullness of the inhalation.

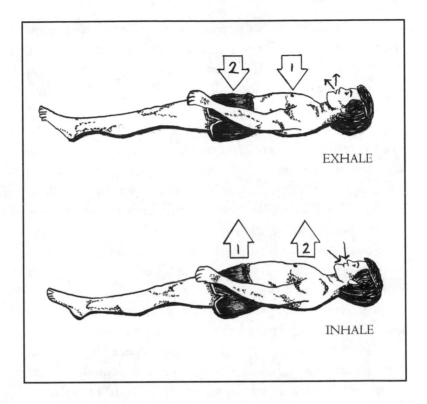

Figure 17. The Complete Yogic Breath

Alternate Nostril Breathing. Pranayama is perhaps best known for its techniques of balancing the two sides of the body, as well as the hemispheres of the brain, with *alternate nostril breathing.* This is not an obscure form of gymnastics to develop muscles in your nostrils. Rather, you alternately press each nostril closed with a finger and hold it closed while inhaling or exhaling through the other, then switch. The breaths are long, deep, and even.

Our nostrils naturally alternate in terms of which is open and which is closed at different times throughout the twenty-four-hour cycle. This is a direct way you can observe the natural, rhythmic balancing process of your energy as it circulates through you. Each nostril feeds one *nadi*, and it is rare that both nostrils are fully open at the same time. Through alternate nostril breathing, however, you can induce a state of balance and harmony between the *nadis*. This is beneficial when you want a better sense of integration or balance emotionally or psychologically. It will also balance both hemispheres of the brain.

You begin each breath on the exhale. Close the right nostril and exhale, then inhale. Close the left nostril and exhale, then inhale. (Try this for a few minutes, and let each exhalation be twice as long as the inhalation.)

Inasmuch as the *nadis* terminate in the nostrils, you are alternately energizing each of the two main *nadis* (energy channels) that rise up through the body. When air enters the right nostril, the right side of the body is activated and vital energy is coursing down the major channel on this side, the *pingala*, symbolized by the sun. When you breathe through the left nostril, you are energizing the *ida*, symbolized by the moon.

In Ayurvedic medicine, *pranayama* is considered a way of integrating a meditative life with rebalancing your vital energy, toward the ultimate goal of maintaining perfect health. However, as a practical matter it can even be used on a momentary basis to change the mood or state that you happen to be in. To do this you simply breathe through the more congested nostril while closing off the one that is more open. This will interrupt the pattern that has been in place, sustaining the mood or state you want to change. With the shift of this pattern, a new state will arise.

CHI KUNG

Like *pranayama*, the traditional Taoist energy practice of *chi kung* also includes breathing as a means of circulating vital energy through the body. As I stated earlier, the inhalation is considered the yang segment of the breath, and the exhalation is considered the yin segment. Hence any full, complete breath helps to balance the energy of the body and bring harmony to it.

Both the breath and the mind can be used to circulate energy, and when used together they create an even more potent force. In the words of San Francisco *chi kung* teacher Ellen Raskin, "When you want to increase the movement of the *chi* that is being directed by the mind, you do so with the breath, and when you bring the movements of *chi kung*, the breath, and the focus of the mind all together, you are 'in the Tao.'"[17]

Being "in the Tao" was a profoundly exhilarating experience for Ann, who for some time had been grappling with the synergy of breath, movement, and mind. One afternoon she was doing her *chi kung* practice near a marsh on the edge of the San Francisco Bay. There came a moment when she realized that she was in a state of fusion or oneness with breath, mind, and movement. At that instant, she looked up and saw a huge egret take off and fly away. "I had the very clear, distinct sensation that he was flying on my breath, and that I was up there in the wind and the sky with him," she states.

By using breath, mind, and movement together, Ann experienced an expanded state of consciousness in which she felt at one with her surroundings.

Another powerful connection was made by Rose, who had a congenital heart problem from which she had been suffering her whole life. She was a very serious meditator and was now also studying *chi kung* with Raskin.

"She came in one day and said that she had finally come to understand the relationship between the breath and the heart—how by working with her breath, she could *calm* her heart," recalls Raskin. "The next week she came in and said, 'By learning to work with my breath and my heart, I am no longer dealing with the heart as a physical ailment. I'm dealing with how to bring love and compassion out of my heart into the world, and I see that it's my *breath* that does it.'"

The Mind as a Catalyst

Both of these traditions teach us that mind and breath work together to direct vital energy through us. Visualization of the movement of vital energy through the body may be used with each breath. As an integration of several traditions, the Japanese subtle energy researcher Hiroshi Motoyama teaches a vitalizing breathing process in which you

1. inhale for a count of two;
2. retain the breath for a count of two;
3. exhale for a count of four; and
4. retain the exhalation for a count of two, before beginning the next breath.

During the moments of holding, your mental intention is to *thoroughly absorb* the energy that has been drawn in.

A variation of this is taught by the energy healer Mietek Wirkus. It involves visualizing and directing each breath along a circular pathway through the body. This pathway corresponds with what in Taoist theory is called the "micro-cosmic orbit." The instructions are as follows:

1. Counting from one to eight: While inhaling a full complete breath, imagine you are drawing energy upward from the sacrum to the back of the head at the level of the third eye.
2. For a count of four: Hold the breath and imagine the energy moving from the back of the head through the pineal gland to the third eye in the forehead.
3. For a count of eight: Exhale thoroughly while imagining that the energy is cascading like a waterfall down the front of your body to the front of your root chakra.
4. For a count of four: Hold the lungs empty and imagine the energy moving from the front of the root to the sacrum.

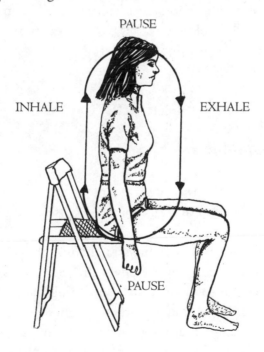

Figure 18. The Microcosmic Orbit

In this process, the third eye is considered the "distribution center" of your energy on the out-breath. When exhaling, you can imagine a third of the vital energy is being directed down the front of the orbit; a third is being directed through the shoulder joints and down the arms into the palms; and a third stays in the third eye to strengthen and sustain it.

Wirkus teaches that by breathing this way, you strengthen your energy field so that it is resilient and able to resist intrusions from other energy sources. You may use this exercise with a series of ten to fifteen breaths, three or four times per day, as a program for the overall strengthening of your energy field.

The breath is clearly the most important influence on our energetic nature on a moment-to-moment basis. In the next chapter we will explore a variety of other means for sustaining and cultivating our vital energy.

EXERCISE

Fire Breathing

This is a power *pranayama* technique for building more energy quickly. Its Sanskrit name is *bastriki,* which means "bellows."

Sit on the edge of a chair, straight upright. On the in-breath reach up and grab the sky with your hands. On the out-breath clench your hands and slowly pull the sky down to shoulder level. After doing a series of these, reach up and clasp your hands high above your head, pointing your index fingers upward in the shape of a steeple. At the same time hold your breath, lock your chin to your chest, and also lock your anal muscles. As you continue holding your breath, feel the charge of energy circulating throughout your body. Then slowly release the out-breath as you continue to absorb the energy. Do this for a few times, then look around to notice whether your senses seem sharpened.

EXERCISE

Chakra Breathing

This is a technique for energizing and strengthening all your chakras. It can also be used to focus on one specific chakra for an area of the body that is having problems.

Inhale slowly and fully, with the mental intention that you are drawing in the vital energy directly through the specific chakra. After taking in a full breath, hold your breath for a few moments while concentrating your attention on that chakra. Imagine that the chakra is absorbing and assimilating the energy, healing and strengthening itself. When you exhale, do so from the specific chakra, and imagine that the air being expelled is carrying with it any dark or dysfunctional energy or residue from that chakra, leaving it fresher, cleaner, and more radiant than before.

Do this with several breaths on each chakra you wish to work with. As a general healing and strengthening practice you could move up through the sequence of all seven chakras.

EXERCISE

With a Partner

Sit facing each other and each of you place your right hand palm down in your partner's open left hand (palm up).

Make eye contact and begin breathing together in an alternate fashion—that is, you exhale while your partner is inhaling and you inhale when your partner is exhaling. On the out-breath direct your energy out your right hand into your partner's left hand, and on the in-breath imagine drawing in the energy through your left hand.

See if you can feel the breath entering and leaving through your hands. Of course it is not the air itself, but the energy, the *prana* or *chi*, that is drawn in with the physical act of breathing.

After a while, you may notice that a charge of energy has built up. Experiment at this time with taking in another deep, full breath and holding it in for a few seconds before releasing it; then resume normal breathing.

EXERCISE

Na Dan *Meditation*

For this *chi kung* exercise begin by putting the focus of your attention on your chest (the middle *dantien*). Imagine a ball of light there, and the breath is coming and brightening the light. As you exhale, consciously move the light down the front of your body, cleansing your energy field. You are using your breath and mind together as a cleansing agent.

EXERCISE

Breathing with Music

Without having to do a formal type of breath therapy, you can experience how the breath and music work together powerfully, just by playing your favorite music and consciously breathing with it. As you do so, make the breath as effective as possible—complete and thorough, full and deep. Imagine that you are inhaling the energy of the music, drawing it into your body, and circulating it throughout your body. Imagine your nostrils and ears are merged into one organ. As you breathe in *prana*, or *chi*, the music has a "potentizing" effect, making it more vibrant and energized.

Try this with different pieces of music to see how music and breath combined can alter your energetic and emotional state.

CHAPTER 6

SUSTENANCE: THE CARE AND NURTURING OF OUR VITAL ENERGY

If the body is nourished and protected by [the] circulation of vitality, how can it possibly become ill?
— THE YELLOW EMPEROR'S CLASSIC OF
INTERNAL MEDICINE (SECOND CENTURY B.C.)

Energy. We want it, and we are drawn to people who radiate it. When we have it, we feel great, and when we don't, we feel as though we're missing out on life. How can we be stewards of our vital energy, cultivating it and manifesting more when we need it?

Walter is one of those people who seems to have boundless energy. He is a successful physician and also a prolific writer. He often arises at three or four A.M. to write and then is able to have a full workday, including travel between offices in neighboring cities. His wife, Tammy, can't understand why he needs only about four or five hours of sleep each night, when she needs eight hours to feel like her real self.

While modern science has virtually no concept of vital energy, let alone a human energy field, Eastern cultures have been teaching how to sustain and nurture it for thousands of years. We Westerners are conditioned to think that energy is something elusive that just sort of happens to us. When it's here, we use it, and when it's not, we wait. In the East, energy is something that can be deliberately cultivated, much the way we would cultivate and nurture the soil of a garden.

TWO KINDS OF ENERGY

To understand how to cultivate vital energy we need to look more deeply at the nature of it. According to Taoist energy theory, we have both *congenital chi* and *acquired chi*. Congenital *chi* translates roughly as "essence" or "sexual essence." Our congenital *chi* underlies our basic constitutional strength and is determined by the energy of our parents, our in utero nutrition, planetary influences at conception, and possibly past-life phenomena.

It cannot be replaced, but is gradually spent over a lifetime. It can be conserved by a healthy lifestyle, meditation, and certain sexual practices; but it becomes depleted through overwork, unhealthy living habits, and sexual excess. Just as a battery gradually is depleted through use, and a generator can restore some power temporarily, as the battery ages it eventually becomes unable to hold any charge at all.

Walter has an abundance of congenital *chi*, but he augments it with acquired *chi*, that which we gain from food, energetic herbs, and air. Acquired *chi* helps to conserve our congenital *chi*, and the two work together synergistically for longevity and personal power.

The marriage of these two kinds of energy explains the

differences in people's energetic resources. All of us are capable of raising the level of our vital energy with the use of acquired *chi* and by conserving our congenital *chi*. In the remainder of this chapter I'll explain how we can care for our vital energy through our patterns of activity and rest, food, energetic herbs, energy practices, and sexual practices.

TIMING IS EVERYTHING

There is a famous story in the Buddhist tradition that speaks to the wisdom of living in harmony with one's natural energetic cycles. A disciple once asked a great enlightened teacher, "Master, what is the difference between you and me?" To which the master replied, "When I'm hungry, I eat. When I'm tired, I sleep."

The idea of living in such a natural relationship with our bodies is alien to most of us in Western culture. Unfortunately our civilization has had the effect of disconnecting us from our nature as energy beings. We live our lives according to the mind and the clock, rather than responding to the natural ebb and flow of our energy.

Through the course of each day, our energy goes through cycles or phases. *Chronobiology* tells us that there are optimal times of the day for the activities of work, play, rest, and eating. If we are aware of these cycles, we can be more productive and more healthy. If we ignore them, we create disharmony in body, mind, and spirit.

RHYTHM AND BLUES

One of the great lessons of chronobiology is that maintaining a *consistent pattern* of mealtimes, activity, rest, exercise, and refreshing sleep is one effective way to maintain optimal energy and health.

We can easily grasp the concept that when an oscillating machine—such as a sewing machine or car engine—is out of rhythm, it wears unevenly and wears out prematurely. This metaphor applies to us when we are energetically out of rhythm, as our bodies wear and age prematurely. Working when the body needs rest, not eating when hungry, or resting when we need exercise are all ways of being "out of rhythm" or "out of sync."

People who are unable to establish and maintain a smooth rhythm of sleep, rest, and activity undergo premature aging and a deterioration of their resistance to illness. I believe that at the heart of such conditions as clinical depression, fibromyalgia, chronic fatigue syndrome, and perhaps even cancer is a constant state of such energetic "arrhythmia" (being out of rhythm) and nonrefreshing sleep. In my clinical practice I have seen people make major progress in these illnesses simply by attending to this issue, when drugs and other treatments did not work.

THE CYCLES OF OUR VITAL ENERGY

In the Indian tradition of Ayurveda, a clear and practical understanding can be found that explains how our vital energy moves naturally through six phases or cycles in each twenty-four-hour period. These are four-hour blocks of time in which one of the three *doshas* predominates in our energetic metabolism. A good metaphor for this is that the *doshas* are woven or braided together like three strands of rope, together constituting our vital energy. At different times of the day, a different strand "pulls more weight" and is predominant as the entire rope snakes its way through our lives.

Morning Kapha: *"Where's the Snooze Alarm?"* The morning period from six to ten A.M. is when *kapha* predominates. In keeping with the nature of *kapha*, this is a time when we feel sluggish and may have a difficult time getting moving. The earlier we get up in this period, the easier it is; and the longer we stay in bed, the more sluggish we'll feel. This is why it feels so refreshing to exercise or use some energy practice at this time—movement directly counteracts the lethargic tendencies of *kapha* and will help us be more productive.

Since moisture, water, and accumulation are characteristics of *kapha*, this is also a time of more congestion, when colds and runny noses are at their peak. In nature, it's the time when morning dew rests on the earth and the fog lays heavily across the land, waiting to be burned off in the *pitta* phase.

The virtue of *kapha* time is that it is a calmer time and helps balance *vata*. It's a good time for *vatas* and *pittas* to do some stretching and yoga, but for *kaphas* it's particularly important to be stimulated and get moving.

Midday Pitta: *Peak Performance.* These characteristics pass as we move further into the *pitta* phase, beginning around midmorning. From ten A.M. to two P.M. is the *pitta* cycle, a time when we heat up. The window of transition from *kapha* to *pitta* in midmorning is a time when our productivity builds to a peak, because the lethargy of *kapha* diminishes and the transformative fire of *pitta* releases a lot of energy that spurs us to outward action.

Pitta tends to burn out and dry out any congestion, and morning *pitta* time is also when our digestive powers are strongest. Noontime, the peak of *pitta,* is when our enzymes and the hydrochloric acid in our stomach peak, making this the best time for the main meal of the day. Anything we eat will be burned more thoroughly and cleanly than at any other time. As a consequence, you are less likely to gain weight from what you eat at this time, while the same meal late in the evening will be burned less completely and will contribute to weight gain. Hence you can lose or gain weight just by changing the *timing* of your meals without changing *what* you eat.

Afternoon Vata: *After the Fire.* From two to six P.M. is a *vata* cycle. In keeping with the understanding that *vata* disperses, this is a time we are more "dried out" on many levels. Congestion and fluids are more likely to have dispersed by this time from the fire of *pitta.* The release of energy during the transformative time of *pitta* leaves us with a lighter, less grounded feeling during *vata* time. Our thinking becomes more scattered. We will have more difficulty concentrating during this period, and this is naturally the worst time to expect children to concentrate in school. They love to play wildly during this period, however, further dispersing their energy.

Late afternoon is a particularly good time for *kapha* people to exercise, before the *kapha* of evening sets in.

Evening Kapha: *Winding Down.* From six to ten P.M. is another *kapha* cycle. This is the time when we begin to wind down, gather ourselves, and calm down for the night. There is a slowness and calmness to the evening time as the rush of the day has passed. As I mentioned earlier, this is not the best time for a big meal, as *kapha* is an accumulation phase. This is when couch potatoes are in their full glory.

Night Pitta: *Restoration.* As *kapha* wanes we move into another *pitta* cycle. This one is different from the one earlier in the day, however. Our digestive organs are again the focus, but this is the time when they clear out, detoxify, and rejuvenate. It is a time of restoration and purification of the body's tissues and not the best time for digestion of new food.

There is an interesting dynamic in moving from the *kapha* to the *pitta* cycle around ten P.M. If we stay up later than ten, the *pitta* energy that would go into restoration is easily diverted into productivity. There will be a price to pay the next day, however, as the ensuing sleep will not be as restorative.

Morning Vata: *Lightness and Clarity.* After we sleep through this restorative *pitta* period, we move into another *vata* phase from two to six A.M. Because our evening meal has been fully processed and our digestive organs have gone through their restoration, gradually our sleeping becomes lighter, and we awaken more easily toward the end of the *vata* cycle. In turn, our minds are most clear and bright in these early hours of the morning, making this the optimal time for meditation and inspiration.

The transition to *kapha* at around six A.M. brings in a steadying and calming effect. We feel both fresh and grounded during this transition time, but the more deeply we move into *kapha*, the more sluggish we are likely to feel.

It's interesting to see how we can take these cycles into account in planning our daily activities. For example, Nancy and Tim have found that when they are having conflict in their relationship, *kapha* time is most conducive to a conciliatory, peaceful resolution, while talking it out during a *pitta* period usually leads them into a more volatile and fiery exchange.

As a hyperactive ten-year-old, Jason has benefited greatly from his teacher's recognition that his symptoms are much less during the morning *kapha* hours than in the afternoon *vata* time. Since they have adjusted their expectations accordingly and given him work at strategic times, he has been doing better in school and his self-esteem seems to be improving.

Some meditative traditions ring the wake-up gong at three or four in the morning to begin spiritual practices, taking advantage of the rarefied energy of early morning *vata*. And one of the secrets known to a few in the business world is that the best time for a business meeting in which major decisions to take action need to be made is during the morning *pitta* time, but not too close to noon, when hunger begins to take over our attention.

THE BALANCE OF ACTIVITY AND REST

The wise timing of rest and sleep may be the single most important thing you can do for sustaining your vital energy. These are the times when all of your biological oscillators and energetic systems are allowed to "reset" themselves, falling back into their natural harmony with one another. In the natural metabolic cycles of the day and night, there are windows of opportunity in which your body can make the most productive use of rest or sleep, giving you the greatest benefits in terms of vital energy and healing and even in slowing the process of aging.

REST

The balancing of activity and rest reflects the natural dynamic balance of yin and yang that pervades the universe. Stillness is yin, and action is yang. If you observe the behavior of animals, you will see that they all go through many cycles of activity and rest during the day. One of the differences between us and them is that animals rest *spontaneously*. We humans, on the other hand, particularly in Western industrialized societies, tend to push ourselves to be active in large blocks of time without interruption for restorative rest.

If we do take rest during the day, particularly in the workplace, it is an arbitrary time and for a set period. Our minds are so strong, and our addiction to productivity so compelling, that we lose sensitivity to our internal energetic state. We do not rest spontaneously, when the natural ebb and flow of our energy might call for it. Thus we seem to insist on having a yang imbalance.

The cost of this lifestyle is a gradual accumulation of stress and the erosion of vital energy and, hence, of our ability to "bounce back" from the stresses and challenges of daily life. It results in the depletion of our adrenal glands, which create hormones to trigger the release of energy in the physical body. Physicians are now beginning to recognize a new syndrome called "adrenal exhaustion," in which people's adrenals are so overworked that their vital energy is very low and they become easily exhausted after stress. The main remedies for adrenal exhaustion are rest, supplementation by energetic herbs, and treatment with hormones that allow the adrenals to regenerate.

THE ULTIMATE ANTIDOTE

The most powerful antidote to adrenal exhaustion is known as the "relaxation response" discovered and named by Herbert Benson, M.D., and his colleagues in 1974.[1,2] They were studying a pattern of changes that occur in people practicing meditation. This pattern of changes has been found to represent a very beneficial state, one that is the mirror opposite of the stress response. It includes reductions in blood pressure, respiratory rate, heart rate, oxygen consumption (burning of fuel), blood flow to skeletal muscles, perspiration, and muscle tension. There is also evidence that it promotes higher levels of melatonin, the hormone that induces sleep and has immune-enhancing and anti-aging effects.[3]

The relaxation response allows all our oscillators to come into harmony—it's like pushing a reset button. This also enhances the immune system and self-repair mechanisms, brings greater energy, and improves emotional well-being. This can have profound impact on health. For example, I recently completed a study of meditation with sixty people with chronic fatigue syndrome. The result was that those meditating at least three times per week were three times more likely to improve over the course of a year than were those who meditated less.[4]

There are many techniques that can be used to produce the relaxation response. In addition to meditation, one which I enjoy is lying down on the floor with my feet elevated on a chair for about twenty minutes, once or twice a day. I have discovered that my body seems to have a threshold of eighteen to twenty minutes, at which time I invariably sense a shift of energy. There arises a sudden sensation I can describe only as "freshness," which comes in a matter of seconds—as if a switch has been turned on. This is a subtle yet profound energetic shift. My mind is suddenly sharper, and my breath moves more easily.

Obviously, adopting a pattern of rest periods during the day will have great benefits for replenishing and maintaining your energetic resources.

SLEEP

Night is yin and day is yang, each flowing eternally into the other. During the yin of night, momentum is building for yang to spring forth in the morning. When the yang energy of sunlight arrives, blossoms burst open, animals become active, the buzz of nature resumes. Then comes a building and a cresting of yang energy during the day, and as the day wanes into the evening, there is a natural return back to the yin of quiet and calm.

As a being of energy, you are part of the energy of nature—even though you may be inside a building. By being active in the day and calm in the night, you are following nature's pattern. Your own energy is, in a sense, ushered along by that of nature—you are moving with the flow rather than resisting it. Conversely, to remain active deep into the night and to be sleeping later into the morning light takes you out of the flow of nature.

This has a definite impact on the quality of your sleep in terms of how refreshing and healing it is. Sleeping eight hours between ten P.M. and six A.M. is going to be more refreshing and energizing than sleeping eight hours between midnight and eight A.M., or between two A.M. and ten A.M. In chapter 3 I explained that the earth's geomagnetic field is more conducive to good quality sleep at night. Another reason is that your pineal gland, the king gland that regulates your sleep cycle and your hormonal system, follows nature's rhythms of darkness and light.

Your pineal gland takes its cue from the fading light of the evening hours and naturally begins secreting melatonin, the sleep hormone, at around eight P.M. in order to prepare you to sleep. Blood levels of melatonin peak between two and four A.M., after which they take a precipitous dive back down toward baseline, as the pineal gland begins to respond to the first rays of the morning light, sensed by the retina through your closed eyelids.[5]

This rise and fall of melatonin levels through the night is paralleled by changes in body temperature, which lowers during sleep to help conserve and rebalance our energy and rises again with the light of daytime.[6]

UNHAPPY OUTCOMES

The importance of maintaining a good rhythm was illustrated in a study of the effects of sleep on the immune system in twenty-three healthy men in their thirties. For each of four days the men's natural killer cell activity was tested. (Natural killer cells are immune cells that attack bacteria, viruses, and tumors.) The men's sleep time during the four days averaged eight hours per night. On the fifth night they were awakened at three A.M. and got four hours less sleep than usual. This one insult to their sleep cycle resulted in a *28 percent decline* in the activity of their natural killer cells the next day, an indication that the immune system's vitality or vital energy had declined appreciably.[7]

I've learned a great deal about sleep from my work with people suffering from chronic fatigue syndrome and fibromyalgia. Some researchers believe that a sleep disturbance plays a key role in these modern maladies, and I agree. These are illnesses in which the person commonly wakes up in the morning feeling as though a truck had run over them—even after twelve or more hours of sleep. The problem is that these people do not adequately experience the deep, restorative phase of sleep called the "delta phase." This is the phase that is most healing for the physical body, and without it the results are fatigue, the tender points of fibromyalgia, a foggy mind, and other symptoms.

This understanding was confirmed by researchers at the Center for Sleep and Chronobiology at Toronto Hospital in Canada. They studied the effects of experimentally induced sleep interruption of a group of medical students. Over several nights, each time the students were going into the delta phase of sleep, they would be deliberately disturbed. The result was that in a few days they developed all the classic symptoms of chronic fatigue syndrome and fibromyalgia.[8]

SLEEP SUPPLEMENTS

Many clinical studies have shown that supplementation with synthetic melatonin can be very helpful. According to Andrew Weil, M.D., "Melatonin is safe and effective for resetting wayward biological clocks."[9] This simple and inexpensive substance is increasingly popular and is available in health food stores. It is a nonaddictive, nondepressant regulator of sleep cycles.

Another well-regarded sleep supplement is valerian root.

This is a natural sedative, though, and is not recommended for long-term use. It is commonly available in health food stores as a tincture to be taken in water at bedtime (about one teaspoon). Melatonin is considered the superior choice for long-term supplementation because of its safety and because the pineal gland's production of it gradually declines with age, perhaps contributing to aging.

LET THE SUN SHINE

In many ancient traditions the sun is worshipped as the source of all life, and this is quite true in the sense that our planet was born from the sun and life on earth could not exist without it. One native American ritual is to exhale your first morning breath into cupped hands and offer it as a gift of gratitude to the rising sun. In Oriental traditions, the sun is held to be a very rich and powerful source of *chi* or *prana,* and we can absorb this directly by receiving the sun's rays.

Spending a few minutes in the early morning sun will help you sleep better at night, because it helps your biological clock align itself with the cycles of nature. It is as if you are helping your pineal gland to say in no uncertain terms, "Yes, no question about it, it's daytime." This helps the pineal to have a clear sense of the distinction between night and day— when to secrete the sleep hormone melatonin and when not to. Also, people suffering from seasonal affective disorder (SAD) usually have abnormally high levels of melatonin during daytime, which is the wrong time. Studies have found that those who receive more morning light improve their condition.[10]

THE ENERGETICS OF FOOD

Beyond its chemical constituents, food contains vital energy. When we eat, we absorb this energy and it feeds our own. Live or freshly harvested foods contain the richest, most robust, most nourishing energy. Foods that are processed, old, stored, cooked and recooked, refrigerated, or frozen have much less vital energy to be passed on.

Imagine the difference in energy between a bite of an apple that is still hanging from the tree and an apple that has been shipped for two months in a dark box from another country far across the ocean. Or imagine eating a freshly prepared chicken that spent its life roaming freely in the countryside, in the sun every day, eating bugs and wild grains; then contrast this with eating a chicken that spent its entire life in one square foot with no room for movement, never seeing the light of day, being fed a chemicalized formula, and being frozen and trucked three thousand miles across the country.

We know intuitively that the energetic qualities of food are what we need.

OUR ANCESTRAL DIET

According to Boyd Eaton, professor of anthropology at Atlanta University, twentieth-century humans have virtually the same genetic makeup as their Paleolithic ancestors fifteen thousand years ago. However, they were fit and lean hunters who lived on a diet of organic vegetables and lean meat from wild game. They never ate cereal grains, and they had no milk after being weaned. "Our ancestors got up to five times the vitamins and minerals we are getting today," he states. "Our ancestral diet is that for which our genetically determined metabolism was originally designed."[11]

Our ancestral diet is available today only in so-called health food stores. Because of the economics of our food industry, we are presented a food supply consisting largely of fast and processed foods. Unfortunately, "fast" and "processed" are euphemisms for "stripped of their original nutritive and energetic qualities." As a consequence, today's chronic illnesses are largely related to a combination of the undersupply of many essential nutritive substances and energies and the overburdening of the body with alien chemicals and toxins.

FOOLING OURSELVES

We feel the negative consequences of this kind of diet on our vital energy each day, and then we may try to compensate with caffeine and foods high in simple sugars. Unfortunately these add to the burden on our body's detoxification system, stress organs such as the pancreas, liver, kidneys, and the adrenal glands, and weaken the immune system.

Sweet foods and caffeine are commonly thought of as sources of increased energy, yet they actually have a paradoxical effect and in many people are the root cause of depletion of vital energy. White sugar gives a temporary energy high because it doesn't require much breaking down and enters the blood and body's cells very quickly, releasing its energy. However, in order to accommodate this sudden infusion of simple sugar in the blood, the pancreas overreacts, releasing a high level of insulin. The net result is that too much blood sugar is *removed*, leading to the perception of an energy "crash," or hypoglycemia (low blood sugar).

Caffeine is a central nervous system stimulant that makes the adrenal glands trigger a sudden release of sugar that is naturally stored in the liver. This sudden jolt creates a similar cascade of events to white sugar in terms of the release of insulin and the ensuing sugar "low," leading many people to feel they need even more coffee. Thus, in addition to triggering the hypoglycemic symptoms, caffeine stresses the adrenals and can lead to adrenal exhaustion. Healthy adrenal glands are what help us cope with the stress of daily life.

Alas, even some so-called natural foods are often processed or altered in such a way as to have many nutrients removed or to have unnaturally high concentrations of natural sugars. Two darlings of the health food industry, concentrated juice drinks and fruit juice–sweetened whole-grain cookies, have an extremely high concentration of natural sugars and introduce an intense sugar shock into the bloodstream, far stronger than the body is designed to metabolize easily. In such high doses, fruit sweetening loses any health advantage over refined sugar.

All these nutritive stresses on the body sap our vital energy; leave vital organs toxified, overstressed, and undernourished; and weaken the body's ability to support the harmonious circulation of vital energy through its organ networks.

Foods as "Energy Tonics"

Traditional Chinese medicine has a rich and exhaustive tradition of understanding the energetic qualities of foods.

Treated quite separately from the matter of herbs, foods themselves are considered "tonics" for different purposes. A tonic is a substance that serves to strengthen and make more resilient, somewhat analogous to our concept of toning muscles. The difference is that in this case what is being tonified are different aspects of our vital energy and our energetic anatomy.

Foods that serve the broad purpose of energy tonics are believed to help people suffering from a general low level of vital energy, or *chi*, which may be attributed to chronic illness, genetic factors, aging, and chronic stress.

A list of traditional energy tonic foods includes some rather interesting dishes that may or may not be familiar to Westerners. Examples include beef liver, bird's nest soup (a delicacy for only the highly motivated), bitter gourd seed, broomcorn, cherries, chicken, coconut, crane meat, dates, eel, fermented glutinous rice, ginkgo, ginseng, goose, grapes, herring, honey, jackfruit, licorice, longan, lotus rhizome powder, mackerel, mandarin fish, octopus, pigeon egg and meat, sweet and white potatoes, rabbit, red and black dates, glutinous and polished rice, rock sugar, shark's fin, shiitake mushrooms, squash, sturgeon, tofu, and white string beans.[12]

As Henry Lu, author of *Chinese Foods for Longevity*, explains, energy tonic foods mostly strengthen the organs of the digestive system, which is the underlying key to generating more energy for the body. By strengthening the furnace, we will get more benefit from whatever fuels are being burned.

A Matter of Taste

In Ayurveda, foods are known to either increase or decrease our *doshas*. Once you understand the energetic qualities of food from the Ayurvedic perspective, you can choose a diet that rebalances you or helps you maintain balance and harmony, and you can minimize intake of foods that aggravate your *dosha*.

For example, if your dosha is *kapha* and you want to watch your weight, you would eat foods that decrease *kapha*, such as spicy foods, green leafy vegetables, and beans. These same foods, however, would increase *vata*, so they would not be so desirable for someone who is primarily *vata*. Dietary therapy is one of the foundations of Ayurveda, and there are specific diets for reducing or "pacifying" each *dosha*, depending on which one is out of balance.

The tastes of foods are what reveals their energetic qualities. There are six tastes: sweet, sour, salty, pungent, bitter, and astringent.

According to Dr. Mary Jo Cravatta of Palo Alto, California, "Everyone should have all six tastes at their main meal but in different proportions, depending upon what *dosha* they need to balance."[13]

When we have a *preference* (short of a strong craving) for certain tastes, this usually indicates that those tastes are needed to balance our predominant *dosha*. In this sense the body in its wisdom is telling us what is needed for balance. On the other hand, extreme cravings or addictions to tastes indicate an underlying *im*balance that would be further aggravated by those tastes.

Table 2 shows the six tastes, their associated foods, and their effects on the various *doshas*.

TABLE 2:
TASTES, FOODS, AND THEIR ENERGETIC EFFECTS

Taste	Foods (examples)	Effects on Doshas: Vata	Kapha	Pitta
Sweet	sugars, milk, butter, rice, breads, pasta	decrease	increase	decrease
Sour	yogurt, lemon, cheese	decrease	increase	increase
Salty	salts	decrease	increase	increase
Pungent	spicy foods, ginger, hot peppers, cumin	increase	decrease	increase
Bitter	green leafy vegetables, turmeric	increase	decrease	decrease
Astringent	beans, lentils, pomegranate	increase	decrease	decrease

By consulting with an Ayurvedic practitioner, you can easily discover an entire dietary system that works for you and your particular constitution. There are also books on Ayurvedic cooking that identify the energetic qualities of complete meal plans.

The ancient Ayurvedic text *Charaka* offered the following practical guidelines for healthful eating:[14]

1. Food needs to be hot (usually cooked).
2. Food needs to be tasty and easy to digest.
3. Food needs to be eaten in the proper amounts, not too much or too little.
4. Food needs to be eaten on an empty stomach, after your last meal has been digested and not before.

5. Foods need to work together and not contradict one another in their actions.
6. Foods need to be eaten in pleasant surroundings with the proper equipment for their enjoyment.
7. Eating should not be rushed.
8. Eating should not be a horrendously drawn-out affair, either.
9. It is best to focus on your food while eating.
10. Eat only food that is nourishing to your particular constitution and that suits your mental and emotional temperament.

THE FIRE WITHIN: DIGESTION

In Taoist theory the region of our body that holds our digestive organs is called the "middle burner," and in Ayurveda the digestive fire is called "*agni.*" These are excellent metaphors for the processes that go on there, for digestion is a process of burning, like a furnace burning fuel to release its energy. The importance of good digestion in nourishing our vital energy cannot be overstated.

A clean-burning and efficient furnace will produce more energy and less waste or residue. For the physical body, this translates into less undigested material that can putrefy in the colon and release toxins to be absorbed, plaguing the body with allergies, food sensitivities, and fatigue. It also means more vital energy, as the source of fuel is completely used and its *chi* is absorbed.

MOTHERLY ADVICE

There are several ways we can enhance our digestion. First, digestion begins in the mouth, with the enzymes in our saliva released through chewing. Mother's admonishment to chew your food thoroughly was excellent advice. In fact, Michio Kushi, the father of macrobiotic cooking, is credited with saying we should "drink our solids and chew our liquids" to get the full benefit from this first stage of digestion. An added benefit is that if we take the time to chew thoroughly, we and our digestive organs are likely to be more relaxed.

When you are stoking a fire, wet fuel takes longer to kindle because the moisture keeps it cool longer. Hence the recommendation not to drink much liquid with a solid meal.

No doubt you have observed that a cold log placed on a fire takes longer to heat up and reach the burning temperature. A fire burns more cleanly if the fuel is already warm. Cold foods are harder to digest and actually stress the digestive organs. Cooked and warm foods are the most easily digested and assimilated. Eating ice cream or drinking iced drinks with or shortly after a meal will only help to put out the fire.

The metaphor of the fire applies to *how much* we eat as well. Pack a wood stove solid, with more fuel than it can process, and no matter how good the fuel is, it will burn less efficiently. This is why it is wiser to eat moderate-sized meals and avoid overeating.

As I mentioned earlier, the timing of eating can make a great deal of difference in our digestion. Ayurveda teaches that midday is the time of strongest and most complete digestion. The digestive fire within, *agni*, parallels the intensity of the sun in the sky. Thus the last meal of the day should be eaten before sundown, as *agni* follows the sun into the night.

Raw or Cooked?

There is an ongoing debate over whether raw or cooked foods are best for our health and vital energy. There are many highly esteemed experts on both sides of this issue. Advocates of raw foods say that cooking above 107 degrees destroys the enzymes that are needed to digest food. They say that this forces the body to rob enzymes from its own tissues to rescue the digestive process, thus depleting the body of its own reserves. Enzymes are needed to break down the food into its chemical components so that their energy can be released in the cells of the body. On the other hand, proponents of cooked food argue that raw food doesn't burn as cleanly—it is difficult to digest and stresses the body. Cooking eases the breakdown process and allows cleaner burning.

Some people take the step of supplementing a diet of cooked foods with digestive enzymes. There are no definitive studies that I am aware of to decide this issue one way or another. You are, of course, free to choose what paradigm feels intuitively right to you. In the Western perspective, enzyme supplementation may make sense because it suggests better digestion from a biochemical point of view. From an Eastern perspective, however, it is the energetic qualities of the food that are important, and enzymes are not part of that paradigm.

STOKING THE FIRE

The Ayurvedic tradition offers us a powerful practice for stoking the digestive fire about twenty to thirty minutes before a meal. Try a few slices of raw ginger sprinkled with lemon juice and a little salt. This will stir the digestive fire, or *agni,* to dramatically improve digestion—your stomach will *feel* like a furnace.

ENERGETIC HERBS AND SUPPLEMENTS

To practitioners of Oriental medicine, Westerners' fascination with supplementing their diets with vitamins, minerals, and other substances is a peculiar idea. This is because in the Oriental view it is the *energy* of our diet that matters, not the *chemistry.* In the words of Bob Flaws, author of *Prince Wen Hui's Cook: Chinese Dietary Therapy,* "[I]f one follows Chinese dietary theory according to its own energetic concepts and principles, one will achieve health without having to consider such materialistic concepts. One will be getting a well-rounded diet even from a Western nutritional point of view."[15]

Herbal supplementation is based on this notion of working with our energy rather than our chemistry. This is the world's oldest approach to medicine, and herbs have been used for such diverse purposes as treating symptoms of disease, strengthening the body, prolonging life, increasing virility and fertility, enhancing the powers of the mind, and promoting spirituality and the growth of consciousness. More recently, research has found herbs to be medically beneficial in heart disease, cancer, and reducing the side effects of chemotherapy.[16]

Tonic herbs serve to stimulate or strengthen our vital energy. They are not taken for medicinal purposes, in that they are not intended to treat disease directly. In cases of illness, a more specific herbal regimen would be appropriate, perhaps complemented by other forms of medicine. Rather, the historic purpose of tonic herbs in the Orient has been a more spiritual one—to generate "radiant health" by tonifying, harmonizing, and regulating vital energy so that the body is a suitable vehicle for attaining spiritual enlightenment.[17]

Of the tonic herbs available, ginseng and licorice have shown some particularly interesting benefits in research.

GINSENG

This famous herb is reputed to boost vital energy, relieve stress, improve mental clarity and concentration, increase athletic performance and endurance, enhance sexual function and immunity, and promote healing in a variety of health conditions. In fact, the term "Panax" in *Panax ginseng,* one variety, has its root in "panacea," which means "cure-all." While some of the traditional hyperbole of the virtues of ginseng may be overstated, it is a potent "adaptogen" in that it promotes the rapid mobilization of vital energy and helps the body cope with stress by supporting the functioning of the adrenal glands.[18] Research has also found it to be an antioxidant[19] and have a protective effect on the liver.[20]

Types of ginseng are distinguished by their active ingredients. Korean, Chinese, and Panax ginseng contain *gin-senisodes*. These forms of ginseng have an overall stimulating effect on the central nervous system. They are not usually recommended for long-term daily use because such stimulation could cause side effects, such as insomnia and anxiety.

American ginseng also contains ginsenisodes but in a different balance, which produces an overall sedating effect on the central nervous system. Thus American ginseng can be taken as a daily tonic, but it does not have the stimulating or energizing qualities of the Korean, Chinese, or Panax varieties.

Siberian ginseng has a different kind of active ingredient, *eleutherosides*. Like the other kinds of ginseng, Siberian is also considered an excellent adaptogen in promoting vital energy and adaptation to stress. However, it has a very low toxicity and thus can be taken daily over long periods, allowing cumulative benefits for vital energy and stamina. It is so well respected in Russia that it is taken by over twenty million Russians and is used regularly by Russian Olympic athletes and cosmonauts. It is becoming increasingly popular in the United States. Clinical research has found it to help people adapt to high and low temperatures, intensive exercise, and other forms of stress.

Siberian ginseng has also been the subject of numerous studies of health benefits. Studies have found it to reduce the incidence of stress-related diseases[21] and improve the status of patients with chronic gastritis, diabetes, and hardening of the arteries. Other studies have found it to speed recovery from surgery and stimulate the immune system in cancer patients[22] and to reduce the toxic effects of cancer chemotherapy and the narcotic effects of sedative drugs.[23]

For all ginseng products, the main criteria for selection should be potency and standardization. The greatest potency is found in *extracts* derived from the plant root. The potency is specified in terms of milliliters or milligrams of the active ingredients. "Standardized" means that the level of active ingredients is guaranteed.

Ginseng can come in a variety of forms. Powder capsules are usually not standardized. Tablets are compressed powders, which may not always contain active ingredients and may not be standardized. Liquid extracts are usually in a base of alcohol or glycerin and may not be standardized. The best choices are paste extracts, which usually contain high levels of active ingredients, are standardized, and have a good shelf life. The paste extracts can be found either in jars or in capsules. Of the two most popular ginsengs, Panax and Siberian, the latter is less expensive.

Licorice Tea (*Ganzahaou*)

An easy and economical treatment for adrenal exhaustion is to take licorice tea several times each day. Licorice tea contains *glycyrrhiza*, a powerful stimulant of the adrenal glands. It functions similarly to adrenocortical hormone and is also a powerful detoxifier of the body, helping to eliminate or detoxify over 1,200 known toxins. This is the most widely used of all Chinese herbs. It is also believed to clean the meridians and allow the *chi* to flow smoothly.[24]

Boiling up the raw herbs is preferable. Chinese licorice (*Glycyrrhiza uralensis*), which has a relaxing effect, is better than American licorice (*Glycyrrhiza glabra*), which can cause nervousness. Glycyrrhiza blocks the breakdown of hydrocortisone in the liver, allowing blood levels to remain higher, slowing down the production of the stress hormone (ACTH) from the pituitary and adrenal glands, thus allowing the adrenals to receive a much needed rest.[25] The licorice root available in capsules is usually the American variety. Tea is preferable because it contains other elements for a synergistic effect.

ASHWAGANDA

Ashwaganda is a favorite rejuvenescent herb from the tradition of Ayurveda. Like ginseng, *ashwaganda* is an adaptogen, but the two are botanically unrelated and their actions are quite different.

Ashwaganda comes from the roots of *Withania somnifera*, a small shrub from India and a member of the nightshade family. It has mild sedative qualities and is reputed to increase sperm count, improve female fertility, and be a sexual tonic with aphrodisiac qualities. It is also used in Ayurveda for reduction of rheumatic swelling and soothing of ulcers.

CHYAVAN PRASH

This is the most famous energy tonic formula from Ayurveda. It is a jellylike fruit compote consisting of *amalaki* fruit, long pepper, bamboo manna, cloves, cinnamon, cardamom, cubebs, ghee, raw sugar, and other herbs. There are also many variations of this popular tonic. *Chyavan prash* has historically been considered helpful for almost any health condition because of its benefits to vital energy. It is widely available in this country through health food stores and Indian markets.

SUMA

This South American herb has been used in the folk medicine of several indigenous peoples for thousands of years. It is used in Brazilian hospitals in treatment of cancer and diabetes and is reputed to be of great benefit for almost whatever ails you. Its Spanish name is *para todo,* meaning "for everything," and it is a powerful adaptogen that counteracts the effects of stress on the body. Herbalists in North America have found it beneficial for premenstrual syndrome, hormonal imbalances, chronic fatigue syndrome, and building vital energy.

This root product from the Amazon basin has become widely available in the United States only recently and can be taken either as a tea or as a powder in capsules.

OTHER TONIC HERBS

There are hundreds of other tonic herbs reputed to help tonify our vital energy. Practitioners of Oriental medicine, whether of Chinese or Ayurvedic form, are well versed in the strategic use of tonic herbs. While there are also many popular books in this field, I recommend that you work with a practitioner who is skilled in this area to learn what is right for your particular energetic condition.

THE MOTHER OF ALL HORMONES

Hormone therapies are increasingly being looked at in Western medicine for helping people with energy deficiencies. Among other functions, hormones govern the creation and metabolism of energy in the cells of our physical body. The most abundant hormone in the human body is DHEA (dehydroepiandrosterone), which is the precursor of other important hormones such as estrogen, progesterone, and testosterone.

There are over four thousand studies suggesting that hormone therapies can promote health and vital energy, particularly as we age. A twelve-year study of 242 men between the ages of fifty and seventy-nine found that supplementation with DHEA was associated with a 48 percent reduction in death from heart disease and a 36 percent reduction in deaths from all causes, other than accidents.[26] Another study examined rates of breast cancer and levels of DHEA in 5,000 women. Those developing breast cancer showed falling levels of DHEA as many as nine years prior to the onset of the cancer.[27]

According to Norman Shealy, M.D., Ph.D., a leading proponent of such supplementation, this is also the most sensitive chemical to the effects of stress.[28] He describes DHEA as a "chemical stress reservoir"—meaning that the lower the reservoir of DHEA, the less we are able to tolerate stress. He argues that the reason so many of us are so low in DHEA is that it is a product of the adrenal glands and we have adrenal burnout or adrenal exhaustion, caused by chronic stress.

You will be hearing a lot more about DHEA in the coming years. Supplementation with DHEA apparently has no negative effects. Fortunately the pure formulation (not to be confused with wild yam extract, which contains some of its precursors) is becoming increasingly available over the counter.

THE TAO OF EXERCISE

Exercise is a very direct way to stimulate vital energy to move through your body. When balanced with adequate rest, regular exercise has a general effect of raising your basic energy level. Conversely, a sedentary lifestyle, in which you are "sitting on" your energy for long periods without moving it through exercise, will tend to diminish it. In essence, energy begets energy: the more you move your energy—within moderation, not to the point of exhaustion—the more you will have.

The Western view of exercise is, however, very different from the Eastern. We tend to focus on strengthening and toning our musculature, becoming more lean, and building aerobic fitness. These are generally beneficial outcomes, and indeed, research has shown that people who undertake regular vigorous exercise live longer.

The Eastern view, in contrast, makes a distinction between two kinds of exercise: *external* and *internal*. The forms we are most familiar with, such as weight training, jogging, and competitive sports, would be considered *external* exercise. Practices that focus on directly cultivating *chi*, or the vital force, such as *chi kung, tai chi*, and *pranayama*, are considered *internal* exercise. They serve to strengthen and refine our vital energy and to tonify our internal organ networks and glands, which are the conduits of our vital energy.

STRONG ON THE OUTSIDE, WEAK ON THE INSIDE

Our Western concepts of exercise are not concerned with the health of our internal organs and glands, other than indirectly through improved blood circulation. Thus a person can have a high degree of aerobic fitness and a beautifully developed physique on the outside, while digestion and the functioning of internal organ networks and glands may remain very poor.

In the Eastern perspective the strengthening and tonification of our vital energy and internal organ networks takes priority over external physique. Those who have cultivated and mastered their *chi*, even though they may have what appears to be little muscle definition, will be inwardly stronger and more fit in terms of their ability to enjoy life and even resist illness. The consequences of these two divergent views of exercise can be illustrated as follows:

Imagine a situation in which two backpackers are trapped and threatened by a rapidly advancing forest fire in a mountainous terrain. One is an experienced and devoted *chi kung* practitioner, while the other is a competitive marathon runner. If the situation calls for them to run for their lives, the runner will likely be more successful in reaching safety, though years of hard training may have left his internal organs stressed and weakened.

On the other hand, if the same two individuals were traveling through Africa and were exposed to an outbreak of *ebola* virus, the *chi kung* practitioner would be more likely to survive the infection because his immune response—fueled by the vital force—would likely be stronger and more able to fend off the virus.

Studies have shown that exercise leads to improved immune functioning, including better natural killer cell activity.[29] However, on closer inspection, the findings indicate that light to moderate exercise, more along the lines of *chi kung*, a form of internal exercise, stimulates the immune system, while intense external exercise, such as long-distance running, may have the opposite effect.[30]

THE BEST OF BOTH WORLDS

Our physical body and our vital energy exist in a complementary relationship. Think of the physical body as the container and the vital energy as the content. This complementarity is described by Roger Jahnke, O.M.D., as follows: *Chi*, or vital energy, is yang; and the physical body, which is "substance," is yin. "Substance is needed to hold the *chi*," he states. "To sustain, support, carry, and conduct that yang you have to have a yin element," and the healthier and stronger the physical body is, the better it is able to do so.[31]

By integrating both kinds of exercise into your life, you can magnify the benefits of each. Vigorous exercise arouses a great deal of *chi*, which seems to exude from one's pores and, in reality, is radiating strongly from all the chakras. If you could see your energy field clearly after exercise, you would see that it is greatly intensified and expanded beyond its normal boundaries.

For this reason it is very beneficial, immediately after jogging, weight training, or any other external exercise, to have a period of internal exercise—such as a few minutes of *chi kung* or *pranayama*—for balancing and consolidating this aroused *chi*. By doing so, you can contain and absorb the additional energy, rather than just going on with your day and letting it all dissipate into the environment around you. This energy can then serve to further strengthen your internal organs and energy systems.

Some Eastern traditions integrate aspects of both inner and outer exercise, by virtue of their refined attention to the breath and vital energy while simultaneously using postures, positions, or movements that challenge and strengthen the musculature. These include certain varieties of yoga and the martial arts, some of which can be quite vigorous and bring aerobic conditioning as well.

Where exercise is concerned, East and West can learn from each other, and the optimal approach is to integrate the best of both worlds.

ENERGY PRACTICES

There are many practices you can use in daily life to stimulate and cultivate your vital energy. Throughout this book I have mentioned several. Now I want to elaborate on some of them and introduce others.

HYDROTHERAPY: BRACE YOURSELF

The first time I went skiing was at Winter Park, Colorado, high in the Rockies outside Denver. At the resort where I was staying there was a huge hot tub, a most welcome sight after a cold and strenuous day on the slopes. One tradition around this particular tub was to step out of it and immediately jump into a deep snow drift, then return to the tub to get heated up again. I didn't know it at the time, but this was a serious experience of hydrotherapy.

Anyone who has had the experience of ending a hot shower with a blast of cold water, or leaping from a hot tub or sauna into a cold swimming pool or snowbank, can testify to the stimulating and "bracing" effects of hydrotherapy. It may feel as though energy is literally exploding through all your pores—and, indeed, the "rush" that you feel is the sudden dramatic increase of vital energy surging through your body.

While hydrotherapy is not customarily thought of as an energy practice, I include it here because it is a surprisingly stimulating and tonifying practice easily available to most anyone. It involves using the extremes of hot and cold moisture to arouse and stimulate the body's vital energy. According to Hector Ramos, a teacher of *"pranic* healing" in Berkeley, California, hydrotherapy has a balancing effect on the chakras.[32]

Many health spas and resorts have hot and cold pools next to each other for this reason. Even the simple practice of splashing cold water on your face first thing in the morning is an experience of hydrotherapy.

This method was brought to the United States in 1896 by Benedict Lust, a German who had cured himself of tuberculosis using hot and cold water treatments. It is used in naturopathic medicine as therapy for many specific ailments. One common form is to use towels that are wrung out in hot and cold water and apply them alternately to the body. In addition to stimulating the flow of vital energy, blood circulation to a certain area can be dramatically increased. In digestive disorders, for example, intense fluctuations in temperature on the surface of the abdomen can serve to improve blood circulation to the stomach, liver, kidneys, and intestines, thereby improving digestion and elimination of metabolic waste. The "toxic load" on all the vital organs is reduced, and the immune system is stimulated.

The simplest way to enjoy the benefits of hydrotherapy on a regular basis is with a daily shower, and many people have discovered this delight on their own. You can easily experiment with this by alternating hot and cold water in the shower a few times to get a sense of the invigorating potential of hydrotherapy.

YOGA: OPENING THE CHANNELS

One of the most direct and immediate ways to experience an infusion of energy is through the practice of yoga. The most commonly practiced form is *hatha yoga*, which consists of specific postures or stretches, called "asanas." We Westerners usually think of the benefits of yoga in terms of developing greater flexibility of muscles and joints. Indeed, these are major benefits, but they are just the tip of the iceberg. From an energetic point of view, yoga asanas actually stimulate the flow of *prana* through our entire energetic anatomy.

This has great importance in healing, since specific illnesses are associated with energy blockages in specific chakras. For example, difficulties in the uterus or prostate, which are centered deeply in the area of the second chakra, are helped by postures that stimulate the flow through that chakra. Hundreds of scientific studies have documented the health benefits of yoga for all kinds of conditions.

In addition to affecting the major chakras, the yogic perspective views the joints of the body as minor chakras. By opening up our joints and making them more flexible, we are opening and allowing greater flow of vital energy through those chakras, contributing to greater flow through the body as a whole. Furthermore, as our muscles, ligaments, and other soft tissue become more flexible, they too are more able to conduct an even and harmonious flow of vital energy through our energetic anatomy.

Thus yoga is clearly not just an "external" form of exercise in the sense of working only with the musculoskeletal system, but is also an "internal" form by virtue of its beneficial impacts on our energy system.

Figure 19: Yoga: Opening the Channels

Yoga as Energy Enhancement. You can get a significant increase in your daily energy level through yoga. This was shown in a study comparing the effects of three different approaches to energy enhancement. One group of subjects used the classic relaxation technique called "progressive relaxation" in which the various muscle groups of the body are relaxed in a sequence. The second group were instructed to visualize an image that represented their current energy level, then modify that image to represent a state of higher energy. The third group performed a sequence of twelve yoga stretches combined with deep breathing and forced exhalation.

Of the three methods, yoga produced a significantly greater sense of both mental and physical energy in the participants, combined with greater feelings of enthusiasm and alertness.[33]

You don't need to practice yoga for a long time to begin to sense these benefits. Even if you've never done yoga before, you will feel the impact on your energy immediately with the very first session, regardless of the degree of flexibility you have. Any attention you give even to slightly increasing your current level of flexibility will be accompanied by a tangible sense of greater energy flowing through your body. Hundreds of yoga classes and groups are available, along with excellent videotape programs, to support you in maintaining a daily practice.

CHI KUNG AND TAI CHI: FOLLOWING THE RIVER

Frances, who has been living with chronic fatigue syndrome for three years, shows us an example of the benefits of energy cultivation. She is participating in a treatment program that employs training in *chi kung*, an Oriental healing art involving breathing, graceful movements, self-massage of acupuncture points, and self-imaging techniques.

Since beginning the program two months ago, Frances has

noticed a gradual improvement in her level of energy and mental clarity and in the quality of her sleep. During the daily exercises she often has sensations of warmth, buzzing, or vibration in her body as the circulation of her vital energy, or *chi*, is stimulated.

What Frances is experiencing is commonplace in China, where millions of people of all ages practice *chi kung* and *tai chi* each morning in public. *Chi kung* is the five-thousand-year-old tradition that is the mother of all martial arts, including the closely related *tai chi*, and both of these are used for health as well as building strength for self-defense. In Shanghai there is even a hospital devoted to treating cancer with these methods.[34]

While there is a great deal of similarity between *chi kung* and *tai chi*, the latter is generally considered to be more movement oriented and the former more stationary, although this is a simplification. Both disciplines contain elements of meditation, relaxation, visualization, movement, postures, and breathing exercises. In the Orient they serve both as forms of exercise for physical fitness and as self-healing tools. *Chi* is always circulating in a person, but in doing these practices, you *accelerate* the flow through your intention and directed action.

The aim is to strengthen the flow of *chi* through the body to promote health and well-being. The benefits require daily practice to accrue. This can be done in a routine that takes as little as twenty minutes per day. Some practitioners of Chinese medicine teach these techniques to their patients, while others will refer to classes taught by specialists.

Over eight hundred studies of the effects of *chi kung* have been published in the Orient, though the discipline has not been studied extensively in the West. Scientists have dis-

Figure 20: Tai Chi: *Following the River*

covered that the practice of *chi kung* increases the amount of ATP (adenosine triphosphate) in the blood,[35] which is known in the West as the key substance that releases energy to fuel our cellular metabolism and muscular activity. Other studies have found *chi kung* practice to increase immune cell counts and enhance their functioning.[36]

• • •

A Matter of Flow. "By moving the body in this fashion, one guides the body's internal energies to flow according to the same natural laws that keep the planets on course and the galaxies propelling through space in harmony. By practicing these energy-guiding exercises, one may unblock and relieve energy congestion in certain parts of the body, and gradually eliminate the stress that has accumulated over the course of time. One may also redirect the flow of vitality so that every muscle, nerve and organ is nourished and tonified.[37]

These are the words of the modern *tai chi* teacher Master Hua-Ching Ni, describing the benefits of *tai chi.* He vividly illustrates the workings of our energetic anatomy as it sends our vital energy through the various meridians, channels, *nadis,* and other avenues of circulation. The key concept he is illustrating, however, is that of *flow* or *movement.* These practices are means of systematically ushering our energy along its pathways.

And a Matter of Balance. Like *chi kung, tai chi* has also been studied as to its health benefits. Recently a study was conducted at Washington University School of Medicine in St. Louis that compared the effects of several kinds of exercise in the elderly. The forms studied included weight training, stretching, endurance, and *tai chi,* which in this study was regarded as a form of "balance training."

The specific aim was to find what method worked best in reducing the occurrences of falling, which is a multibillion-dollar health problem in the elderly. The study followed over two thousand elderly people at eight treatment centers and compared the number of falls with their peers who did not exercise. The programs lasted between ten and thirty-six weeks, and the participants were followed for four years.

Of all the forms of exercise used, *tai chi* had the best

outcome because it reduced fall-related injuries by 25 percent over the four years. This study was reported in the prestigious *Journal of the American Medical Association*.[38]

It's interesting that to the Western mind, the graceful movements of *tai chi* are viewed as mechanical and balance related, suggesting an external form of exercise. The real roots of the practice are, of course, as an internal exercise: the flow of vital energy is the focus, and external balance is but one of many results of this inner process.

THE ADVENTURE OF FOLLOWING YOUR INTUITION

It is one thing to use an energy practice as taught by someone else and quite another to invent on your own a practice that works for you. All of the famous traditional ways of working with energy were invented by pioneers and adventurers, people who attuned to their own energy and explored until they found systematic ways of working with it. Then they packaged these approaches into systems of thought, which became traditions that were passed down the ages—but all had their origins in this intuitive approach to self-discovery.

I encourage you to follow an intuitive approach as well. Who knows? What you discover simply by attuning to your own energy, playing with it, and moving your body in creative ways may well turn out to be the next "four-thousand-year-old tradition" someday.

BALANCING WITH EARTH ENERGY

The yogis who lived in caves did so not only to be physically removed from the marketplace, but also to be immersed deep in the energy field of the earth. Being in a cave can have a very "grounding" effect. I once had the opportunity to spend some time in a cave along the Ganges while traveling in India. The feeling was one of being completely enveloped in the womb of the earth, and the silence was overwhelming. I was amazed to discover what a tremendously deepening and balancing experience was possible.

Of course you don't have to go to India to experience this. There are caves and caverns everywhere, and the true enthusiast can even take a shovel and simply dig a hole in the ground to have this experience. In some indigenous cultures the earth is used for healing in a very literal way. People would dig a hole in the ground and immerse the sick person in it for a time, with only the head exposed, to absorb earth energies for healing.

Another effective way to absorb earth energy is simply to lie on the ground. I like to lie facedown, spread-eagle and motionless. After twenty to thirty minutes you will sense a palpable balancing and harmonizing in your energetic state. (A complete exercise for this is described at the end of chapter 3.)

Finally, the tradition of *chi kung* includes many references to absorbing energy from nature. One of the more well-known practices, which I described in chapter 3, is to embrace a tree and exchange energy with it, thereby absorbing fresh energy from the earth through its roots.

SEX AND VITAL ENERGY

In chapter 4 I discussed how Christine and Alan discovered the joys of tantric lovemaking. As they found, the relationship between our sexual behavior and our vital energy is very important for those who seek to cultivate their energy and promote health. In Taoist energy theory, sex can serve to either *enhance* or *deplete* our vital energy, and sexual vitality is also considered a good indicator of overall health and immunity to disease.[39]

To understand this more fully we need to recall that there are two aspects to our vital energy: congenital *chi,* also called *jing,* and acquired *chi.* As I stated earlier, we are born with a limited reservoir of congenital *chi,* or *jing,* which cannot be replaced.

In addition to the general wearing down of our reserves through life, there are two specific means through which we lose *jing.* Women lose it through menstruation and men through ejaculation. These two experiences are analogous in terms of the felt impact on one's energy, although for men ejaculation brings a more acute and instantaneous experience of loss compared to the more drawn-out experience of menstruation for women.

WHY MEN FALL ASLEEP

The male orgasm involves an outward explosion and release of *jing,* whereas the female orgasm is an inward explosion. When a man ejaculates he is releasing vital essence or energy, which is carried out of his body by the ejaculatory fluids. In the Taoist perspective, sperm carries the man's *jing*, or sexual essence. As explained by Daniel Reid, semen forms "a functional bridge between organic matter and pure energy.... Vitality is thus a functional fusion of biochemicals and bioenergies...."[40]

The temporary feeling of depletion that men have after ejaculation is thus a true representation of what has happened. As men age and their natural reservoir of *jing* diminishes, their recovery period after ejaculation—before they are capable of another erection and ejaculation—increases.

Men who use tantric sexual practices that involve semen retention—that is, intercourse without ejaculation—do not experience this depletion of vital essence and in fact feel more energized afterward. It is like having their batteries recharged or receiving an infusion of vital energy, rather than the feeling of depletion. Plus, they are able to have intercourse more often, for longer periods, and enjoy more potency in the process.

The experience of greater potency is attributable to three things. First, the sexual glands and organs are not being depleted of vital essence during ejaculation. Second, they are being strengthened and tonified by the muscular exercise involved in intercourse. Third, a great deal of vital energy is being aroused and stirred up, and then, since it is not being discharged, it is circulated and reabsorbed throughout the body.

WHY WOMEN DON'T

Women do not lose vital essence during orgasm because it is not being expelled out of the body, as is the case for the male. The female orgasm is more of an implosion than an explosion. However, as I just mentioned, women do lose *jing* during menstruation through the loss of blood—like semen, another vital fluid and bridge between organic matter and vital energy.

There are esoteric teachings in Taoist theory that explain how women, like men, can dramatically reduce the depletion of *jing*. The female counterpart to male semen retention is the reduction and cessation of menstruation, which can be attained through learning specific techniques of circulation and cultivation of energy. (This is described in Mantak Chia's *Taoist Secrets of Love: Cultivating Female Sexual Energy*[41] and his other writings.)

It is important to point out here that the cessation of menstruation in these cases is due not to any pathological condition, as we would assume in the West, but rather to an exceptionally high level of cultivation of vital energy and the ability to conserve it and channel it to higher centers in the body's energetic anatomy. This will not make sense to Western-trained physicians, who, without an understanding of its energetic aspects, can see cessation of periods only as a disease state.

Taoist and tantric sexual practices teach how to move and circulate the energy throughout the body, rather than simply allowing it to stagnate in the sexual organs, so this energy can be absorbed and transformed into health-giving *chi*. This latter point is particularly important. If the charge of sexual energy is aroused and then left "unmoved," so to speak, congestion in the sex organs will naturally develop. However, simply by learning to draw the aroused energy upward and circulate it through the body's various energetic pathways, and then using the breath and visualization to help direct this, the energy is easily circulated.

A Cure for Impotence

In the Taoist tradition, male impotence is considered a result of depletion of *jing* through excess release of semen. One of the most effective therapies for impotence is frequent intercourse with the same woman, without *any* emission of semen, several times a day for ten days. The recommended position for intercourse is the female-superior position so the man can rest passively below, quietly allowing the stimulation and secretion of vital hormones to restore the health and potency of his sexual organs.[42] Thereafter, according to Taoist teachings, he should adopt a sexual lifestyle of minimal or no ejaculation in order to maintain potency, a gratifying sexual life, and optimal health.

By understanding these issues, women can ultimately improve their own sexual enjoyment and at the same time help their men become better lovers, be happier, and be healthier.

Prostate Health

It is noteworthy that we are facing epidemic rates of prostate cancer at this time in history. Ordinarily we explain such trends in terms of bad diet, lack of exercise, environmental toxins, and perhaps genetic vulnerability. However, no studies have looked at the possibility of a relationship between sexual activity and prostate cancer.

While this may seem farfetched at first, it seems plausible that as our average life span has lengthened and our culture has become less preoccupied with the demands of physical survival in daily life, there have been more opportunities for sexual expression over a lifetime than in prior generations.

Since our culture is obsessed with the notion that orgasm and ejaculation are the "logical" outcome of every sexual encounter, it is possible that Western men living at the end of the twentieth century have "burned out" or depleted their vital essence more than their forebears, weakening the prostate in the process.

Prostate health is poorly understood in Western medical circles—so much so that some conventional physicians recommend more frequent ejaculations for men who are experiencing prostate disorders. In the Eastern perspectives, of course, this advice will serve only to weaken and deplete the very resources needed for health and healing. What would be recommended instead would be either no sexual activity or the cultivation of techniques for circulating sexual energy through the body rather than discharging it. In addition, tonifying herbs would be used for strengthening the sexual organs and specifically the prostate.

All forms of life are endowed with a genetically programmed life cycle ending in death—from the tiniest microbe, which might survive for just a few minutes or days, to the giant sequoia tree, which can live two thousand years but still must eventually die. Our genetic heritage is believed to allow for a potential life span of around 120–140 years, and it is through our lifestyles that we dramatically cut this short to the 70–80 years that is most common in the West.

This is premature aging, and it is caused by the premature depletion of our vital energy over time. It is our vital energy that allows regeneration of our bodily tissues and recovery from the "wearing" effects of stress on our bodies. Clearly the care and nurturing of our vital energy is the all-important issue in slowing the aging process, as well as in maintaining radiant health.

EXERCISE

The Art of Waking Up

Perhaps you can relate to the experience of having to get up at four A.M. to make a trip, after which your energy isn't quite "you" for the rest of the day. Or perhaps you have experienced the grogginess that comes from staying in bed much later than you needed to, with the result that your energy seems to be a little lower throughout the day.

As you get to know your own energetic cycles more intimately, you will discover that there is an optimal moment for you to get up each morning. Choosing this moment is like a surfer choosing the right moment to mount a wave. If you get on the wave when it is peaking, its momentum will carry you far into the day. If you get on the wave too soon or too late, you will not get the benefit of this momentum.

Let's consider how your energy flows early in the morning. While you are still asleep, your biological clock is sensitive to low-intensity light coming through your closed eyelids. There are direct neural pathways from your retinas into your pineal gland, and the presence of light is noted in its subtlest stages, triggering a cascade of neurochemical and energetic events preparing you to awaken. The natural process of the sunrise is dim light progressing slowly into brighter light, bringing more light into your room and giving you a smooth transition to wakefulness.

You can discover the optimal time to get up by attuning closely to your energy in these early moments. When you first realize you are awake, begin to pay close attention to your eyes and your breathing, and you'll notice that they signal some distinct stages for your energy as a whole. The first thing you may notice is that while you are awake you are still in a groggy, twilight kind of state. Your energy is not yet fully aroused, but it is building.

In this initial stage you may notice that your eyelids seem resistant to opening, as if their natural preference is to remain closed. You may also notice that your breathing is not yet flowing lightly but still feels somewhat heavy.

As you continue to rest, the energy in your eyes and your breathing will shift subtly. You will eventually cross a threshold where a feeling of freshness in the energy in and around your eyes will emerge. Your eyelids now want to remain open, and it actually takes a little effort to keep them closed. You will also notice that your breathing takes on a quality of lightness, effortlessness, and pleasant refreshment.

These subtle cues signal that your vitality has reached a peak. This is the crest of a wave, the optimal time to get up. If you stay in bed beyond this window of time, you will notice that they will change again. The energy in your eyelids will shift back toward the more lethargic state in which it is easier to keep them closed than open, and your breathing will become heavier again. The crest of the wave has passed, and it will then be more and more difficult to get up.

EXERCISE

Awakening Your Chi

A traditional Taoist *chi kung* practice for stimulating and awakening your *chi* in the morning, or any time you might feel sluggish, is "hitting." This involves spending a few minutes rapidly and rhythmically hitting or slapping the entire length of your body with your hands, as if playing it like a bongo drum. This is done standing, and you start with your feet and ankles, rhythmically hitting up the length of the inside of your legs, then down the outside. Then up through the hips, abdomen, chest, and back. Then up and down the arms, shoulders, neck, and around the head. You are essentially following and stimulating the major acupuncture meridians, awakening the flow of *chi* throughout your body. This will leave you feeling more awake and vitalized and has a similar effect on your energy as does splashing cold water on your face.

Another practice is that of rubbing the all-important kidneys, atop which sit the adrenal glands. (The kidneys are located midway up the back on either side of the spine.) In terms of the five elements and their organ networks, the kidney network "consolidates and stores the *chi* that initiates and keeps life growing,"[43] and it is especially helpful to stimulate the kidneys to release this energy in the morning or any time you want an infusion of more energy moving through you.

CHAPTER 7

COURTING THE SPIRIT: SUBTLE ENERGIES IN PRAYER, MEDITATION, AND HEALING

If you lay aside the obstruction, then the spontaneous occurrence happens, because the Spirit pervades all things.
—HIGH STAR (LAKOTA SIOUX)[1]

When the gross physiology is made calm, then we can work with the subtle energy and subtle physiology.
—HIS HOLINESS THE DALAI LAMA[2]

When we enter into prayer, meditation, or spiritual healing activity we are entering into a kind of courtship of the Spirit. We seek an experience of direct partnership with the Divine because these activities are all concerned with union or communion across dimensions. It is no coincidence that the words "holy," "whole," "hale," "health," and "healthy" all have their roots in the Greek *holos*, meaning "oneness with all that is." And since energy is the medium of the Spirit, we experience energy in many ways at these times.

There's a Sufi saying that prayer is when you talk to God

and meditation is when God talks to you. Though we may bring different intentions to these two pursuits, in practice they are often commingled and can bring similar energetic experiences. While meditation is traditionally thought of as passive and receptive, and prayer as active and engaging, the distinction blurs the more closely the two activities are examined. This is expressed in the words of the seventeenth-century Carmelite monk Brother Lawrence, who wrote that prayer is "the practice of the presence of God,"[3] which certainly encompasses both. They are two sides of the same coin.

FILLED WITH THE SPIRIT

While repeating the Lord's Prayer after a particularly poignant sermon one Sunday morning, Maureen found herself with an overwhelming sensation of tingling and warmth in the heart and throat centers, a sensation of glowing light inside, and the perception that "Divine Energy" or the "Holy Spirit" was moving through her. What she experienced is not at all uncommon, particularly among religious traditions that encourage passionate involvement in worship.

"The Bible says very clearly that the body is the temple of the Holy Spirit. That's where the Lord will work," explains Reverend Samuel Celovsky, pastor of Christ Tabernacle Church in Santa Rosa, California. "God touches not only our minds, but also our emotions, and all of our senses. The response can be in many ways. You feel goose bumps and other sensations. Many times there is warmth, and a strong sense of joy. None of this is self-generated."

The sense of joy he refers to can be overwhelming and seems to be the predominant theme in the rise in popularity of "laughing revival" services in England and Canada, where it is called the "Toronto blessing." After the service begins with the normal hymns, prayers, and Bible readings, a prayer is offered inviting the Holy Spirit to visit the revelers. This is followed soon by people laughing, and as the laughter becomes more energized, people fall to the floor, shaking, sobbing, roaring, and laughing uncontrollably. These kinds of experiences are part of a long-standing Pentecostal tradition that only began to decline in the 1950s.[4]

Energetic phenomena also occur, of course, in private individual prayer. As singer/songwriter Dan Seals, a practitioner of the Baha'i faith, states in Jim Castelli's *How I Pray*, "[S]ometimes when I pray, I get shivers physically: the hair on my arms stands up. . . . And then sometimes my heart feels like it's getting bigger in my chest; it's swelling or it's dilated."[5]

In the same book Carole Mu'min, a Muslim businesswoman and community activist, describes her sense of connectedness to the Creator during prayer as "like an electrical charge; it's not just space or air. There's a connection between you and your Creator. . . . Sometimes when I get ready to begin prayer, I can't even pray because the reality of what is about to happen is so overwhelming, I just kind of cry; I am that filled up."[6]

THE POWER OF EXPECTANCY

"The energy and power that occur are the work of the Spirit. When we submit ourselves to the movement of the Spirit, the internal experience we have is the presence of the Lord," continues Celovsky. "The Bible says this is what will happen to those who believe, but the Lord is not going to force anything on us. Somewhere there has to be that acceptance, and the *expectancy* that something is going to happen."

The power of expectancy is apparent as Celovsky recounts the story of a woman who came to the church with some heavy burdens in her heart because of some family situations. "I said, 'Let me pray with you.' And I prayed, 'Lord, would you touch her right now with your presence,' and bam, she just raised her hand and fell backward. I hadn't even touched her. There were other people around who caught her as she fell. Then she said there was an intense heat in her body, and tears of joy flowed. She was filled with the Holy Spirit."

DOING NOTHING

Surprising energetic experiences can also arise spontaneously through the sedate, calm practice of meditation. Such was the case for Esther, who reflects on her first long retreat practicing mindfulness meditation:

"My first retreat was for ten days in Yucca Valley. About four or five days into it there came a moment when I suddenly felt this explosion in my chest. I knew enough that I didn't have a heart attack, but it was like this incredible experience of light. I realized later it was an opening, and I think it was my chest releasing whatever that blocked energy was. When it opened it had a sensation of light and space.

"The sensation was something like relaxing into love," she continues. "I was being overcome by love and I realized that *it* was finding *me*, I wasn't finding *it*. . . . It was somewhat of a surrender."

During another sitting, Esther recounts, "At one point I had an orgasm, which was rather strange. I was just sitting there, and it happened all of a sudden. It started very local, and then it diffused throughout my body, became bodywide."

Meditation also has a way of bringing up old pains: "I have an old neck injury on one side. Something else that happens to me quite regularly is that if I sit long enough, the pain will turn to this delightful, lovely iciness, and then it will just diffuse. The whole area then becomes very supple and feels very good. Something just releases and it feels good.

"I was a pretty blocked-up person," Esther concludes, "so I could sit a long time and keep on releasing. I have a very 'God-based' nature, and I really believe those experiences are given to me by the grace of God, and it's for me to just not obstruct it."

The sensation of energy being released is very common as we sit in silence, watching the body and its energy field, as was also the case for Sarah:

"The first time I sat down to meditate, after a while I started to have a 'rippling' sensation in my face. It was like I was having a facial, and I felt my flesh just rippling. It seemed to last for ten or fifteen minutes. I just sat with it and I just thought it was amazing. Meditation was new to me, and I thought, This must be what meditation is, but of course it never happened again. I think it had to do with a major release in my body." She adds, "I often get really warm while I'm sitting. I think the heat is from my energy, which just intensifies during the meditation process."

RAPTURE AND ECSTASY

It was the afternoon of the twelfth day of a retreat when I suddenly started seeing a flickering light behind my closed eyes. My heart began to race, and I felt a warm flush seemingly enter through my right shoulder and move across my chest and down my arms, accompanied by feelings I can only describe as elation and bliss. I could feel the temperature changing slowly as it moved down my arms, until my hands became hot. These sensations stayed around for a few minutes as I continued to maintain my attention on the breath. (I knew from past experience that the feelings would pass immediately if I started thinking about them.) Gradually the feelings faded out.

My experience fits the description of what some mystical traditions call "rapture"—what the American Vipassana teachers Jack Kornfield and Joseph Goldstein describe as "a delightful energetic experience that can result from steady concentration and a composed mind."[7] Elsewhere Goldstein states, "Ecstasy can mean different things, and it can come from many different causes. In the course of meditation practice, ecstatic feelings often flood our consciousness when our mind is pure, bright, and luminous. Although they may be wonderful feelings, they arise because of certain conditions and will inevitably pass away."[8]

From the yogic perspective, it might also be described as an experience of Kundalini energy. Kundalini is the primal energy described in yogic theory that rises from the base of our spine and is associated with the opening of our chakras and the expansion of consciousness.[9]

These experiences are addressed in the writings of John Selby, a teacher of Kundalini meditation, as follows: "[I]n this calm state of consciousness, we can observe and participate in the infinite lifeforce as it flows through our bodies. And with regular meditation, we come to experience a most remarkable phenomenon directly at the center of our own being—*the bright flash of illumination that brings us into immediate contact with the divine force of creation that animates all of life*[10] (italics added). Is this flash of illumination a direct experience of such contact?

The Cabala refers to an all-encompassing state of awareness believed to be the initial light from which the universe was created. This light, the *ohr ain sof*, can be accessed through specific meditations that are part of Jewish mystical tradition. The thirteenth-century mystic Abraham Abulafia was one of the first to advocate for a more direct experience of God through meditative and contemplative practices, and heat and light were regarded as products of this experience. According to Rabbi Ruvi New of Atlanta, "The great Jewish meditators were known to generate lots of heat as a result of the concentration that was involved" in these practices.

The meditations are intended to help the meditator unite with the glory of God and become a vessel for the "light" of God. These teachings are embodied within the Thirty-two Sacred Paths of Wisdom and the Tree of Life. In fact, the Tree of Life is a map of the pathways through which spiritual energy flows into the world.

You Are the Transducer

But how can it be that simply sitting still can generate such a range of experiences—from openings of the heart to orgasms to rippling skin to heat—especially when the whole practice is centered around "nondoing," as in some forms of meditation? Here we have strong indications that simply by consciously intending to bridge to another dimension, a chain of events seems to be set in motion that can alter us on an energetic level.

That happens because *we become transducers.* In Chapter 1 I explained that a transducer is any device that converts energy from one form into another—like a microphone converting sound vibrations into electrical impulses. I noted that the human body contains a transducer system (comprising our endocrine glands, our nervous system, and our own biofield) to which these systems are coupled and that this is what allows us to detect subtle energies.

In spiritual practices *the whole person* becomes a transducer. We are converting energy from another dimension, the spiritual, into energy of this dimension, which we can experience throughout our body as light and all the other sensations I have described.

How our energy can shift and change is described beautifully by Joseph Goldstein of the Insight Meditation Society in Barre, Massachusetts, who writes:

> As we deepen concentration through sustained meditation, the whole nature of our experience changes; we see reality in different ways. One of the compelling discoveries for me in meditation practice has been the ongoing experience of this mind-body as an energy system.
>
> In the beginning of our practice we have a strong sense of the body feeling solid, both when we sit in meditation and when we move around in our daily lives. But as practice goes on, and as concentration gives us more penetrating per-

ception, our experience of this solidity quite naturally fades and disappears. Instead we begin to feel and know the body as an energy field, a continuous flow of sensations.

One way to understand this energy flow is to see that we experience it differently as we focus our attention on different centers in the body. If we direct our awareness to our heart center, we will feel the sensations one way. If we are focused on the sexual center, we will experience different kinds of feelings. We might also place attention on the throat, the brow, the crown of the head, or anywhere else. I was quite surprised when I realized that this is all the same energy stream, simply felt as different energetic "flavors" at different places in the body.

Besides feeling the energy system we call mind-body at different centers, we can also experience sensations of energy at different vibrational frequencies. As we practice and the concentration becomes stronger, the frequency of the flow of sensations becomes finer. It is as if we keep raising the frequency of the mind-body oscillator until the flow of sensations becomes very smooth and refined. Sometimes the sensations become so refined that they disappear, and all we remain aware of is the flow of consciousness.[11]

CHANTING: THE POWER OF RESONANCE

At a Benedictine monastery in France in the 1960s, a place known for hundreds of years for the beautiful chanting of its monks, a decision was made to replace the daily practice with other more practical activities. Shortly thereafter the monks, who had previously maintained good health on three or four hours of sleep per night, began experiencing fatigue and more illness. They were given more time to sleep, and even their diet was changed, but the trend toward malaise and ill health continued. When the practice of chanting was resumed a few years later, there was a remarkable turnaround in the health and general well-being of the monks in just a few months.[12]

According to the renowned French physician and ear specialist Alfred Tomatis, who worked with the monks, the resonance of the sounds in chanting produces rich overtones of higher frequencies, and these have the effect of stimulating and charging the brain with electrical potential. (Conversely, sounds in the lower-frequency ranges have the effect of drawing down our energy.[13]) Thus the monks were missing an important source of energy by discontinuing their practice—a source that helped maintain a state of coherence and balance in their overall energy field.

One of the most powerful spiritual practices in terms of altering our energy, chanting is in a sense a form of prayer, as it involves the sometimes rhythmic repetition of words or sounds intended to carry a meaning or accomplish a purpose. Rather than focusing on the choiceless awareness that characterizes meditation, it is an active process whose purpose is usually to alter the mind-set of the person doing the chanting.

The Christian Gregorian chants serve to instill a sense of awe, reverence, and gratitude—both in those doing the chanting and in those listening. In the Hasidic Jewish tradition, chanting is used to prepare for deeper, more effective prayer. It is deemed necessary by virtue of its opening the heart and readying it for the fullest experience of prayer possible.

Shamanic traditions the world over use chanting to create altered states of consciousness and to bridge our material reality with that of the spiritual. The spiritual energies or forces are then able to traverse this bridge in order to do their healing work.

The chanting of a word or sound, which may be done verbally or silently in the mind, may also be used to focus the mind as well as to attune to a certain frequency that is associated with a spiritual goal.

STIMULATING THE CHAKRAS

In addition, specific chants can resonate with and stimulate specific chakras. This is based on the notion that each chakra is an oscillator with its own frequency of pulsation. Hence a specific sound frequency will resonate with that particular chakra, thus balancing it and reducing its variability. For example, "ohm" or "aum" is regarded as the original sound of the unfolding universe. You can experience this right now by setting down the book and just repeating the sound "ohm" or "aum" for a few minutes. You'll most likely feel a direct resonance in your heart region and discover the relaxing effects of this sound.

Chanting can be most powerful when there is a dynamic interplay between the *meaning* of the words of the chant and the *resonance* their sounds create in the chakras. While the sound vibration alone may be enough to stimulate the previously mentioned effects in your chakras, these effects can be enhanced if the chant carries a heartfelt meaning for you. This is because through the mind-heart connection (to be discussed in more detail), loving or appreciative thoughts themselves have an effect on the heart center.

As we have already seen, the heart is the most powerful energy center in the body and tends to bring all the others into entrainment with it. Thus, focusing on thoughts of love or appreciation, even without voicing them, has been found to bring the heart into coherence. To give voice to these thoughts in a way that resonates with the energy centers of the body can add impact and make for an extraordinarily potent combination.

THE MIND-HEART CONNECTION

"I did a lot of *metta* when I went on my vacation to Santa Fe to visit my cousin and her husband. I would sit and do *metta* for a while each morning. I had expected that I'd get bored, but the longer I did it, the more people came into my awareness whom I wanted to include," states Penny, who had recently taken a class on a form of meditation called *metta*.

Metta is a Buddhist practice in which you repeat intentions of goodwill toward yourself, others, and the world at large. It bridges meditation and chanting, and its power comes from the repetition, which serves to focus the mind and intention on a central thought or theme, in effect shutting out distracting thoughts and giving your full mental energy to the intention at hand.

"On my own, I found myself wanting to include people I'd had conflicts and difficulties with, including my father, with whom I've always had a very painful relationship. The more I did it, the more love I felt—my heart felt more and more expansive, which became a wonderfully pleasurable experience.

"The feeling would carry over into my day, and I would look forward to doing it again the next day. It also made it easier to be with my cousin and her husband, who in the past had been very difficult and demanding. It was much easier for me to just accept them rather than be in conflict with them. We ended up having this wonderful trip together, and he even became more loving in the process."

There are many ways to practice *metta*, which is sometimes also called a "loving-kindness" meditation. (There is a guided exercise in this at the end of this chapter.) One form is as follows:

May I be peaceful.	*May all beings be peaceful.*
May I be happy.	*May all beings be happy.*
May I be well.	*May all beings be well.*
May I be safe.	*May all beings be safe.*
May I be free from suffering.	*May all beings be free from suffering.*

These words are repeated slowly, with pauses between phrases for contemplation and absorption of the intention. It is a common practice in this tradition to "do *metta*" as a formal spiritual practice daily, and there are even meditation retreats in which this constitutes the whole practice day in and day out for a week or more. The emphasis is not so much on sound vibration as on being absorbed in the repetition of the mental intention. Practitioners universally report that such practice opens the heart and creates deep feelings of peacefulness and harmony.

HEAD-HEART ENTRAINMENT

Take a moment right now to think of someone who has touched your life deeply in a positive way and whom you genuinely appreciate. Picture this person in your mind's eye, and as you do so bring your attention to your heart. You have just caused a shift in the energy field of your heart.

One of the goals of spiritual practices across traditions is a sense of integration and oneness within oneself. On the physiological level this takes the form of coherence and entrainment occurring in our energy systems. And this is not something that takes years of practice to experience.

I've explained earlier that simply feeling sincere appreciation increases coherence in the energy field emanating from the heart. This was discovered when researchers at the Institute of HeartMath were studying the effects of a stress-reduction technique called "Freeze-Frame."

The technique, developed by Doc Lew Childre, founder and president of the institute, could actually be described as a very quick and effective variation of *metta* meditation. It involves consciously disengaging from unpleasant emotional and mental reactions, shifting your attention to the heart region, and focusing on feeling appreciation or similar positive emotion toward someone. It is a one-minute technique originally developed as a stress-reduction tool, and its steps are described in the exercises at the end of this chapter.

What is fascinating about the Freeze-Frame research is that it has been found to increase coherence in the heart energy field, which then more easily pulls our other oscillators into entrainment. This is called "frequency pulling," and it affects your brain waves as well as your breathing pattern. Thus your brain waves can be agitated and incoherent when you start, but because the heart is a stronger oscillator than your brain, it will pull your brain waves into entrainment and coherence. Likewise, your breathing will become calm and steady.[14]

As I stated earlier, such head-heart entrainment leads to a shift in perception and reduces the levels of anxiety, fear, and depression, with corresponding increases in clarity, buoyancy, intuitive awareness, and inner peace. These benefits are aptly summarized by William Tiller, a collaborator in the research:

> My own experience has been that when applied intentionality is focused through the human heart into the life process, an increased rate of structural refinement occurs and, thus, the more rapidly does one's consciousness expand. It is the focused feeling of love, across its broad spectral band, that opens key structures in the heart. . . .[15]

THE ENERGETICS OF POSTURE
AND CONCENTRATION

Richard was one of the early students of Maharishi Mahesh Yogi, the founder of transcendental meditation (TM). He has been practicing TM for thirty years and often meditates four to five hours per day—sometimes more.

"In the last few years I have been experiencing an extremely powerful sense of Kundalini energy moving up my spine," he states. "My spine feels like a hose, and the sensation is like 'turgor pressure.' That's a biological term for the pressure of moisture within the stem of a plant that keeps the plant erect. When a plant leans over from dehydration, it's lacking in turgor pressure, and when you add water the pressure returns and makes it upright. That's the only way I can describe the energy. It just seems to snap me right up.

"The pleasure and joy I experience with this energy are so compelling that I sometimes feel I can't get enough. I can meditate for eight or nine hours at a time if I have the opportunity. The bliss that I was seeking in all the great loves of my life, or from going out in the ocean in my boat or being in nature, I get in meditation as this energy moves up my spine."

The upright posture has clearly been a key for Richard in opening up the flow of Kundalini energy. In Chapter 5 I noted the Buddha's basic instructions for meditation included the following: "One goes to the forest, to the foot of a tree, or to an empty room, sits down cross-legged in the lotus position, holds one's body straight, and establishes mindfulness in front of oneself."[16]

We Westerners tend to think of sitting upright without back support—either cross-legged on a cushion or on our knees, perhaps supported by a low bench—as a prescription for discomfort. However, the mystics taught these postures for practical energetic reasons. In fact, one of the important functions of yoga is to help us release tension so that we can sit upright more comfortably and calmly for spiritual practices.

When we lie down, our energy is easily dispersed throughout our body, and this position does not support the kind of concentration we want in a spiritual practice. To sit upright against a chair is an improvement, but it still allows a great deal of our energy to be dispersed to our extremities, and contributes to feelings of restlessness or agitation.

To sit upright *without* back support, however, requires us to draw energy toward the musculature that supports us against gravity. These muscles are located along the spine, and the more we are able to draw our energy to the region of the spine, the finer is our concentration and the more centered we can become.

The mystics taught that as a final consequence, when we reach a delicate state of balance in relation to gravity, the energy that is being employed along the spine in holding us up can then be drawn farther inward, actually *into* the spine, where it can be concentrated for the benefit of building consciousness. At this point of perfect balance in terms of outward posture, we are then just hanging on our bones and ligaments with no muscular effort. To allow greater concentration on the flow of our Kundalini upward from the base of the spine is the goal of the upright sitting posture, and Richard is reaping the benefits of this practice after many years.

It can take a lot of work and strong intention to develop the ability to use posture to actually support one's spiritual practice. In long meditation retreats I have experienced all manner of painful sensations as a result of attempting to remain still and find a posture that works effortlessly. One of the most common complaints is pain in the knees and legs. However, take heart. To endure suffering is not the point. In one retreat I asked the contemporary Buddhist meditation teacher Venerable Ayya Khema how important it was to maintain stillness through excruciating pain. Her response was that it's okay to move if you do so mindfully, adding: "Enlightenment happens in the mind, not in the legs."

THE HANDS IN PRAYER AND MEDITATION

When I was taught as a child to fold my hands in prayer, I took it as a gesture of humility or submission. However, there are real energetic aspects to this. When we hold our palms together we are completing a circuit of energy extending from the heart down the arms and through the chakras in the center of the palm of each hand. As I explained in chapter 2, the palm chakra of the right hand is normally giving off energy and that of the left is receptive to it.

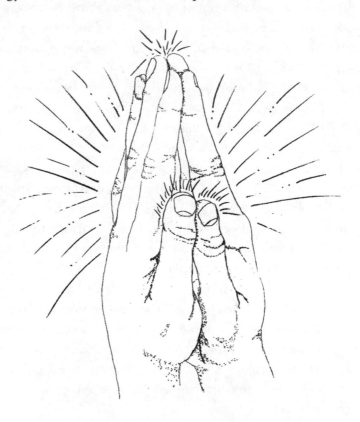

Figure 21: Prayerful Hands: Completing the Circle

The completion of this circuit has a powerful influence in terms of *containing* rather than *dispersing* our energy—and whatever other energy may be visiting us. There seems to be something "holy" about putting our hands together, and in fact, in an energetic sense we are more "whole" by doing so.

There is also a subtle difference between having the fingers intertwined and extending them so that their tips are also touching, completing a circuit. Since the fingertips are lesser chakras, there is even more completion of energetic circuitry with this pose. You can experiment with various ways of positioning your hands during prayer and meditation and notice the energetic differences.

THE INFLUENCES OF THE *DOSHAS*

While each of us has a predominant *dosha*, our vital energy comprises all three *doshas*. This becomes readily apparent during prayer and meditation, as we get to experience the effects of all three in some very tangible ways.

Vata: *Monkey Mind. Vata*, the quality of rapid movement or dispersion, corresponds with the agitation and hyperactivity of the mind we often encounter when attempting to be still and meditate. While we sit with our intention to be calm and focused on the present moment, the "monkey mind" ceaselessly flits and jumps from one thought to another, cycling through an unending montage of ideas, worries, obsessions, and desires, all the while dispersing our energy mentally. This often leads to feelings of frustration with the process as one realizes how helpless one can be to control the mind, and is why the Indian mystic Osho once described the experience of meditation as "one insult after another." Of course, this is a perfect opportunity to practice compassion for yourself.

Kapha: *Lethargy. Kapha* shows its influence as the opposite extreme to monkey mind. The lethargy and sleepiness with which we sometimes struggle during meditation are an expression of *kapha*, the quality of heaviness, density, and holding—a slowing down of energy. You may be sitting there with your mind relatively calm and suddenly find yourself about to keel over, jerking your head back up from your chest, perhaps with a tinge of embarrassment if you're sitting in a group. Finding balance between the *vata* and *kapha* aspects of our energy during meditation is one of the practice's great challenges.

Pitta: *Heat and Fire. Pitta,* the fiery energy that transforms, manifests its influence through experiences of insight and breakthroughs of awareness that arise seemingly out of the blue from calm states. We may also experience *pitta* in the form of tingling, heat, or burning sensations, as we open to new and powerful energies such as the rising of Kundalini through the body. People with excess *pitta* may even have difficulty being calm because of strong energetic experiences that continuously absorb their attention.

Clearly, imbalance in any of the three *doshas* can manifest as specific difficulties during meditation practice. This is why other aspects of lifestyle such as diet, stress, exercise, and sleep habits, which collectively determine our general state of balance among the *doshas* before we even sit down, have direct impact on our experience of meditation. Things that aggravate *vata*, such as coffee, would obviously not be a good idea just before meditating. Eating a heavy meal would obviously contribute to difficulty with *kapha* and sleepiness.

Attempting to meditate in the hot sun or a room that is too warm will obviously aggravate *pitta*.

If you can associate a particular difficulty you commonly have during meditation with one of these imbalances, then you can take steps to rebalance it before you even sit down, thereby helping your meditations to be more fruitful.

THE RELAXATION RESPONSE

"Meditating has changed my entire life. I feel relaxed and healthy all the time." These are the words of a sixty-two-year-old man with high blood pressure who has recently taken up the practice of meditation. He is a participant in a study of the effects of transcendental meditation and relaxation training on blood pressure among elderly African Americans. In the study over a hundred people, ranging in age from fifty-five to eighty-five, were assigned to one of three groups: those who meditated twice a day, those who used progressive muscle relaxation exercises, or those who simply modified their diet and exercise patterns.

For those practicing meditation, the reductions in blood pressure were more than twice as great as in those using the progressive muscle relaxation, which was itself also significantly beneficial. This particular man's blood pressure declined fourteen points and remained stable. The study, published in the medical journal *Hypertension,* showed that the meditation and relaxation training can reduce hypertension as much as the drugs ordinarily used to treat it.[17]

This is but one of hundreds of studies showing the medical benefits of spiritual practices. The key to such benefits appears to be the relaxation response. Both prayer and meditation have been found by Dr. Herbert Benson and his colleagues at Harvard Medical School to result in the relaxation response. This is a state in which there is an increased coherence between the right and left hemispheres of the brain, as well as a plethora of other beneficial changes, including increased immunity and reductions in blood pressure, respiration, heart rate, oxygen consumption, and muscular tension.[18]

BRAIN WAVE CHANGES

Another physiological change that occurs during such practices is in our brain waves. When we are in the process of falling asleep, certain kinds of brain waves called "alpha" and "theta" increase in number, power, and synchronicity. We normally pass through this stage in just a few *seconds* on our way to deep sleep, but in meditation we can remain in that territory for a long time. What's interesting is that these waves allow us to bridge the conscious and subconscious for long periods of time. This is illustrated in the experience of Sarah, who recalls:

"I had a time when I'd been sitting on a long retreat, and I began to get information that seemed like past-life experiences. When the sitting was over and I was doing walking meditation, it was as though there were no interruption, no ending of the sitting and beginning of the walking. It was all continuous."

In that special state we can experience feelings of extreme peace and a heightened sense of self-awareness. Occasionally we have moments of reverie, extraordinarily vivid and inspiring mental imagery, and the unfolding of unconscious material. There can even be rhythmic high-voltage surges in brain wave activity, leading to what we call "peak experiences" of clarity, bliss, or spiritual energy.

These experiences are not limited to the relatively calm, passive states of meditation or prayer. They can also happen in shamanic rituals, which include drumming, chanting, and singing. Studies have found that the rhythmic auditory stimulation of these activities may also increase the production of alpha and theta waves.[19]

WHEN THE LIGHT SHINES

Experiences of light are common in spiritual practices. What might be happening in our bodies at these times? Scientists have come up with some intriguing observations.

We know that one of the effects of profound relaxation, such as occurs in deep states of meditation, is stimulation of the *parasympathetic nervous system,* which slows down all our bodily processes, including heart rate, respiration, blood pressure, and oxygen consumption.[20]

When the parasympathetic system is highly stimulated, there can be a reduction of blood flow to the occipital lobe in the brain. Through a variety of neurological pathways, this in turn leads to the *perception of white light in the visual field,* even though the eyes are closed. Hence, in deep meditation you can be teetering on the brink of low blood pressure in the brain, and in moments of extreme relaxation the white light will appear. This is also the explanation that has been applied to perceptions of white light that people have during near-death experiences.

This feeds into a further explanation of the perception that light or energy is spreading throughout your body during certain ecstatic meditative experiences. According to neurological research, following a sudden reduction of blood circulation to the brain, there is also a sudden and extreme decrease in vascular tension throughout the body. But to compensate, the body's *sympathetic nervous system* kicks in and creates a very rapid *increase* in blood flow, as if the body is responding with a protective mechanism to restore blood pressure. The increase in blood flow begins at the center of the body and expands outward, paradoxically bringing a profoundly pleasant feeling of relaxation. This can easily be perceived as light or energy suffusing the body and flooding us as it moves from the center outward.

Another factor in this experience is a simultaneous release of *endomorphins* ("endogenous morphine"), neuropeptides created by the brain, which bring feelings of bliss and ecstasy.

What about the visions that some people have during such experiences? These may also be explained by research indicating that when the sympathetic nervous system is overstimulated, we can have memories and visions. If the dance continues, and the parasympathetic system kicks in to balance this, we again have deep, sudden relaxation and see the white light. Thus, through the alternate stimulation of the two systems, we activate what August Reader, M.D., calls the "near-death reflex," which leads to experiences of white light, release of endorphins, sensations of energy flowing through us, and visions.[21]

BODY AND SPIRIT IN TANDEM

When I first came across this information I found it disheartening. I wanted to believe that such energetic experiences that I have had in meditation were authentic spiritual experiences and not just physiological anomalies of low blood flow to the brain. Had I been deceiving myself?

Hence I was glad to come across a counterargument to this physiological explanation. Peter and Elizabeth Fenwick, authors of *The Truth in the Light*,[22] have written extensively about experiences of the light in near-death experiences, and it seems that their analysis may also apply to experiences of light in meditation or prayer. They argue that if an experience is caused strictly by interrupted oxygen flow to the brain, known as "cerebral anoxia," then the person is unlikely to maintain consciousness and be able to remember the experience. Cerebral anoxia produces disruption and disorganization of brain function. This is certainly *not* consistent with the sense of clarity and profound insight that people tend to report with these experiences.

This view is supported in the research on near-death experiences, including her own, by Yvonne Kason. Kason asserts that "the awakening of latent spiritual energy is the biopsychospiritual basis of near-death experiences. This spiritual energy is known in various sacred traditions as holy spirit, vital winds, chi, dumo fire, and in the yogic tradition, kundalini."[23] The evidence suggests that the light seen in meditative and near-death experiences is the same and the same dynamics are at play.

As is usually the case when there are alternative explanations for something, both may be true. In this case, it seems reasonable that there is a mutual reinforcement between spiritually attuned states of consciousness and physiological changes in the body. It may be a "chicken or egg" question as to which comes first. I believe that they are *parallel and complementary processes*. It may be that each can occur without the other, but when they occur together the effects are enhanced.

ENERGY AND HEALING

"I always pray privately before seeing a patient," explains Gwenlyn, who works in a neurology and pain clinic in the Midwest. "I ask that I work in clarity and that whatever happens is for the highest good, and that nobody will be hurt in any way. I ask for the presence of my Higher Self and the patient's Higher Self, and any angels of high-level guides that can assist the process. I also ask for the presence of the over-arching light of Christ."

As means of "tapping into" spiritual resources, prayer and meditation are an integral part of energy-based healing. Whether healing is something to be "done" by a so-called healer or is simply something a person seeks to receive directly on his own from Spirit, these practices clear the way for receptivity—opening the channels of communication across dimensions.

Gwenlyn is one of an emerging genre of modern-day healers now working quietly and discreetly in many main-stream health care institutions. She is trained and certified in the appropriate professional disciplines, but her healing work takes her and her patients well beyond the mundane. She recounts the story of Claire, who came to her with severe headaches:

> She'd had surgery for skin cancer on her chest a couple of years ago. It had been a huge lesion, but it was now healed. She'd been having these headaches and nobody could figure out what was going on. I was working in the energy field around her neck, and she said, "It feels like there's a rope in there that's just all twisted, and it's felt

that way since the surgery because they pulled a whole lot of skin and muscle down from my neck to fill in the space in my chest."

So I worked with unwinding the energy in that area and it just released. She hasn't had any pain there since we did that and hasn't been able to feel the rope. The muscle energy pattern just simply released.

I also worked with the scar tissue on her chest. There was a raised ridge of scar tissue. I put my hand behind her and directed energy from my fingertips toward where the scar was, and I put my top hand over the scar. She could feel the intense heat, which is not unusual in energy work, and I could feel the scar softening. The scar softened and the tissue around the scar also softened. When we were done she could feel a lot more mobility and not as much pulling in that area in her chest.

THE DIVINE BLUEPRINT

Gwenlyn was working with Claire's energy field in order to promote healing of her physical body. In chapter 2 I noted that according to yogic theory, there are several layers to our energy field. While the details aren't so important here, what matters is that our energy field seems to contain a blueprint for our perfect health, and if we can just tap into this blueprint, perhaps with the help of a healer, it can guide us on our way. This was illustrated in the work Gwenlyn did with a woman named Ellen:

Due to a work injury, Ellen was having severe pain in her neck and right shoulder. She had been using acupuncture and biofeedback for about a year but was still immobilized on her right side. She couldn't lift her right arm and had been unable to cook for a long time. Nothing seemed to work.

I worked with her own energy. I did some manipulation of her arm, but I followed *her* energy in that joint. I wasn't channeling energy, but I was following her energy. Her arm started to move spontaneously, and all I was doing was supporting that movement. It was totally effortless for her, and her arm was moving in all directions. I just had two fingers on her arm, just following it around. She was waving it all around like a ballerina.

It unwound the bound energy pattern in her shoulder, and she had total mobility with no pain. Neither one of us could believe it. I took her out to show the nurses that this woman had complete range of motion, and the nurses couldn't believe it, and her doctor's jaw just dropped.

We simply allowed her own body's energy to guide the healing. We let her energy body do the directing. My instruction to her was, "Let's just see what your shoulder wants to do, and we won't do anything more than what your shoulder tells us to do." So she relaxed, and I made contact with her arm, and I just became very relaxed. I tried to blend with her energy. Our energy fields became blended together, and there was no other direction on my part.

Her energy body moved the arm in the way it needed to in order to release an energy block. This was absolutely astonishing. Her eyes got real big and she kept saying, "I can't believe it, I can't believe it." She went and showed her minister, and this was a permanent cure.

The idea that our energy field "knows" what to do seems remarkably consistent with some religious notions that there exists a Divine Plan for our evolution. Is the etheric template about which the yogis speak this Divine Plan? Spiritual healing is clearly working with some "guiding patterns" to effect changes on the physical level, bringing the physical into alignment with a subtle blueprint.

A Lasting Impression

Practitioners of energy healing believe that the etheric body can be damaged by trauma to the physical body, which makes an imprint on the energy field. Gwenlyn offers an illustration in the case of Patricia, who had been having low back pain for about three years:

Through scanning her energy field, I found a real painful area, where it felt to me as if there were some kind of needle sticking in her. I asked her to tell me about what might have caused that. She said when her child was born she had a saddle block, which is an injection in the spine to deaden the lower pelvis. I had a very sharp needlelike sensation in my hand, and she could distinctly feel the trajectory of the needle itself—the tissue still had that memory.

> I just pulled my hand through her aura with the intention of pulling it out, and it's as if the needle just followed my hand. It was painful for me, too, because when you do that work you feel it also. As soon as the injection site was cleared her back pain just dissolved, and she hasn't had it since.

Spiritual healing is usually directed at healing and strengthening some aspect of the energy field, regardless of the cause of the disturbance. When healing at the energetic levels is complete, healing on the physical level will follow if it is possible. Spiritual or divine energy from the outer layers can be brought to bear on the inner layers to repair or strengthen them, so that they in turn can successfully guide the healing on the physical level.

Given the amazing results that appear to be possible on a one-to-one basis, what is the potential for healing effects when a whole group of people focus their healing intentions on one person?

COLLECTIVE INTENTION

Howard, seventy-two, was suffering from metastatic prostate cancer and was living in constant pain despite the medication he had been prescribed. He described the pain as "like 2 five-pound weights hanging from my testicles."

He was in the third day of a seven-day group retreat at the Cancer Support and Education Center in Menlo Park, California, with his wife, Bonnie. The participants were undergoing group therapy for coping with the stress of cancer and were also learning techniques of mind-body medicine to cope with symptoms and promote healing.

This particular afternoon, when it was apparent that he was in great discomfort, I asked if he would like to receive some direct support from the other group members, to which he agreed. I asked him to sit in the middle of the circle, and the other eight participants brought their chairs close around him. I then instructed the others each to gently place one hand on Howard, close their eyes, and, in their own way, begin visualizing the pain leaving Howard's body.

Figure 22: Collective Intention and Laying On of Hands

As we sat there with eyes closed and maintaining contact with him, we went around the circle with each person in turn slowly describing out loud his own personal imagery of the pain leaving Howard's body. It took about thirty minutes to make it all the way around the circle.

At the end of this exercise, Howard was beaming. He reported that he was completely pain free, for the first time in months. Three days later he was still pain free.

Was the relief of his pain simply a result of the power of suggestion, or did something happen on an energetic level? Studies have found that when one person contacts another person's energy field with a healing intention, *with or without contacting their physical body*, a state of coherence and synchrony between the brain waves of the healer and the recipient develops—they literally become unified in one energetic field.[24] Other studies have found this kind of communion to reduce the severity of pain,[25] reduce anxiety,[26] heal wounds more rapidly,[27] and even raise the level of hemoglobin in the recipient's blood.[28]

To me this experience showed that all support groups could be easily transformed into healing groups. We all have the potential to be a healing presence for one another, if we will just set our intention to do so and follow a few simple guidelines. I believe that in Howard's case the collective intentionality of the group, coupled with their direct energetic and physical contact with him, transformed the energetic dynamics that were creating pain in his body.

We have no way of knowing what happened on the physiological level to his disease process or the mechanisms that were leading to his perception of pain. However, as I see it, what mattered here was that Howard had the clear intention to receive, the others had the clear intention to give, and the images formed in the minds of the participants were somehow "potentized" by the collective intentionality of the group. A strong, coherent field of energy was created, he received it, and it had a lasting impact on the coherence of his own field for an extended period, overriding the forces of incoherence being produced by the disease process.

WITHOUT CONTACT

The healing power of collective intention can also be expressed without direct physical contact. In *Chicken Soup for the Soul,* Reverend Mark Victor Hansen recounts the story of a seventeen-year-old girl dying of leukemia. She had been given just a few more days to live and through the Make-a-Wish Foundation had requested the opportunity to attend one of his sermons before she died.

Hansen welcomed the girl and her parents into a seminar with over a thousand other attendees. During the course of the afternoon, he asked the audience if they would like to learn a healing process, to which they eagerly agreed. As Hansen tells it, "I taught the audience how to vigorously rub their hands together, separate them by two inches, and feel the healing energy. . . ."

Hansen later addressed the audience as follows: "This morning I was introduced to Amy Graham, a seventeen-year-old, whose final wish was to be at this seminar. I want to bring her up here and let you all send healing life-force energy toward her. Perhaps we can help. She did not request it. I am just doing this spontaneously because it feels right."

Hansen continues: "Amy's dad led her up onto the stage. She looked frail from all of the chemotherapy, too much bed rest, and an absolute lack of exercise. . . . I had the group warm up their hands and send her healing energy, after which they gave her a tearful standing ovation.

"Two weeks later she called to say that her doctor had discharged her after a total remission. Two years later she called to say she was married."[29]

Here again we have evidence of the ability of a collective energy field to profoundly alter that of an individual. In Amy's case, it appears that what she received from the group gave her own energy field the strength to overcome a supposedly fatal disease process that was out of control in her body. The power of collective intention is again demonstrated, this time in saving a life.

AND THE *CHI* FOLLOWS . . .

Collective healing intention is also at the heart of the work in a hospital in China where healing is based on energy alone. In the city of Qinhuagdao, the Wahzhan Zhineng Chigong Clinic and Training Center houses over four thousand patients and personnel but uses no drugs. Rather, it uses *chi kung* and other forms of energy healing to treat its patients.

One component of the program there is group healing sessions, in which the *chi kung* teacher synchronizes the minds of the group to invoke a strong collective energy field. This energy field is formed by the collective intention of the group and is a deliberate way of using the potential of a shared energy field for the benefit of each individual.[30]

EVIDENCE FOR HEALING THROUGH TOUCH AND PRAYER

We all have native healing abilities. We are all healers, and as subtle energy researcher Charles Tart, Ph.D., observes, it is only our cultural blinders and prejudices that keep more of us from functioning as healers.[31]

One researcher who has made an exhaustive study of energy healing is Daniel Benor, M.D., an American psychiatrist and healer. "Spiritual healing by the laying on of hands or by prayer/meditation has been practiced for as long as recorded history," he states. "The Bible is replete with tales of unusual cures by the prophets, Christ, and the Apostles. Virtually every known culture has included healers among its health care professionals." If this kind of healing were a drug, it would be accepted easily on the basis of its scientific evidence, for there are hundreds of studies documenting its medical effects.[32]

Benor is actually referring to two very different kinds of energy healing. In one, the healer's energy field is in direct contact with that of the recipient—as in the laying on of hands. The other is "remote" healing, in which the healer and recipient are at a distance beyond the reach of their energy fields—as in distant prayer or meditation. In the latter case, the healer's influence must be reaching the recipient through some other dimension beyond the physical.

Examples of healing research include studies of the effects on plants, animals, and humans. In a study of the effects of healing on fungus and bacteria, a group of ten people was able to inhibit the growth of fungus cultures by concentrating on them for a few minutes from a few feet away.[33]

Another study found similar effects when the people were several *miles* from the cultures.[34]

Another study involved sixty people not known to have any special healing abilities. Merely by their conscious intention they were able to alternately stimulate or impede the growth of bacteria.[35]

Even human cells have been shown to be affected by conscious intention of people around them. Researchers at the Mind Science Foundation in Houston found that volunteers could significantly decrease the normal rates of hemolysis (the body's routine way of destroying old red blood cells).[36]

A famous British healer, Matthew Manning, was able to cause a drastic alteration in cancer cell cultures in two different ways. One was to simply hold his hands near the cells, and the other was to direct his intention from a distant room.[37]

From the plant kingdom we also have fascinating evidence of our ability to have an impact. In one study, a saline solution was poured on plant seeds to inhibit their growth. Then one set was worked with by healer Oskar Estabany, who was able to overcome the inhibiting effects of the saline solution, and the plants grew more quickly.[38]

Another study involved handing wounded mice in a paper bag to a healer. The mice receiving a healing treatment showed significantly faster wound healing than those not receiving the treatment. The mice were then subjected to near freezing temperature overnight. Nearly two-thirds of those treated by the healer survived, while only 14 percent of the others did.[39]

The acclaimed healer Rabbi Abraham Weissman was able to consistently reduce the growth rate of cancerous tumors in mice. According to Weissman, "As I became adept at working with the energies I began to realize that although I believe I am channeling from God, you might believe that you are channeling from Buddha, the wind, or the sun, and it would be the same energy source. I also found that you cannot impose a healing on anybody."[40]

TOUCH

When most of us think of spiritual healing we usually associate it with the age-old practice of the laying on of hands. The reality is that we all have performed this act countless times spontaneously in our daily lives without giving it a second thought. A bump on the head or a bump or bruise anywhere else on the body is usually met with the laying on of a hand to soothe or protect. We do not have to conjure up the conscious *intention* to soothe or protect, for it's already there. Nor do we think about the fact that our hands are conduits of healing energy from the heart, which is channeled through our palm chakras, or that by touching the wound we are sending energy through it that can clear out trauma and restore energetic balance to that area.

As children we knew how good it felt to have Mother or Father touch us when we were in pain, and we spontaneously tend to reach out to touch others around us who are suffering. Taking another's hand, placing a loving hand on someone's shoulder, are ways we naturally express our caring. It's not just psychological support, for something energetic is transferred. When we touch another, we are completing a circuit by connecting energy fields and creating a larger, joint energy field. This allows the other to draw upon our resources and allows us to give support in the form of energy, or what we colloquially call "strength."

All this seems self-evident, yet it is the basis for many

highly developed traditions of healing practice and, more recently, scientific studies documenting real physiological benefits. The healing power of touch has not gone unrecognized in the medical literature. Articles have appeared documenting miraculous cases of cure by the laying on of hands, including spontaneous disappearance of an abdominal tumor.[41]

Therapeutic Touch. In terms of formal scientific studies, the most closely examined form of this kind of healing is called Therapeutic Touch. It was developed in the 1970s by Delores Krieger, Ph.D., R.N., a professor at New York University, and

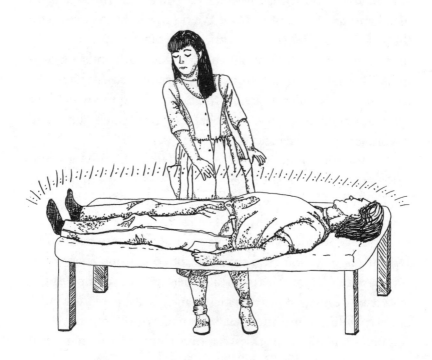

Figure 23. Therapeutic Touch

Dora Kunz, a natural healer, but is a contemporary interpretation of several ancient healing traditions.

This practice is so highly regarded that at Columbia Presbyterian Medical Center in New York City, Mehmet Oz, M.D., a cardiovascular surgeon, invites healers into his operating room to use it on patients while they are undergoing surgery. It is based on the principle that the human energy field extends beyond the skin and the practitioner can use the hands as sensors to locate problems in it that correspond with problems in the physical body. Disease is seen as a condition of energy imbalance or disorder or of blocked energy flow. Assessment is done by passing the hands over the body from head to toe about two to four inches above the surface.

The practitioner then serves as a conduit for universal energy, consciously and actively transferring energy into the recipient. The hands are used to direct and focus the energy, sometimes in rhythmical, sweeping motions. The method is initially taught "off body," meaning the practitioner's hands do not touch the physical body, though later, with experience, physical contact may also be used.

Since it is not necessary to touch the physical body (what is being touched is the energy field), this method is especially helpful in situations where the patient may not be able to tolerate contact (as with postsurgical patients or burn victims). Sessions last up to thirty minutes and can be done sitting or lying down, fully clothed.

Many compelling studies of Therapeutic Touch have documented its effects. One study examined the healing of identical surgically inflicted minor wounds in the shoulders of forty-four male college students. Twenty-three received Therapeutic Touch treatments, and twenty-one did not. Neither group was aware of the purpose of the experiment, and those treated were not aware they were being treated.

After eight days the treated group's wounds had shrunk an average of 93.5 percent compared with 67.3 percent for those untreated. After sixteen days the figures were 99.3 percent and 90.9 percent.[42]

Another study looked at the effects of Therapeutic Touch on the nervous system. The subjects, a group of meditators, were not informed of the true nature of the study in order to control for the effects of placebo and expectation. Each was wired from several points on the surface of the body to an electromyograph to record the amount of muscular tension during the course of the experiment.

They then meditated while, unknown to them, behind their backs they were being given Therapeutic Touch. The practitioners giving the treatments also gave alternate "mimic" sessions in which they simply moved their hands through the air without a conscious intention of having a therapeutic effect on the meditators.

The findings were that when the practitioners' conscious intention was to use Therapeutic Touch, the meditators showed a significant *decrease* of muscular tension as measured by electromyography, while the practitioners sent cold, uncaring energy, the muscle energy along the spine *increased* as the person "bristled" at the intrusion. These findings indicate that the treatment had a measurable effect on the nervous systems of the meditators.[43]

Power to the People. Therapeutic Touch is another example of a healing technique that does not require a lot of formal training. It can be learned by most anyone and used effectively with family members or loved ones. In fact, one of the leading researchers and teachers of this method, Janet Quinn, Ph.D., R.N., of the University of Colorado School of Nursing, has created a videotape home-study course for family care givers (see Appendix).

DISTANT HEALING THROUGH PRAYER

One of the most common ways we function as healers is through our prayers. Prayer not only has impact on the one who is praying, it can also affect others at a distance. According to Dr. Larry Dossey, author of *Healing Words*, prayer is part of a new "non-local medicine," which he sees as the next great step beyond psychosomatic medicine.[44]

Healing the Heart. Dr. Randolph Byrd, a cardiologist at San Francisco General Hospital, showed the value of non-local medicine in a controlled study of the effects of distant prayer with nearly four hundred coronary care patients. Half received routine care only, and the other half, unknown to them, were also prayed for by name by various Protestant and Catholic prayer groups throughout the country. The study was designed to high scientific standards, and neither the patients nor medical staff knew which group the patients were in.

The outcomes were striking. Those who were prayed for had significantly less congestive heart failure, need for diuretics, cardiopulmonary arrest, or incidence of pneumonia. They were five times less likely to require antibiotics and three times less likely to develop pulmonary edema. None of the prayed-for patients required intubation (an artificial airway for mechanical ventilation), while twelve of the others did. Also, fewer of those who were prayed for died during the follow-up period.[45]

That distant prayer was found to have these effects seems to offer irrefutable evidence of the existence of multiple dimensions of reality. Clearly, in the purely physical time-space dimension, the distances between the patients and those doing the praying were too great for any kind of "energy" to be directly transmitted across physical space between their bodies. Remember, one of the important prin-ciples of the physics of energy is that the farther it gets from its source (like a radio signal from its transmitter), the weaker it gets until it trails off to nothing.

Since it is implausible that any energy emanating from the bodies of those doing the praying was physically reaching the patients across the miles, this must be a cross-dimensional phenomenon. That is, the praying was done in one place, but its influences were somehow carried through another dimension, only to "reenter" and manifest in the energy fields of the recipients. I think this cross-dimensional explanation is the only way that we can make any sense of the effects of distant prayer.

Can distant prayer also be a resource in AIDS and cancer? Elizabeth Targ, M.D., a psychiatrist at the University of California, San Francisco, is heading up a rigorous scientific study of the distant effects of prayer on the immune systems of AIDS patients. Preliminary indications are that this inter-vention may hold promise, and plans for the future include extending this work to serve women with breast cancer. On the opposite coast, Harvard's Mind/Body Medical Institute has also embarked on a major study of distant healing through prayer, as have other universities in the United States and Europe, further legitimizing this area with serious research.

Love across the Miles. While the previous studies are con-cerned with medical outcomes, a study that took place high in the Sierra Mountains of Northern California looked directly at the effects of distant prayer on our energetic anatomy. Twenty-one people were randomly assigned to treatment or control groups for 2 thirty-minute periods. They were all told that the study was examining the effects of sitting without back support, and all participants sat upright on backless chairs or benches. Electromyographic (EMG) recordings were made on the forehead and several points on the spine (cervical, thoracic, and lumbosacral). (An EMG measures the amount of electromagnetic radiation emanating from the muscles, an indication of nervous system activity and muscle tension. The muscles are considered "end organs" of the nervous system.)

Both groups were instructed simply to sit quietly, looking out the window at the Sierras. Meanwhile, two hundred miles away in the San Francisco Bay area two healers were using prayer to send love to the subjects in the experimental group only. There were large and significant reductions in EMG activity in the thoracic and lumbosacral regions compared with results in the control subjects who were not prayed for. This means there was a significant reduction of tension and increase in relaxation in those parts of the body during and following the distant prayer treatment.[46]

According to Jeffrey Cram, Ph.D., of Sierra Health Institute, who headed up the study, yogic theory suggests that the reduction of muscle energy required to hold up the spine while being prayed for may result from the body's energy withdrawing from the surface *into the nadis or primary chakra centers*. The thoracic region, which experienced a 50 percent drop in muscle tension at the surface, corresponds with the heart chakra. Hence it is evident that the heart was the energy center most altered by being prayed for—as would be predicted in the ancient yogic teachings known as the Vedas, as well as in other spiritual traditions.

What can we glean from this study? One important consideration is that the people receiving treatment were sitting quietly, perhaps in a near meditative state. It may be that had they been actively engaged in some demanding activity, the prayer would not have had the same effects. It seems reasonable that their passive, receptive state at the time of the prayer may have somehow helped the prayer to have its impact. However, in the study of cardiac patients, the medical benefits were not dependent on this kind of patient participation.

It is also noteworthy that both of these studies point to the heart, as if the heart center is somehow the portal or antenna through which distant prayer enters to impact the body. In the first study, the effects were seen in the heart's physiology; in the second, its energy field. The findings are, of course, consistent with all our imagery of the heart as being the seat of the soul and the key to our health and well-being.

An interesting dialogue is now under way about whether what is sent during prayer should be considered a form of energy. Nevertheless, studies like these and others have helped open many eyes and minds to the effects of prayer and the spiritual dimensions of healing.

It was a cool spring afternoon as Arlene and John walked across the grass of the Boston Common. John, who has epilepsy, suddenly began to sense the aura that precedes a grand mal seizure. They immediately stopped walking and he lay down on the ground, with her kneeling beside him. She spontaneously put her hands on him—one on his heart and one on his abdomen. "I just centered myself and visualized being with him as he moved through his seizure," she recalls. "I visualized our energies being together and supporting him and loving him, sending love to him, just being a loving presence for him.

"While normally he would have had major convulsions with wild thrashing, this time he moved through his seizure very easily with only a minimal amount of twitching, and it was over within a minute."

On another occasion they were sitting in a restaurant when he felt the aura of a seizure coming on. This time, she states, "I just sat very quietly without touching him, and looked into his eyes as he was going into it. I began to focus on being a loving presence again. He was able to move through the whole seizure sitting upright."

Most of us have been led to believe that epileptic seizures, long considered "electrical storms" in the brain, cannot be halted or mitigated once they are in progress. The sufferer loses consciousness, and the most we can do, we are told, is to protect him from harm until the storm passes. Yet Arlene and John have shown both of these beliefs to be invalid. What's even more amazing is that after each of these events John reported that he had been aware of Arlene's energy during the seizure and was able to remain conscious of what was happening. This is unheard of with a condition that is supposed to involve a complete loss of consciousness.

Like most of us, Arlene was not trained as a healer, nor had she received any preparation in working with energy. Yet what she did spontaneously and intuitively turned out to have a profound effect on John's energetic state. Her actions illustrate once again the magic that resides within us all: our energy can become a transformative force for ourselves and others when guided by a loving heart.

We need no special training, for we all have these gifts. We are all healers.

EXERCISE

*The Freeze-Frame Technique**

This simple technique can be used in one minute. Try it when you are feeling stressed or out of balance.

1. Recognize the stressful feeling, and Freeze-Frame it (take a time-out).
2. Make a sincere effort to shift your focus away from the racing mind or disturbed emotions to the area around your heart.
3. Recall a positive, fun feeling or time and attempt to reexperience it.
4. Using your intuition, common sense, and sincerity, ask your heart what a more efficient response would be, one that would minimize future stress.
5. Listen to what your heart says in answer to your question.

The emphasis is on actually feeling the feeling, rather than having this be an intellectual experience.

---

*The Freeze-Frame Technique® steps listed here are a condensed version of the complete Freeze-Frame technique and instructions found in the book *Freeze-Frame®—Fast Action Stress Relief*, by Doc Lew Childre (copyright Planetary Publications, 1994). Freeze-Frame is a registered trademark of the Institute of HeartMath, Boulder Creek, California.

EXERCISE

A very powerful, heart-strengthening form of *metta* meditation is as follows:

1. Visualize someone for whom you have very loving feelings, and for a few minutes concentrate on feeling and projecting these feelings to this person. Try to feel the love and appreciation as thoroughly and completely as you can, letting them suffuse your whole being.
2. Next, visualize someone toward whom you have feelings that are warm but not as strong as for the first person. As you focus, bring to this second person the same degree of love and appreciation you felt for the first person.
3. Next, visualize someone you have neutral feelings toward—nothing strong either way. As you focus on the person, bring the same intensity of love and appreciation you felt for the first two people to the third.
4. Now visualize someone you have some difficulty with, perhaps whom you dislike but not very intensely. Bring to this person the same feelings of love and appreciation.
5. Finally, visualize someone you have a strong dislike for, and again, as you focus on this person, bring the same degree of love and appreciation you felt for the others. It may be helpful to focus on the person's heart as you do this.

NOTES

---

1. SUBTLE ENERGY: MEDIUM OF THE SPIRIT

1.   Lao-tzu, in Feng, G., and J. English, trans. 1972. *Tao Te Ching.* New York: Vintage Books, p. 14.

2.   Muktananda, S. 1979. *Kundalini: The Secret of Life.* South Fallsburg, N.Y.: SYDA Foundation.

3.   Klivington, K. A. 1992. If spirit matters, it must do something that mind and body cannot. *Advances* (Winter) 8(1):32–3.

4.   Green, E., and A. Green. 1989. *Beyond Biofeedback.* New York: Knoll Publishing Co., p. 304.

5.   Pavek, R. 1994. Biofield Therapeutics. In *Alternative Medicine: Expanding Medical Horizons.* Bethesda, MD: National Institutes of Health.

6.   Tiller, W. Personal communication.

7.   James, W. 1960. In Gardner, Murphy, and Robert Ballou, eds. *William James on Psychical Research.* New York: Viking Press, pp. 6–7.

2. EMBODIMENT: OUR ENERGETIC ANATOMY

1.   Beinfield, H., and E. Korngold. 1991. *Between Heaven and Earth: A Guide to Chinese Medicine.* New York: Ballantine, p. 29.

2.   Barinaga, M. 1992. Giving personal magnetism a whole new meaning. *Science* 256:967.

3.   Green, E., Parks, P., Green, A., et al. 1992. Gender differences in a magnetic field. *Subtle Energies* 3(2):65–104.

4.   Becker, R. 1992. Modern bioelectromagnetics and functions of the central nervous system. *Subtle Energies* 3(1):69.

5.   Blakemore, R. 1975. Magnetotactic bacteria. *Science* 190:377; Beason, R., and J. Nichols. 1984. Magnetic orientation and magnetically sensitive material in a transequatorial migratory bird. *Nature* 309:151; Walker, M., et al. 1984. A candidate magnetic sense organ in the yellowfin tuna, *thunnes albacares. Science* 224:751.

6.   Pavek, R. 1993. Biofield therapeutics. In *Alternative Medicine: Expanding Medical Horizons.* A report to the NIH on alternative medical systems and practices in the United States, prepared by members of the Ad Hoc Advisory Committee to the Office of Alternative Medicine, NIH, p. 140.

7.   Stone, R. 1986. *Polarity Therapy.* CRCS Publications, Sebastopol, Calif.

8.   For information contact: Progen, 319 Spruce St., Redwood City, CA 94063, phone (800) 321-AURA.

9.   For a full discussion of the subtle bodies, see: Brennan, B. *Hands of Light.* Bantam, 1987.

10.   Wright, S. M. 1991. Validity of the human energy field assessment form. *Western Journal of Nursing Research* 13(5):635–647.

11.   Wang, P., Hu, X., and B. Wu. 1993. [Displaying of the infrared radiant track along meridians on the back of human body]. *Chen Tzu Yen Chiu Acupuncture Research* 18(2):90–3, 89. Hu, X., Wu, B., Wang, P. 1993. [Displaying of meridian courses traveling over human body surface under natural conditions.] *Chen Tzu Yen Chiu Acupuncture Research* 18(2):83–9.

12. Yan, Z., Chi, Y., Wang, P., Cheng, J., Wang, Y., Shu, Q., and G. Huang. 1992. Studies on the luminescence of channels in rats and its law of changes with "syndromes" and treatment of acupuncture and moxibustion. *Journal of Traditional Chinese Medicine* (December 12) (4):283–7.

13. Jackson, A. 1992. Energetic medicine: a new science of healing: interview with Dr. Hiroshi Motoyama. *Share International Magazine* 11(7):5–7.

14. Sugano, H., and S. Uchida. 1994. A new approach to the studies of subtle energies. *Subtle Energies* 5(2):143–69.

15. For information about availability of the AMI, contact the California Institute for Human Science, 609 South Vulcan Ave., Suite 201, Encinitas, CA, 92024; (619) 634-1771.

16. Hu, X., Wu, B., Xu, J., and J. Hao. 1990. [Studies on the low skin impedance points and the features of its distribution along the channels by microcomputer. I. Observation on the reliability of the measurement.] *Chen Tzu Yen Chiu Acupuncture Research* 15(3):232–8; and Hu, X., Wu, B., Huang, X., and J. Xu. 1992. Computerized plotting of low skin impedance points. *Journal of Traditional Chinese Medicine* (December 12)(4):277–82.

17. McCraty, R., Atkinson, M., and G. Rein. (1993). ECG Spectra: the measurement of coherent and incoherent frequencies and their relationship to mental and emotional states. *Proceedings of the Third Annual Conference, International Society for the Study of Subtle Energies and Energy Medicine.* Monterey, Calif., pp. 44–48.

18. McCraty, M. A., Atkinson, M., and A. Tiller. New electrophysiological correlates associated with intentional heart focus (1994). Unpublished manuscript, Institute of HeartMath, 14700 West Park Ave., Boulder Creek, CA 95006.

19. Rein, G., Atkinson, M., and M. A. McCraty. (1994). The physiological and psychological effects of compassion and anger. Unpublished manuscript, Institute of HeartMath, 14700 West Park Ave., Boulder Creek, CA 95006; McClelland, D., and C. Kirshnit. The effect of motivational arousal through films on salivary immunoglobulin. *Psychology and Health*, 1988, 2:31–52.

20. Bailey, A. A. *A Treatise on White Magic: The Way of the Disciple.* New York: Lucis Publishing, 1979, p. 469.

21. Adapted from Barbara Brennan's *Hands of Light*, Bantam, 1987.

22. Motoyama, H., and R. Brown. *Science and the Evolution of Consciousness: Chakras, Ki, and Psi.* Brookline, Mass.: Autumn Press, 1978, pp. 93–98.

23. Electronic evidence of auras, chakras in UCLA study. *Brain/Mind Bulletin* (March 20, 1978) 3(9); Miller, R. Bridging the gap: An interview with Valerie Hunt, Ed.D. *Science of Mind* (October, 1983).

24. Jackson, A. 1992. Energetic medicine: a new science of healing: interview with Dr. Hiroshi Motoyama. *Share International Magazine* 11(7):5–7.

25. Vilenskaya L. Personal communication.

26. Rein, G., Atkinson, M., and R. McCraty. In press. The physiological and psychological effects of compassion and anger. *Journal of Advancement in Medicine.*

27. Frawley, D., and V. Lad. 1986. *The Yoga of Herbs.* Twin Lakes, Wisc.: Lotus Press, p. 10.

28. For a more thorough explanation, see: Vasant Lad's *Ayurveda: The Science of Self-Healing, A Practical Guide* (Santa Fe: Lotus Press, 1984) or Deepak Chopra's *Perfect Health: The Complete Mind/Body Guide* (New York: Harmony Books, 1991).

29. Green, E., and A. Green. 1977. *Beyond Biofeedback.* Knoll Publishing Company, Inc.

30. Copyright Maharishi Ayur-Ved Products International, Inc. Used by permission.

3. *SPIRITUS MUNDI:* SUBTLE ENERGIES IN NATURE AND THE ENVIRONMENT

1. Bolen, J. S. 1994. *Crossing to Avalon.* HarperSanFrancisco, p. 31.

2. Hou, T. Z., Re, Z. W., and M. D. Li. 1994. Experimental evidence of a plant meridian system: II, the effects of needle acupuncture on the

temperature changes of soybean (Glycine max). *American Journal of Chinese Medicine* 22(2):103–10.

3. Hagens, B. Personal communication. Also see W. S. Becker and B. Hagens, The Rings of Gaia, in J. A. Swan (ed.), *The Power of Place*. Wheaton, Ill.: Quest Books, 1991, pp. 257–79.

4. Leviton, R. 1992. Ley lines and the meaning of Adam. In D. H. Childress, ed., *Antigravity and the World Grid*. Stelle, Ill.: Adventures Unlimited Press, p. 142.

5. Michell, J. 1972. *The View over Atlantis*. New York: Ballantine, p. 26.

6. Ibid., p. 25.

7. Betz, H. 1995. Unconventional water detection: Field test of the dowsing technique in dry zones: part 1. *Journal of Scientific Exploration* 9(1):1–43.

8. Graves, T. 1986. *Needles of Stone Revisited*. Glastonbury, England: Gothic Image Publications.

9. Freeman, M. 1995. Sacred waters, holy wells. *Parabola* (Spring):57.

10. Vortex patterns anchor Schwenk's theory of flow. *Brain/Mind Bulletin* (January–February 1996):3.

11. Cox, A. 1967. Magnetic field reversals. *Scientific American*:44–54; Gubbins, D., and Bloxham, J. 1985. The secular variation of the Earth's magnetic field. *Nature* 317 (October 31).

12. Nakagawa, K. 1976. Magnetic field deficiency syndrome and magnetic treatment. *Japanese Medical Journal* 2745 (December 4).

13. Bonlie, D. Unpublished data. Address: Dean Bonlie, D.D.S., President, MagnetiCo Inc., #107, 5421 11th St. NE, Calgary, Alberta T2E 6M4 Canada; (403) 730-0883.

14. For more information, contact the Time Research Institute, P.O. Box 620198, Woodside, CA 94062.

15. Radin, D., and J. Rebman. 1996. Lunar correlates of normal, abnormal and anomalous human behavior. *Subtle Energies* 5(3):209–38.

16. Friedman, H., et al. 1965. Psychiatric ward behavior and geophysical parameters. *Nature* 205:1050.

17. Friedman, H., et al. 1963. Geomagnetic parameters and psychiatric hospital admissions. *Nature* 200:626.

18. Becker, R. 1990. Geomagnetic activity and violent behavior. *Subtle Energies* 1(2):65–79.

19. Persinger, M. A., and G. B. Schaut. 1988. Geomagnetic factors in subjective telepathic precognitive and postmortem experiences. *Journal of the American Society for Psychical Research* 82:217–35; Persinger, M. 1985. Geophysical variables and behavior: XXX, intense paranormal experiences occur during days of quiet, global, geomagnetic activity. *Perception & Motor Skills* 61:320–22; and Becker, R. 1992. Electromagnetism and psi phenomena. *Journal of the American Society of Psychical Research* 86:1–17.

20. Persinger, M. A., and S. Krippner. 1989. Dream ESP experiments and geomagnetic activity. *Journal of the American Society for Psychical Research* (April) 83:101–16.

21. Krippner, S. Personal communication.

22. Roos, P. A. 1991. Light and electromagnetic waves: The health implications. *Journal of the Bio-Electro-Magnetics Institute* 3(2):7–12.

23. Ott, J. 1973. *Health and Light.* Old Greenwich, Conn.: The Devin-Adair Co.

24. Light therapy. In *Alternative Medicine: The Definitive Guide.* 1993. Puyallup, Wash.: Burton Goldberg Group, pp. 320–1.

25. Editorial. 1991. Excessive sunlight exposure, skin melanoma, link to vitamin D. *International Journal of Biosocial and Medical Research* 13(1):13–14.

26. Lefkowitz, E. S., and C. F. Garland. 1994. Sunlight, vitamin D, and ovarian cancer mortality rates in U.S. women. *International Journal of Epidemiology* 6(December 23):1133–6.

27. Reported in Environment News Briefs, *Spectrum* 39 (November–December 1994):14.; and *Acres USA* (August 1994).

28. Gauquelin, M. 1988. Is there a Mars Effect? *Journal of Scientific Exploration* 2(1):29–51.

29. Ertel, S. 1988. Raising the hurdle for the athletes' Mars Effect:

Association co-varies with eminence. *Journal of Scientific Exploration* 2(1):53.

30. For a fascinating discussion of the possibilities, see *The Passion of the Western Mind* by Rick Tarnas. Harmony Books, 1991.

31. Wertheimer, N., and E. Leeper. 1979. Electrical wiring configurations and childhood cancer. *American Journal of Epidemiology* 190(3):273–84.

32. For a review of studies, see: Maxey, E. S. 1991. Perspective: A lethal subtle energy. *Subtle Energies* 2(2):55–72.

33. Michaud, L., and M. Persinger. 1985. Geophysical variables and behavior: XXV, alterations in memory for a narrative following applications of theta frequency electromagnetic fields. *Perception & Motor Skills* 60:416–18.

34. Reichmanis, M., Perry, F., Marino, A., and R. Becker. 1979. Relationship between suicide and the electromagnetic field of overhead power lines. *Physiology, Chemistry and Physics* 11:395–403; Wilson, B. 1988. Chronic exposure to ELF fields may induce depression. *Bioelectromagnetics* 9:195–205.

35. Reported in *Science News* (March 18, 1995).

36. Wilson, B. W., et al. 1988. Effects of electric blanket use on human pineal gland function. Preliminary report in *Proceedings of the DOE/EPRI Contractor's Review*, Phoenix, Ariz. (October 30–November 3), Washington, D.C., U.S. Department of Energy, Office of Energy Storage and Distribution.

37. Maxey, E. S. 1991. Perspective: A lethal subtle energy. *Subtle Energies* 2(2):55–72.

38. Startling link found between Alzheimer's, EMF's. *Brain/Mind Bulletin* (August 1994): 1. This article reports findings to be published in a forthcoming issue of *Neurobiology of Aging.* The findings were reported at the fourth International Conference on Alzheimer's Disease and Related Disorders, Minneapolis, 1994.

39. Savitz, D., and D. Loomis. 1995. *American Journal of Epidemiology* 141:123–4.

40. Reported in *Science* (January 27, 1995).

41. Reiter, R. J. 1994. Melatonin suppression by static and extremely low frequency electromagnetic fields: Relationship to the reported increased incidence of cancer. *Reviews of Environmental Health* 10(3–4):171–86.

42. Molis, T. M., et al. 1995. Melatonin modulation of estrogen-regulated proteins, growth factors, and proto-oncogenes in human breast cancer. *Journal of Pineal Research* 18(1):1–11.

43. These devices are commercially available from Clarus Systems Group, 1120 Calle Cordillera, San Clemente, CA 92673; (800) 425-2787.

44. Connecting mind, nature. *Brain/Mind Bulletin* (July 1995):1.

45. Leakey, R. 1995. *The Sixth Extinction.* New York: Doubleday, p. 271.

46. In Roszak, T. 1995. *Ecopsychology: Restoring the Earth, Healing the Mind.* San Francisco: Sierra Club Books, pp. 168–9.

47. In Simos, M. 1979. *The Spiral Dance.* San Francisco: HarperCollins Publishers.

4. Two or More Together: Subtle Energies in Relationships

1. Reed, H. 1996. Close encounters in the liminal zone: experiments in imaginal communication. Part I. *Journal of Analytical Psychology* 41:81–116.

2. Ibid., 41:86.

3. Gerber, R. *Vibrational Medicine: New Choices for Healing Ourselves.* Santa Fe: Bear & Co., 1988.

4. Jahnke, R. 1991. *The Most Profound Medicine.* Santa Barbara: Health Action Publishing.

5. Grinberg-Zylberbaum, J., Delaflor, M., Sanchez, M. E., et al. 1992. Human communication and the electrophysiological activity of the brain. *Subtle Energies* 3(3):25–43.

6. Dossey, L. 1992. But is it energy? Reflections on consciousness, healing, and the new paradigm. *Subtle Energies* 3(3):69–82.

7. Gough, W. C., and R. L. Shacklett. 1994. The science of connectiveness: Part I: Modeling a greater unity. *Subtle Energies* 4(1):60.

8. The Holy Bible, Luke 8:45–6.

9. McCraty, R. 1996. The electricity of touch. Paper presented at the International Society for the Study of Subtle Energies & Energy Medicine Sixth Annual Conference, Boulder, CO, June 24; and personal communication.

10. Kiecolt-Glaser, J., Fisher, L., Ogrocki, P., et al. 1987. Marital quality, marital disruption, and immune function. *Psychosomatic Medicine* 49:13–34.

11. Medalie, J. H., and U. Goldbourt. 1976. Angina pectoris among 10,000 men: Psychosocial and other risk factors. *American Journal of Medicine* 60:910–21.

12. Bruhn, J., Chandler, B., Miller, C., et al. 1966. Social aspects of coronary heart disease in two adjacent ethnically different communities. *American Journal of Public Health* 56:2493–2506.

13. Spiegel, D., Bloom, J. R., Kraemer, H. C., E. Gottheil. 1989. Effects of psychosocial treatment on survival of patients with metastatic breast cancer. *The Lancet* (October 14):888–91.

14. McClelland, D., and C. Kirshnit. 1988. The effect of motivational arousal through films on salivary immunoglobulin. *Psychology and Health* 2:31–52.

15. For a helpful guide to tantric lovemaking, see: Muir, C. and C. *Tantra: The Art of Conscious Loving.* San Francisco: Mercury House, 1989. There are also many other popular books available on this subject.

16. Schlitz, M. 1996. Intentionality and intuition and their clinical implications: A challenge for science and medicine. *Advances: The Journal of Mind-Body Health* 12(2):58–65.

17. Schlitz, M., and S. LaBerge. 1994. Autonomic detection of remote observation. *Research in Parapsychology.* Zingrone, N., Parker, A., and D. Biernam, eds. New Jersey: The Scarecrow Press.

18. Braud, W., and M. Schlitz. 1991. Consciousness interactions with remote biological systems: Anomalous intentionality effects. *Subtle Energies* 2:1–57.

19. May, E., and L. Vilenskaya. 1992. Overview of current parapsychology research in the former Soviet Union. *Subtle Energies* 3(3):45–67.

20. Braud, W., and M. Schlitz. 1991. Consciousness interactions with remote biological systems: Anomalous intentionality effects. *Subtle Energies* 2(1):1–46.

21. Braud, W. 1995. *Journal of the American Society for Psychical Research* 89:103–15.

22. For a complete booklet describing this process, *When You and I Are One: Close Encounters in the Imaginal Zone*, send $5 to Henry Reed, Ph.D., 503 Lake Dr., Virginia Beach, VA 23451. Dr. Reed also conducts training programs in imaginal communication. For information write or call (800) 398-1370.

5. IN-SPIRATION: THE BREATH-ENERGY CONNECTION

1. Arberry, A. L., trans. 1968. *Mystical Poems of Rumi.* University of Chicago Press, p. 10.

2. Khan H. I. 1962. *The Sufi Message of Hazrat Inayat Khan*, vol. 7. London: Barrie & Rockliff, p. 104.

3. Leboyer, F. 1975. *Birth without Violence.* New York: Knopf, p. 51.

4. Rama S., Ballentine, R., and A. Hymes. 1979. *The Science of Breath: A Practical Guide.* Honesdale, Penn.: The Himalayan Institute, p. 100.

5. Beinfield, H., and E. Korngold. 1991. *Between Heaven and Earth: A Guide to Chinese Medicine.* New York: Ballantine, p. 121.

6. Ibid., p. 117.

7. Warburg, O. 1966. *The Prime Cause and Prevention of Cancer.* Lindau Lecture, Wurzburg, Germany, K. Triltsch.

8. Gordon, T., and W. B. Kannel. 1970. The Framingham Study: An Epidemiological Investigation of Cardiovascular Disease. Sections 1–26, Bethesda, Md., National Heart and Lung Institute.

9. Cullen, K., et al. 1983. Multiple regression analysis of risk factors for cardiovascular disease and cancer mortality in Busselton, West Australia: A thirteen-year study. *Journal of Chronic Diseases* 36:371–7.

10. Collinge, W. Undated. Evocative breath therapy and immunoenhancement: A pilot study. Manuscript submitted for review.

11. Taylor, K. 1994. *The Breathwork Experience: Exploration and Healing in Nonordinary States of Consciousness.* Santa Cruz, Calif.: Hanford Mead Publishers, p. 51.

12. Ibid., p. 47.

13. Ibid., p. 3.

14. Weil, A. 1972. *The Natural Mind.* Boston: Houghton Mifflin.

15. Grof, S. 1996. Remarks made in a workshop lecture on holotropic breathwork, February 25, San Rafael, Calif.

16. Kornfield, J., ed. 1993. *Teachings of the Buddha.* Boston: Shambhala, pp. 70–72.

17. Raskin, E. Personal communication.

6. SUSTENANCE: THE CARE AND NURTURING OF OUR VITAL ENERGY

1. Benson, H., Beary, J., and M. Carol. 1974. The relaxation response. *Psychiatry* 37:37–46.

2. Benson, H. 1975. *The Relaxation Response.* New York: Avon Books; and 1985. *Beyond the Relaxation Response.* New York: Berkley Books.

3. Meditation may boost melatonin. *Brain/Mind Bulletin,* 21:9, June 1996, pp. 1–2.

4. Collinge, W., Yarnold, P., and E. Raskin. 1996. Functional status and behavioral medicine practice predict 12-month improvement in chronic

283

fatigue syndrome. Study presented at the bi-annual scientific conference of the American Association for Chronic Fatigue Syndrome, San Francisco, October 14.

5.   Strassman, R., Qualls, C., Lisansky, J., and G. Peake. 1991. Elevated rectal temperature produced by all-night bright light is reversed by melatonin infusion in men. *Journal of Applied Physiology* 71:2178–82.

6.   Saarela, S., and R. Reiter. 1993. Functions of melatonin in thermoregulatory processes. *Life Sciences* 54:295–311.

7.   Irwin, M., Mascovich, A., Gillin, J. C., Willoughby, R., Pike, J., and T. L. Smith. 1994. Partial sleep deprivation reduces natural killer cell activity in humans. *Psychosomatic Medicine* (November–December) 56(6):493–8.

8.   Moldofsky, H. Sleep, neuroimmune and neuroendocrine functions in fibromyalgia and chronic fatigue syndrome. *Advances in Neuroimmunology* 5(1):39–56.

9.   Weil, A. 1995. *Spontaneous Healing.* New York: Knopf.

10. Editorial. 1987. Winter blues? Try a little morning light. *Bioenergy Health Newsletter* (December, 7); Gutfield, G. 1993. The new science of rays and rhythms—cutting edge light therapies that can brighten your health. *Prevention* 45(2), 67–71; 116–123.

11. Reuters News Service. 1995. Eat like a cave man. Report from an international nutrition conference in London, October 26.

12. Lu, H. 1990. *Chinese Foods for Longevity: The Art of Long Life.* New York: Sterling Publishing Company.

13. Mary Jo Cravatta, D.C., Palo Alto, Calif., personal communication.

14. Sharma, R. K., and V. B. Dash (trans.). 1976. *Charaka Samhita,* vols. I and II. Chowkamba Sanskrit Series Office, Varanasi, India.

15. Flaws, B., and H. Wolfe. 1983. *Prince Wen Hui's Cook: Chinese Dietary Therapy.* Brookline, Mass.: Paradigm Publications, pp. 23–4.

16. For a summary of research see: Collinge, W. 1996. *The American Holistic Health Association Complete Guide to Alternative Medicine.* New York: Warner Books, Inc.

17. Teeguarden, R. 1984. *Chinese Tonic Herbs.* Tokyo: Japan Publications, Inc.

18. Bombardelli, E., Cirstonni, A., and A. Lietti. 1980. The effect of acute and chronic (panax) ginseng saponins treatment on adrenal function: biochemical and pharmacological. *Proceedings of the Third International Ginseng Symposium* 1:9–16.

19. Feng, L. M., Pan, H. Z., and W. W. Li. 1987. Antioxidant action of panax ginseng. *Chung Hsi I Chieh Ho Tsa Chih* (May) 7(5):288–90.

20. Jikino, H., et al. 1985. Antihepatotoxic actions of ginsenosides from panax ginseng roots. *Planta Medica* 52:62–4.

21. Berdyshev, V. V. 1981. Effect of the long-term intake of cleutherococcus on the adaptation of sailors in the tropics. *Voenno Meditsinskii Zhurnal* (May) 5:57–8 (published in Russian).

22. Kupin, V. I., and E. B. Polevaia. 1986. Stimulation of the immunological reactivity of cancer patients by eleutherococcus extract. *Voprosy Onkologii* 32(7):21–6 (published in Russian).

23. Medon, P. J., Ferguson, P. W., and C. F. Watson. 1984. Effects of eleutherococcus senticosus extracts on hexobarbital metabolism in vivo and in vitro. *Journal of Ethnopharmacology* (April) 10(2):235–41.

24. Teeguarden, R. 1984. *Chinese Tonic Herbs.* New York: Japan Publications.

25. Kennedy, R. 1995. *The Thinking Person's Guide to Perfect Health.* Rohnert Park, Calif.: Context Publications.

26. Barrett-Conner, E., et al. 1986. A prospective study of dehydroepiandosterone sulfate, mortality and cardiovascular disease. *New England Journal of Medicine* 315(24):1519–1524.

27. Bulbrook, R. D., et al. 1971. Relation between urinary androgen and corticoid excretion and subsequent breast cancer. *Lancet* ii:395–8.

28. Shealy, N. 1985. Activating the Ring of Fire. Talk given at the Seventh Conference on Treatment and Research of Experienced Anomalous Trauma (TREAT VII), San Rafael, Calif., April.

29. Fiatarone, M. A., et al. 1989. The effect of exercise on natural killer

cells activity in young and old subjects. *Journal of Gerontology* 44:M37–45; and Makinnon, L. T. 1989. Exercise and natural killer cells: What is their relationship? *Sports Medicine* 7:141–9.

30. Fitzgerald, L. 1988. Exercise and the immune system. *Immunology Today* 9:337–9.

31. Jahnke, R. Personal communication.

32. Ramos, H. Personal communication.

33. *The Yoga Research Society Newsletter,* 3(13).

34. Eisenberg, D. 1985. *Encounters with Qi: Exploring Chinese Medicine.* New York: W. W. Norton & Company.

35. Wang, Z., et al. 1988. A preliminary study of the relationship between qigong and energy metabolism: the changes of blood ATP content in qigong masters in the qigong state. *Proceedings of the First World Conference for the Academic Exchange of Medical Qigong,* Beijing, China, p. 58.

36. Koar, W. H. 1995. Meditation, T-cells, anxiety, depression and HIV infection. *Subtle Energies* 6(1):89–98; Chegwen, H., Huahao, L., and L. Jifeng. 1990. Analysis of the therapeutic effect of qigong on myasthenia gravis in 40 patients; and Lo, J., He, C., Lu, H., and L. Wand. 1990. Analyzing changes of peripheral blood cell population and immune functions in 31 nasopharyngeal carcinoma (NPC) patients treated with radiotherapy and qigong. *Proceedings of the Third National Academic Conference on Qigong Science* November, 32 Guangzhou (Canton), China, pp. 94–5.

37. Oriental secrets of health, happiness and longevity: an interview with Master Hua-Ching Ni. *Spectrum* no. 37 (July–August 1994): 28.

38. Province, M., et al. 1995. *Journal of the American Medical Association,* May 3.

39. Reid, D. 1994. *The Complete Book of Chinese Health and Healing.* Boston: Shambhala, p. 340.

40. Ibid., p. 377.

41. Chia, M., and M. Chia. 1984. *Taoist Secrets of Love: Cultivating Female Sexual Energy.* New York: Aurora Press.

42. Reid, D. 1989. *The Tao of Health, Sex and Longevity.* New York: Fireside, p. 332.

43. Beinfield, H., and E. Korngold. 1991. *Between Heaven and Earth: A Guide to Chinese Medicine.* New York: Ballantine, p. 121.

7. COURTING THE SPIRIT: SUBTLE ENERGIES IN PRAYER, MEDITATION, AND HEALING

1. In Castelli, J., ed. 1994. *How I Pray.* New York: Ballantine, p. 66.

2. As quoted by meditation researcher Frank Echenhoffer, Ph.D. Personal communication.

3. Lawrence, B., and R. J. Edmonson, trans.; Helms, H. M., ed. 1985. *The Practice of the Presence of God* [1692]. Orleans, Mass.: Paraclete Press.

4. Woodward, K. L. 1995. The giggles are for God. *Newsweek* (February 20): 54.

5. In Castelli, J., ed. 1994. *How I Pray.* New York: Ballantine, p. 147.

6. Ibid., pp. 99–101.

7. Goldstein, J., and J. Kornfield. 1987. *Seeking the Heart of Wisdom: The Path of Insight Meditation.* Boston: Shambhala.

8. Goldstein, J. 1994. *Insight Meditation: The Practice of Freedom.* Boston: Shambhala, p. 120.

9. Greenwood, B. 1990. *Energies of Transformation: A Guide to the Kundalini Process.* Cupertino: Shakti River/Transpersonal Learning Service.

10. Selby, J. 1992. *Kundalini Awakening: A Gentle Guide to Chakra Activation and Spiritual Growth.* New York: Bantam Books, p. 8.

11. Goldstein, J. 1994. *Insight Meditation: The Practice of Freedom.* Boston: Shambhala, p. 51.

12. Le Mée, K. 1994. *Chant: The Origins, Form, Practice and Healing Power of Gregorian Chant.* New York: Bell Tower.

13. Tomatis, A. 1991. *The Conscious Ear: My Life of Transformation through Listening.* Barrytown, N.Y.: Station Hill Press.

14. Tiller, W. A., McCraty, R., and M. Atkinson. 1996. Cardiac coherence: a new, noninvasive measure of autonomic nervous system order. *Alternative Therapies in Health and Medicine* 2(1):52–65.

15. Tiller, W. 1994. Commentary. *Subtle Energies* 5(3):254.

16. Kornfield, J., ed. 1993. *Teachings of the Buddha.* Boston: Shambhala, pp. 70–72.

17. Sheppard, B., Staggers, F., et al. 1995. *Hypertension* 26:820–7.

18. Benson, H. 1984. *Beyond the Relaxation Response.* New York: Times Books.

19. Wright, P. A. 1995. The interconnectivity of mind, brain, and behavior in altered states of consciousness: focus on shamanism. *Alternative Therapies in Health and Medicine* 1(3):50–6.

20. For a summary of this research see: Wright, P. A. 1995. The interconnectivity of mind, brain, and behavior in altered states of consciousness: focus on shamanism. *Alternative Therapies in Health and Medicine* 1(3):50–6.

21. Reader, A. L. 1995. The internal mystery plays: the role and physiology of the visual system in contemplative practices. *Alternative Therapies in Health and Medicine* 1(4):54–63.

22. Fenwick, P. and E. 1995. *The Truth in the Light.* London: Hodders/Headline.

23. Kason, Y. 1994. Near-death experiences and kundalini awakening: exploring the link. *Journal of Near-Death Studies* 12(3):143–157.

24. Fahrion, S. L., Wirakis, M., and P. Pooley. 1992. EEG amplitude, brain mapping, & synchrony in & between a bioenergy practitioner & client during healing. *Subtle Energies* 3(1):19–52.

25. Redner, R., Briner, B., and L. Snellman. 1991. Effects of a bioenergy healing technique on chronic pain. *Subtle Energies* 2(3):43–68.

26. Heidt, P. 1981. An investigation of the effect of therapeutic touch on the anxiety of hospitalized patients. *Nursing Research* 30:32–7.

27. Wirth, D. 1990. The effect of non-contact therapeutic touch on the healing rate of full thickness dermal wounds. *Subtle Energies* 1(1):1–20; Grad, B. 1965. Some biological effects of the laying on of hands: review of experiments with animals and plants. *Journal of the American Society for Psychical Research* 59:95–171.

28. Krieger, D. 1973. The relationship of touch with the intent to help or to heal, to subject in vivo hemoglobin values: a study in personalized interaction. *The Proceedings of the Ninth American Nurses Association Research Conference.* American Nurses Association, New York, pp. 39–58.

29. Canfield, J., and M. V. Hansen. 1993. *Chicken Soup for the Soul: 101 Stories to Open the Heart and Rekindle the Spirit.* Deerfield Beach, Fla.: Health Communications, Inc., pp. 40–42.

30. Reported by Luke Chan, a teacher associated with the Wahzhan Zhineng Chigong Clinic and Training Center and living in the United States. Chan is the author of *101 Miracles of Natural Healing* based on the work of the Center and available from him at 9676 Cincinnati-Columbus Road, Cincinnati, OH 45241; (513)-777-0588. Chan also leads training excursions to the Center twice per year from the United States.

31. Tart, C. 1985. Subtle energies, healing energies. *Interfaces: Linguistics, Psychology & Health Therapeutics* 12(1):3–10.

32. Benor, D. 1990. Survey of spiritual healing research. *Complementary Medical Research* 4(1):9–33.

33. Barry, J. 1968. General and comparative study of the psychokinetic effect on a fungus culture. *Journal of Parapsychology* 32:237–43.

34. Tedder, W., and M. Monty. 1980. Exploration of long-distance PK: a conceptual replication of the influence on a biological system. *Research in Parapsychology* 1980:90–93.

35. Nash, C. B. 1982. Study of remote mental healing. *Medical Hypotheses* 8:481–90.

36. Braud, W. 1989. Distant mental influence on fate of hemolysis of human red blood cells. *Research in Parapsychology* 1988:1–6.

37. Braud, W., Davis, G., and R. Wood. 1979. Experiments with

Matthew Manning. *Journal of the Society of Psychical Research* 50(782):199–223.

38. Grad, G. 1965. Some biological effects of laying-on-of-hands: a review of experiments with animals and plants. *Journal of the American Society of Psychical Research* 59:95–127.

39. Tart, C. 1985. Subtle energies, healing energies. *Interfaces: Linguistics, Psychology & Health Therapeutics* 12(1):3–10.

40. Review confirms "healing" effects. 1991. *New Sense Bulletin* 16(8):1–2.

41. Suhr, G. M., Lushington, J. A., Jr., and B. G. Brogdon. 1991. A miraculous cure: spontaneous disappearance of abdominal tumor after "laying on of hands" [letter]. *American Journal of Roentgenology* 157(6):1355.

42. Wirth, D. 1990. The effect of non-contact therapeutic touch on the healing rate of full thickness dermal wounds. *Subtle Energies* 1(1):1–20.

43. Wirth, D. P., and J. R. Cram. 1993. Multi-site electromyographic analysis of non-contact therapeutic touch. *International Journal of Psychosomatics* 40(1–4):47–55.

44. Dossey, L. 1994. Healing, energy, & consciousness: into the future or a retreat to the past? Address given at the fourth annual conference of the International Society for the Study of Subtle Energies and Energy Medicine, Boulder, CO, June 17.

45. Byrd, R. 1988. Positive therapeutic effects of intercessory prayer in a coronary care unit population. *Southern Medical Journal* 81:826–9.

46. Wirth, D. P., and J. R. Cram. 1995. The psychophysiology of non-traditional prayer. *Proceedings of the International Society for the Study of Subtle Energies and Energy Medicine*, Fifth Annual Conference, Boulder, CO, p. 20.

APPENDIX

RESOURCES

International Society for the Study of Subtle Energies and
    Energy Medicine (ISSSEEM)
356 Goldco Circle, Golden, CO 80401
Phone (303) 278-2228, Fax 279-3539
Internet: http://www.vitalenergy.com/ISSSEEM
E-mail: 74040.1273@compuserve.com

ISSSEEM is one of the leaders in the effort to synthesize traditional wisdom and shamanic knowledge about subtle energies with scientific theory and study it with scientific method. Designed as a bridge between scientifically inclined intuitives and intuitively inclined scientists, ISSSEEM supports experimental exploration of the phenomena long associated with the practice of energy healing. Through conferences, a quarterly magazine, *Bridges*, and a peer-reviewed scientific journal, *Subtle Energies*, the society serves its members and strives to stimulate theory, research, and discussion in the larger scientific community.

HealthWorld Online
Internet: http://www.healthy.net

This is the Internet's largest and most comprehensive natural health and wellness site. Provides a wealth of information about varieties of energy medicine, alternative health care resources, diseases and alternative treatments, and interactive forums in specific health care issues including mind/body medicine, women's health, and public health. Offers an opportunity to dialogue with William Collinge in the forum on Mind/Body Approaches to Chronic Illness.

Nurse Healers Professional Associates
1211 Locust St.
Philadelphia, PA 19107
(215) 545-8079

NHPA is an international membership organization for nurses that provides referrals to practitioners and teachers of Therapeutic Touch.

HaelanWorks
3080 Third St.
Boulder, CO 80304
Phone/Fax (303) 449-5790
E-mail: janetquinn@aol.com

Provides training in Therapeutic Touch and other energy healing modalities for both the lay public and health care providers. Video program available: "Therapeutic Touch: A Video Home-Study Course for Family Care Givers." Directed by Janet Quinn, Ph.D., R.N.

The SHEN Therapy Institute
20 YFH Gate Six Road
Sausalito, CA 94965
Phone (415) 332-2593, Fax 331-2455
E-mail: SHENmaker@MSN.com

Offers training and certification programs nationally and internationally in SHEN Therapy, a form of hands-on biofield therapeutics. Developed and directed by scientist and researcher Richard Pavek, a consultant to the Office of Alternative Medicine, National Institutes of Health.

Institute of Noetic Sciences (IONS)
475 Gate Five Road, Suite 300
Sausalito, CA 94965
Phone (800) 383-1394, Fax (415) 331-5673.
Internet: http://www.noetic.org

Founded by *Apollo 14* astronaut Edgar Mitchell, IONS is a nonprofit organization that supports research and education on consciousness, human potential, personal and social transformation, and many other endeavors related to subtle energy and healing. Members receive the *Noetic Sciences Bulletin* and *Noetic Sciences Review* quarterly, and *Noetic Sciences Resource* three times per year.

The Institute of HeartMath
P.O. Box 1463
Boulder Creek, CA 95006
Phone (800) 450-9111
E-mail: hrtmath@netcom.com
Internet: http://www.webcom.com/hrtmath

This nonprofit center of research and training has a twofold mission: (1) to study the effects of heart function on mental and emotional balance, personal efficiency, immune system health, and intelligence; and (2) to use this research to develop and teach practical skills that will enable people to cope more quickly with modern-day stress, enhance performance and health, and access a more complete intelligence in both professional situations and personal life. Workshops and customized training programs are conducted both at their Boulder Creek retreat center and on-site at workplaces and organizations worldwide.

INDEX

Abulafia, Abraham, 231
Acquired *chi*, 174–75, 216
Activity, 180–86
Acupuncture points, 31–35, 39
Adams, Marsha, 80–81
Adrenal exhaustion, 181
Afternoon *vata*, 178
Agape. See Altruistic love
Aging, 220
Agni, 193, 194–95, 196
AIDS, prayer and, 266
Alleo-biofeedback, 134
Alpha brain waves, 246–47
Alternate nostril breathing, 163–64
Altruistic love, 35, 128
Alzheimer's disease, 99–100
American ginseng, 198
AMI (apparatus for meridian identification),
    32–33
Ancestral diet, 187–88
Antibody immunoglobulin A (IgA), 153–54
Asanas, 208
Ashwaganda, 200
Astral body, 29
Astringent taste, 192
ATP (adenosine triphosphate), 212
Aura, 28, 29
Autonomic nervous system, 133–34
Auw centers, 35

Ayurveda
    digestion and, 196
    doshas, 50–52, 57, 118, 177, 191
    energetic nature and, 8
    five elements, 49–50
    foods and, 9, 191–93
    vital energy and, 176
    See also Pranayama

Bailey, Alice, 36
Balance training, 213
Baptism, 155
Barometric pressure, lunar cycle and, 83, 84
Bastriki, 168
Becker, Robert, 24
Beinfield, Harriet, 23, 150
Benedictine monks, 12, 234
Benor, Daniel, 259
Benson, Herbert, 182, 245
*Between Heaven and Earth: A Guide to Chinese
    Medicine* (Beinfield and Korngold), 150
Betz, Hans-Dieter, 69
Beyond Biofeedback (Green), 16
Biofeedback, 53
Biofield, 17–19, 26–31
    equivalent terms for, 18–19
Bitter taste, 192
Blood pressure, 245, 247

295

Body, spirit and, 248–49
Bolen, Jean Shinoda, 59
Bonlie, Dean, 79
Brain waves, 246–47
Braud, William, 135
Brazilian low, 75
Breast cancer, 266
  DHEA and, 202
Breath
  anatomy of, 148–52
  complete yogic, 162–63
  energy connection, 143–71
  full, 151–52
  health and, 152–54
  in meditation, 158–60, 170
  mind and, 166–68
  as oscillator, 151
  as regulator, 149
  spirit and, 145–46
Breathing, 21
  alternate nostril, 163–64
  chakra exercise, 169
  in Eastern culture, 149–50
  fire exercise, 168–69
  immune system and, 153–54
  with music, 171
  with partner, 142, 170
  in Western culture, 146–47
  yoga and, 149, 162–63
Breathwork, 143, 154–58
Breathwork Experience, The (Taylor), 155
Buddhist tradition, 159–60, 175, 236, 240
  See also Metta
Byrd, Randolph, 265

Cabala, 35, 231
Caffeine, 188, 189
Cancer
  electromagnetic fields and, 99
  oxygen and, 152
  prayer and, 266
  sunlight and, 90
  See also specific cancers
Castelli, Jim, 227
Celestial body, 29
  influences of, 81–92
Celovsky, Samuel, 226–28
Centers of energy, 35–45
Cerebral anoxia, 249

Chakras, 35, 36–39
  breathing, 169
  opening and closing of, 41–43
  palm, 43–44, 55, 242, 261
  spinning, 39–40
  stimulating, 235–36
  yoga and, 208–9
Chanting, 12, 234–36
Chi. See Vital energy
Chi kung, 7, 33, 53, 60, 114, 161, 165–66,
    170, 203–5, 210–15, 222
Childre, Doc Lew, 238
Children, 117–18
Chinese culture, 7, 13, 65–66, 94
  five elements, 49–50
  foods, 189–90
  herbs, 196–200
  vital energy, 10, 31–34
  See also Chi kung; Feng shui; Tai chi; Taoist
    tradition
Chronic fatigue syndrome, 10
  meditation and, 182
  sleep and, 185
Chronobiology, 175–76
Chyavan prash, 200
Circles, 98
Cohen, Michael, 103
Collective intention
  with contact, 254–57
  in Hawaii, 138
  without contact, 257–58
Communication
  imaginal, 110, 140–41
  intuitive, 115–16
Complete yogic breath, 162–63
Concentration, posture and, 239–41
Congenital chi, 174–75, 216–19
Conn, Sarah, 103
Conscious intention, 260, 261
Consistent pattern, 176
Cram, Jeffrey, 267
Cravatta, Mary Jo, 191
Creepy feeling, 133
Crisis calls, lunar cycle and, 83, 86
Crown (of head) chakra, 38, 43

Dalai Lama, 225
Dantien, 35
Death rates, lunar cycle and, 83, 86

INDEX

Depression, 99
DHEA hormone, 202
Diet
  ancestral, 187–88
  Eastern culture, 196–201
  weight and, 10–11
  Western culture, 196
  See also Food
Digestion, 193–96
Digestive fire. *See Agni*
Direct communication, 115
"Direct current" magentic energy, 74
Diseases
  electromagnetic fields and, 99–102
  See also specific diseases
Divine blueprint, 251–53
Doshas
  Ayurveda and, 50–52, 57, 118, 177, 191
  determining, 57–58
  influences of, 243–45
  relationships and, 118–24
  See also Kapha; Pitta; Vata
Dossey, Larry, 116, 265
Dowsing, 15, 66–70, 71
Dragon currents, 65
"Drop picture" method, 73

EAR (electromagnetic activity report), 81
Earth
  ecopsychology and, 102–7
  energy fields, 20, 74–81
  influences of, 12–13
Earthquakes, 79–81
Eastern culture
  breathing in, 149–50
  diet, 196–201
  exercise in, 203–6
  sexual relationships in, 129–31
  vital energy in, 31–33, 114
Eaton, Boyd, 187
Ecopsychology, 102–7
Ecstasy, 230–33
Einstein, Albert, 2
Ejaculation, 216, 217
Electromagnetic fields (EMFs)
  diseases and, 99–102
  earth's, 74–81
  energetic anatomy and, 23–24
  heart's, 5, 132

man-made, 98–102
  sexual relationships and, 132
Electromyograph (EMG), 38, 267
Elements, 48–52, 70
Eleutherosides, 198
EMFs. *See* Electromagnetic fields
EMG. *See* Electromyograph
Emotional body, 29
Endomorphins, 248
Energetic anatomy, 20, 23–58
Energetic types, 8
Energy, subtle, 1–22
Energy centers, 35–45
Entrainment, 46–48
  head-heart, 238–39
Environment. *See* Ecopsychology
Ertel, Suitbert, 91
Estabany, Oskar, 260
Etheric body, 29, 63, 65
Evening *kapha*, 178–79
Exercise(s), 203–6
  awakening *chi*, 222–23
  breathing, 168–71
  dosha, 57–58
  energy, 55–56, 139–40
  Freeze-Frame, 270
  imaginal, 140–41
  for lovers, 141–42
  in natural setting, 106–7
  See also Yoga
Expectancy, 227–28
Expiration, 146
External exercise, 203, 206, 209
Eyes, 43, 44–45

Family, 117–18
Female orgasm, 216, 217–18
Feng shui, 13, 93–98
  cures, 96–97
  geometry and, 98
  subconscious and, 95–96
Fenwick, Elizabeth, 249
Fenwick, Peter, 249
Fibromyalgia, 185
Fingertip chakra, 243
Fire, 70, 244–45
Fire breathing exercise, 168–69
Five elements, 48–52, 70
Flaws, Bob, 196

Food
  Ayurveda and, 9, 191–93
  as energy tonic, 189–90
  raw or cooked, 195
  tastes of, 191–93
  See also Diet
Fraser-Smith, Anthony, 81
Frawley, David, 49
Freeman, Mara, 73
Freeze-Frame technique, 238, 270
Full breath, 151–52

Ganzahaou. See Licorice tea
Gauquelin, Michel, 91
Geomagnetic field, 74–81, 215
Geometry, 62–63, 98
Gerber, Richard, 113
Ginseng, 197–99
Ginsenisodes, 198
Glastonbury Tor (England), 72
Glycyrrhiza, 199
Goldstein, Joseph, 230, 232
Graves, Tom, 71
Great Pyramid of Giza, 63
Green, Elmer, 16
Grof, Stanislav, 155–57
Grounding effect, 215
Group
  collective intention, 254–58
  power of, 136–38

Hagens, Bethe, 62–63
Hands
  feeling energy with, 55–56
  holding, 125–26
  in prayer and meditation, 242–43
Hansen, Mark Victor, 257
Hatha yoga, 208
Hawaii, collective intention in, 138
Headaches, 14–15
Head-heart entrainment, 238–39
Healing, 21
  collective intention and, 254–58
  energy and, 14, 250–54
  from meditation, 228–41, 243–47, 271
  from prayer, 259–61, 265–69
  sexual, 9–10
  from touch, 261–64

Healing Words (Dossey), 265
Health
  breath and, 152–54
  light and, 89–90
  love and, 4–5, 127–28
  prostate, 219–20
  radiant, 40, 197
Heart, 35–36, 42
  center, 42
  chakra, 38
  DHEA and, 202
  electromagnetic field of, 5, 132
  energy, 125–26
  entrainment and, 47–48
  mind connection, 236–39
  prayer and, 267–68
  soothing of, 4–5
Heat, 244–45
Herbal supplements, 196–202
High blood pressure, 245
Hills, 105–6
Holotropic breathwork, 143, 154–56
Hopi Indians, 66
Hormones
  DHEA, 202
  stress, 199
  in Western culture, 201–2
How I Pray (Castelli), 227
Hubble Telescope, 75
Hugging, 7
Huna tradition, 35
Hunt, Valerie, 38
Hydrotherapy, 206–8
Hypertension, 245
Hyperventilation, 156–57

Ida, 37, 149, 164
IgA. *See* Antibody immunoglobulin A
Imaginal communication, 110, 140–41
Imaginal zone, 112
Imagination, 110–11, 140
Immune system
  breathing and, 153–54
  hydrotherapy and, 208
  sleep and, 184–85
Impotence, 41, 219
Indian tradition, 8, 31–32, 34, 49, 176
  See also Ayurveda
Infants, 117

INDEX

In-spiration, 143–71
Inspiration, 146
Institute of HeartMath, 4, 36, 47, 53, 125, 238
"In sync", 45–48, 187
Intention
  collective, 138, 254–58
  conscious, 260, 261
  power of, 134–36
Internal exercise, 203, 206
Intimacy, 8–9
Intuition, 214

Jahnke, Roger, 205
James, William, 20
Japan, magnetic field deficiency syndrome in, 77–78
Jewish tradition, 231
Jing. See Congenital chi

Kabbal, Jeru, 157
Kapha, 8, 50–52, 58, 180
  evening, 178–79
  and kapha, 120–21
  lethargy, 244
  morning, 177
  and pitta, 120
  tastes and, 191–92
  and vata, 119
Kason, Yvonne, 249
Ketheric body, 29
Khan, Hazrat Inayat, 145
Khema, Ayya, 241
Kisses, 5–6
Klivington, Kenneth, 16
Kornfield, Jack, 230
Korngold, Efrem, 23, 150
Krieger, Delores, 262
Krippner, Stanley, 89
Kundalini energy, 230–31, 239–41
Kunz, Dora, 263
Kushi, Michio, 194

Lad, Vasant, 49
Lakota Sioux, 62
Lansing, Willy, 66–67
Lao-tzu, 1

Lawrence, Brother, 226
Laying on of hands, 255–56
Leakey, Richard, 103
Leboyer, Frederick, 147
Lethargy, 244
Leukemia, 99, 257–58
Leviton, Richard, 62
Ley lines, 65, 72
Licorice tea, 199–200
Light, 247–49
  health and, 89–90
  seasonal affective disorder and, 89, 93, 186
Livesay, Gerald, 33
Lottery payouts, lunar cycle and, 83, 87
Love
  altruistic, 35, 128
  health and, 4–5, 127–28
  seizures and, 268–69
Low blood pressure, 247
Lu, Henry, 190
Lunar cycle, 83–87
Lung, 150, 151
Lung–mei, 65
Lust, Benedict, 207

Macrobiotic cooking, 194
Magnetic field. See Electromagnetic fields; Geomagnetic field
Magnetic field deficiency syndrome, 78
Male orgasm, 216
Malillumination, 89
Manning, Matthew, 260
Marma points, 34
Marriage, 127
Mars Effect, 91
Mary Line, 72
McCraty, Rollin, 47, 125
Meditation, 21
  breath in, 158–60, 170
  hands in, 242–43
  healing from, 228–41, 243–47
  metta, 271
  posture for, 240–41
  transcendental, 239
Melanoma, 90
Melatonin, 99, 101, 184, 185–86
Menstruation, 216, 218
Mental body, 29
Meridians, 31–34, 39, 65, 149

Metta, 236–37, 271
Metz, Katherine, 94, 96, 97
Michael Line, 72
Michell, John, 65
Microcosmic orbit, 167
Midday *pitta*, 177–78
Mind
 breath and, 166–68
 heart connection, 236–39
 monkey, 243–44
 non-local, 54, 116, 133
 vital energy and, 52–55
Monkey mind, 243–44
Moon, 81–88
Morning *kapha*, 177
Morning *vata*, 179
Morton, Janhavi, 118
Motoyama, Hiroshi, 32, 38, 166
Mountains, 105–6
Muktananda (Swami), 3, 17, 19
Mu'min, Carole, 227
Music, 171
Mutual funds, lunar cycle and, 83, 87

Na dan meditation, 170
Nadis, 32, 37, 65, 70, 149–50, 164, 267
Natural foods, 189
Natural killer cells, 127, 184, 205
Natural light, 89
Natural Mind, The (Weil), 156
Nature, 59–61
 See also Ecopsychology
Near-death experiences, 249
Near-death reflex, 248
Negative ions, 92–93
Neuromagnetics, 24
New, Ruvi, 231
Ni, Hua-Ching, 213
Night *pitta*, 179
Night sleep, 183–84
Non-local mind, 116, 133

Orgasm, 216–18
Oriental culture. *See* Chinese culture; Eastern
 culture
Oscillator, 46, 138, 182
 breath as, 151
Ott, John Nash, 89

"Out of sync", 176
Ovarian cancer, 90
Oxygen, 152
Oz, Mehmet, 263

Palm chakras, 43–44, 55, 242, 261
Panax ginseng, 197–98
Parasympathetic nervous system, 247, 248
Pavek, Richard, 17, 26–27
Periodic Table of the Elements, 48–49
Pets
 health and, 4–5
 returning home, 24
Pineal gland, 184
Pingala, 37, 149, 164
Pitta, 8, 50–52, 57, 180
 heat and fire, 244–45
 and *kapha*, 120
 midday, 177–78
 night, 179
 and *pitta*, 123–24
 tastes and, 192
 and *vata*, 121–22
Planets, 91–92
Plato, 62
Pneuma, 145
Polarity therapy, 27
Posture, 239–41
Power centers, 70–74
Power lines, 99–101
Prakriti, 50–51
Prana, 145, 162, 186, 208
Pranayama, 162–64, 168, 203
Pranic healing, 39, 207
Prayer, 21
 in AIDS and cancer, 266
 hands in, 242–43
 healing from, 225–27, 265–69
 yoga and, 267
Progressive relaxation, 209
Prostate cancer, 219–20, 254
Psychotic behavior, 83, 85
Pungent, 192

Quinn, Janet, 264

Radiant health, 40, 197
Radin, Dean, 82, 88

INDEX

Rama Prasad (Swami), 149
Ramos, Hector, 39, 207
Rapture, 230–33
Raskin, Ellen, 165–66
Raw foods, 195
Reader, August, 248
Rebman, Jannine, 82, 88
Reed, Henry, 110–12, 140
Reid, Daniel, 217
Relationships, 8–9, 21, 109–42
  balance in, 113
  communication wavelength in, 115–16
  doshas and, 118–24
  energy exchange in, 125–26, 139
  energy explosions in, 114
  family, 117–18
  group, 136–38
  love, 127–28
  remote influence in, 132–36
  touching and, 124–26
  See also Sexual relationships
Relaxation, progressive, 209
Relaxation response, 159, 182–83, 245–46
Remote influence, 132–36, 259
Resonance, 234–36
Respiration, 146, 147
  See also Breath; Breathing
Respiratory capacity, 153
Rest, 180–86
Rhythm, 176, 184
Rings of Gaia, 62–65
Roszak, Theodore, 102

Sacred sites, 70–74
SAD. *See* Seasonal affective disorder
Salty taste, 192
Schlitz, Marilyn, 135
Schwenk, Theodore, 73–74
Science of Breath, The (Prasad), 149
Seals, Dan, 227
Seasonal affective disorder (SAD), 89, 93, 186
Seizures, 268–69
Selby, John, 230
Semen, 217, 218, 219
Sexual healing, 9–10
Sexual relationships/practices, 141–42
  Eastern versus Western, 129–31
  electromagnetic fields and, 132
  falling asleep after, 216–18

tantric, 129–32, 216, 218
  vital energy and, 216–20
Shamanic tradition, 235
Shealy, Norman, 202
Shen Therapy, 27
Shushumna, 37, 149
Siberian ginseng, 198
Sixth Extinction, The (Leakey), 103
Skin cancer, 90, 250
Sleep, 173
  after sex, 216–18
  and *feng shui*, 13, 96
  immune system and, 184–85
  night, 183–84
  supplements, 185–86
Sour taste, 192
Spirare, 146
Spirit
  body and, 248–49
  breath and, 145–46
  energy connection, 2–4
  medium of, 1–22
  prayer, meditation, and healing, 225–71
Square, 98
Starhawk, 105
Stone, Randolph, 27
Stonehenge (England), 71
Stress hormone, 199
Subconscious, 95–96
Subtle bodies, 28–30
Sufi tradition, 145, 225
Sugar, 188–89
Suicide
  electromagnetic fields and, 99
  lunar cycle and, 83, 85
Suma, 201
Sun, 88–90, 186
Sweet taste, 192
Sympathetic nervous system, 248

Tai chi, 33, 53, 210–14
Tantric sexual practices, 129–32, 216, 218
Taoist tradition, 162, 165
  breathing in, 149–50, 167
  digestion in, 193
  energy centers, 35
  exercise, 203–6

(*Taoist tradition, continued*)
 five elements in, 49
 vital energy in, 174, 218–19
 See also Chi kung; Tai chi
Targ, Elizabeth, 266
Tart, Charles, 259
Taste, 191–93
Taylor, Kylea, 155
Tea, 199–200
Therapeutic Touch, 14, 30, 262–64
Theta brain waves, 246–47
Throat chakra, 38, 42–43
Tiller, William, 19, 101, 102, 239
Timing, 175–80
TM. *See* Transcendental meditation
Tomatis, Alfred, 234
Touch, 21
 healing from, 261–64
 relationships and, 124–26
Transcendental meditation (TM), 239
Transducer, 16–17, 231–33
Tree of life centers, 35
Trees, 59–60, 61

Vaginismus, 41
Valerian root, 185–86
Vata, 8, 50–51, 57, 180
 afternoon, 178
 and *kapha*, 119
 monkey mind, 243–44
 morning, 179
 and *pitta*, 121–22
 tastes and, 191–92
 and *vata*, 122
View over Atlantis, The (Michell), 65
Vipassana, 159, 230
Vital energy, 10, 21, 25–26
 awakening, 222–23
 breathing and, 158
 care and nurturing of, 173–223
 collective intention in, 258
 cycles of, 176–80
 exercise and, 204–5
 explosion of, 114

flow of, 31–33, 61
foods and, 190
hugging and, 7
mind and, 52–55
sex and, 216–20
sun and, 186
Vitamin D, 90

Waking up, 221–22
Warburg, Otto, 152
Water
 dowsing for, 15, 67–70, 71
 flow, 73–74
 See also Hydrotherapy
Wavelength, 115–16
Weight, 10–11
Weil, Andrew, 156, 185
Weissman, Abraham, 260–61
Wertheimer, Nancy, 99
Western culture
 breathing in, 146–47
 diet, 196
 elements in, 49
 energy in, 2, 16, 20, 23, 66
 exercise in, 203–4
 hormones in, 201–2
 posture in, 240
 rest in, 181
 sexual relationships in, 129–31
 timing in, 175
White light, 247–48
Wilson, Edward, 103
Wirkus, Mietek, 27, 166, 168
Withania somnifera, 200
Women, 216–17
Wright, Susan, 30

Yoga
 breathing and, 149, 162–63
 chakras and, 208–9
 as energy enhancement, 209–10
 prayer and, 267
 See also Pranayama

ABOUT THE AUTHOR

William Collinge, Ph.D., is a teacher, researcher, and writer in the fields of subtle energy and integrative medicine. For over a decade he has served as a guide in self-healing and personal transformation for people with serious illness. He is also the author of *The American Holistic Health Association Complete Guide to Alternative Medicine* and *Recovering from Chronic Fatigue Syndrome: A Guide to Self-Empowerment*. He has led seminars and retreats across North America, Hawaii, and New Zealand.

For information on programs, tapes, and other materials, phone or fax (800) 745-1837. E-mail address is collinge@healthy.net.